SHAKESPEARE'S THEATRE

Second Edition

Peter Thomson

London and New York

First published in 1983
by Routledge & Kegan Paul plc

First published in paperback by Routledge & Kegan Paul in 1985
Second edition first published in 1992 by Routledge
11 New Fetter Lane, London EC4P 4EE

Simultaneously published in the USA and Canada
by Routledge
a division of Routledge, Chapman and Hall, Inc.
29 West 35th Street, New York, NY 10001

Set in 10/12 pt Garamond by Intype, London
Printed and bound in Great Britain by
T J Press (Padstow) Ltd, Padstow, Cornwall

British Library Cataloguing-in-Publication Data
Thomson, Peter
Shakespeare's theatre. – 2nd ed. –
(Theatre production studies)
I. Title II. Series
792.0942164

Library of Congress Cataloging-in-Publication Data
Thomson, Peter
Shakespeare's theatre/Peter Thomson. – 2nd ed.
p.   cm. – (Theatre production studies)
Includes bibliographical references and indexes.
1. Shakespeare, William, 1564–1616—Stage history—To 1625.
2. Theaters–England–London–History–17th century. 3. Theater–
England–London–History–17th century.   4. Globe Theatre
(Southwark, London, England) 5. Chamberlain's Men (Theater company)
I. Title. II. Series.
PR3095.T48   1992
792'.09421'2–dc20   91–33770

ISBN 0–415–07311–1
ISBN 0–415–05148–7 pbk

This book is dedicated to my sister Jean
and to the memory of our parents.

CONTENTS

ILLUSTRATIONS

⸱ ACKNOWLEDGEMENTS

For permission to reproduce illustrations, I am grateful to: Aerofilms Ltd (Plate 2), the Royal Library, Stockholm (Plate 3), the University Library, Utrecht (Plate 4), the Trustees of the British Museum (Plates 8, 12, and 13), the National Portrait Gallery (Plate 9), the Honourable Society of the Middle Temple (Plate 10), and the Marquess of Bath (Plate 11). I am grateful, also, to my daughter Kate for the line drawing reproduced as Plate 1, and to Jenny Bell and Tony Addicott, who made the model photographed for Plates 5, 6, and 7. Copyright in each instance remains with the owners of the original.

I would also like to thank the various people who helped in the writing of the book. Christopher Brown spotted a chink, but had the tact to keep quiet about any other blemishes. Professor Peter Wisemen advised me on a detail that would otherwise have confused me. Stewart Trotter boosted me with his interest in the theatrical usefulness of the early chapters. Michael Hattaway allowed me to read in typescript his own contribution to the present series, *Elizabethan Popular Theatre*. John Russell Brown made several important suggestions about ways of improving the book: I have tried to follow them. Finally, Eve Elwin and Sally Connely gave me a refuge and looked after me during a crucial period of writing. They, and my colleagues in the Drama Section at Exeter University who had to take on extra work during my term off, enabled me to complete the work.

INTRODUCTION

Shakespeare belonged to a successful theatre company. This book is about that company during its ten best years. Part I looks at the planning and personnel, the financing, the repertoire, and the Globe Theatre itself. Part II sets three of Shakespeare's greatest plays in the theatrical context that has been explored in Part I. I have tried throughout to record my sense of the risks taken and the compromises made by a company which was, by any reckoning, adventurous and, sometimes by the skin of its teeth, prosperous. Theatre historians too often neglect the hand-to-mouth instantaneousness of much theatrical decision-making. We should not assume that a solution to a staging problem, once found, would be mechanically applied in every future situation. It is the resourcefulness of Shakespeare's company, its magnificent adaptability, that has most impressed itself on me during the writing of this book.

Page references in Henslowe's *Diary* are to the readily available edition by R. A. Foakes and R. T. Rickert (Cambridge, 1961). Line references in *A Yorkshire Tragedy* are to the Malone Society Reprint (1973), in Ben Jonson to the Herford and Simpson text (Oxford, 1925–52), and in Shakespeare to the one volume Oxford edition, edited by W. J. Craig (1919). For quotations from other dramatists, I have used available modern editions. The reader should not find it hard to trace them. The spelling of all quotations from plays has been modernised. Elsewhere I have retained the old spelling except where it seemed likely to obscure the meaning. I make no apology for this. The old spelling increases, for me, the 'present tense' of the writing. I hope it does so for others.

Part I
THE COMPANY

1

THE LORD CHAMBERLAIN'S SERVANTS

1597 was a bad year for the professional theatre in London. The Lord Mayor and aldermen of the city had been hostile to the professional companies since they began to engage public interest around the middle of the sixteenth century. Not only were plays liable to contain lewd or even inflammatory material, not only were the gatherings of people in theatres, gamehouses, inns or public halls a threat to public order and health, worst of all, these players were under aristocratic protection, and could hope to sidestep the law and cock a careful snook at the civic authorities. By 1597, the predominantly Puritan officers of the Guildhall were seeking to limit courtly privilege within the City of London. It was an opposition that, under the insensitive Stuarts, would eventually lead to civil war. Even in her dotage, the last of the Tudors was more supple. So it was that Queen Elizabeth and her Privy Council responded to a letter from the Guildhall, dated 28 June 1597 and requesting 'the present stay and final suppressing of . . . stage plays, as well at the Theatre, Curtain, and Bankside as in all other places in and about the City', with an astonishing compliance. Was this the end of fifty years of wrangling? If the Court were to withdraw its support from the players, if they were to be allowed no longer the protection of nobleman's livery, they would immediately become liable under the 1572 'Act for the punishment of Vagabonds and for Relief of the Poor and Impotent'.[1] Clearly, the context and the aftermath of the Privy Council's order that all the theatres in and around London be immediately demolished demand attention.[2]

When James Burbage had provided England with its first purpose-built playhouse, the Theatre, in 1576, he had the good sense to build it in Shoreditch, about half a mile north of the Bishop's Gate of the City of London, outside the jurisdiction of the Lord Mayor. The site is a little to the north of today's Liverpool Street Station. The Curtain was built nearby in the following year, also in the grounds of the dissolved Holywell priory. The City fathers did not like the proximity of these new playhouses, and would no doubt have fancied their chance of influencing the justices of Middlesex to do something about them, had it not been for the abiding

3

bugbear of aristocratic privilege. James Burbage, for example, had been a leading member of the company of players licensed as Lord Leicester's Men. Leicester was formidable enough, but the status of the company was further strengthened by the award of a royal patent in 1574. Burbage sensed his opportunity and built his Theatre. There was an immediate problem. During the 1570s, the religious drama of England was finally suppressed, and Burbage, together with all his contemporary theatrical entrepreneurs, found himself searching for a new drama to replace it. The quest was sufficiently successful to encourage further theatre-building, south of the river this time. Of the theatre in the village of Newington, not far from the area now familiar to users of the Bakerloo and Northern Lines of the London Underground as Elephant and Castle, very little is known.[3] The Rose, built in the Liberty of the Clink, just south of what is now Southwark Bridge but was then open river, was overseen by the shrewdest of all the theatrical speculators, Philip Henslowe. In or shortly after 1587 it became the home of the Lord Admiral's Men. The Swan, built in 1595 or 1596, was the last of the theatres to be built before the Privy Council order. As we would expect, it was sited outside the City's jurisdiction, in the Liberty of the Manor of Paris Garden, just south of what is now Blackfriars Bridge, but was then open river. It was because of the presentation there, in July 1597, of a new play by Nashe and Jonson that the Privy Council was brought into its unlikely alliance with the City fathers.

Thomas Nashe was a combative man, thirty years old but already a veteran pamphleteer. He had been engaged, on the anti-Puritan side, in the Marprelate Controversy of 1589. Eight years later, he provided the Earl of Pembroke's Men, playing at the Swan, with a new play called *The Isle of Dogs*. The fervent Nashe had as his equally pugnacious collaborator on this lost text, Ben Jonson. Either openly, or by inference, *The Isle of Dogs* criticised the government of the country, and of the City of London too. It was, we presume, the immediate cause of the Lord Mayor's July complaint to the Privy Council. It certainly provoked the council, not only into concord with the Guildhall, but also into instructing the Middlesex justices[4] to investigate the writing and performing of 'a lewd plaie that was plaied in one of the plaiehowses on the Bancke Side, contanygne very seditious and sclanderous matter.' Ben Jonson and various members of Pembroke's Men were imprisoned (Nashe may have taken refuge on the continent – he lacked Jonson's resistance to deviousness), and the Privy Council issued the order that *ought* to have spelled the end of the still-youthful professional theatre of England:

Her Majestie being informed that there are verie greate disorders committed in the common playhouses both by lewd matters that are handled on the stages and by resorte and confluence of bad people, hathe given direction that not onlie no plaies shalbe used within London or about the city or in any publique place during this tyme of sommer, but that also those playhouses that are erected and built only for suche purposes shalbe plucked downe.

At first reading, this excerpt, like the document as a whole, looks unequivocal enough, but Professor Wickham's detailed analysis has provided it with a sub-text as surprising and as hopeful as the one Portia finds in Antonio's bond. Those interested in the Tudor genius for regulating the relationship between the left and the right hand are advised to read that analysis. It will be sufficient here to emphasise three of the major factors leading to the preservation of the professional stage at the end of the sixteenth century:

1 The continuance of aristocratic protection. It is of particular interest that the patrons of the two leading companies, the Lord Admiral and the Lord Chamberlain, were both members of the Privy Council.
2 Queen Elizabeth's pleasure in the plays performed for her at Court.
3 The acceptance by the Privy Council, and its assumption of the general acceptability, of the need for the theatre companies to rehearse in public the plays they would later perform in courtly seclusion.

A gloss on each of those points will provide a background for many of the subsequent considerations of this book:

1 Whilst it is true that aristocratic patronage of the professional theatre outlasted the 1597 order, it is also true that the order represented an attempt to limit that patronage. The Privy Council seems to have intended to save two companies of players, and two companies only. One of these, the Lord Admiral's Men, was well settled in Philip Henslowe's Rose Theatre on the South Bank. The other, the Lord Chamberlain's Men, may have been settling into Burbage's Theatre in Shoreditch, but it was not yet settled there. It was, perhaps, the shock of the 1597 order that urged this company, the one to which Shakespeare belonged, into a new cohesiveness. However gratified by the Privy Council letters of 19 February 1598, licensing the Admiral's and the Chamberlain's Men 'to use and practise stage playes', the alert leaders of the two companies would not have missed the hardening of attitudes implicit in an act of parliament of the same month. Its effect was to limit the right to maintain a company of actors to barons or to persons 'of greater Degree'.
2 It was fortunate for the actors that James I also took pleasure in court performances of plays; but his fondness was possessive, and his patronage accelerated the professional theatre's drift away from its popular audience. Queen Elizabeth died in March 1603. On 19 May, James translated the Chamberlain's Men into the King's Men. Through his

first parliament, he removed even from barons the right to maintain a company of actors. Under the Stuarts, theatrical performance was to be primarily and emphatically a royal pastime.

3 A profession that owes its preservation to the court, and whose survival in law is based on the provision of performances at court, will base much of its thinking on the requirements of the court. It would have been eccentric of the Chamberlain's/King's Men after 1597 to evolve in the Globe a stagecraft too complex or too particular to be adapted to performance in the makeshift 'fit-up' theatres of the royal residences. The need for flexibility, and the advantages of simplicity, should never be overlooked in speculation on Elizabethan and Jacobean performance styles.

The years of crisis between 1597 and 1604 saw the beginning of the end of the 'popular' theatre. They also saw, despite the appearances of 1597, the end of civic influence over the progress and control of the theatre. The loss of all traces of Puritan interest in the drama may not have worried the actors at the time – on the contrary, they were probably delighted – but it helped stunt the growth of the English theatre. The Puritans' respect for the individual, and their determination to re-examine moral precepts, were first swallowed and then rejected by the greedy Jacobean court. But that is another story, and one which could not have been predicted in 1597. Our concern is with a particular group of people who, in 1597, must have felt themselves to be on the edge of the abyss, but who were in fact on the threshold of a glorious decade.

We can name the eight leading members of the Lord Chamberlain's Men in August 1597 with moderate confidence. They were Thomas Pope, Augustine Phillips, William Kempe, John Heminges, Richard Burbage, William Shakespeare, William Sly, and Henry Condell. The first six of these held shares in the company. The system of self-government so far had been a simple one. The sharers financed each production and divided the takings proportionately. The profits could be used in a variety of ways, and there were presumably company meetings to determine them; but the owner of the theatre would have to be paid for the use of his building (customarily, his payment amounted to half of the gallery receipts), and the hired men – actors, musicians, wardrobe-master (tire-man), prompter (book-keeper), stage-hands – would need their weekly wage. The female roles were played by boys, some or all of whom were apprenticed to actors in the company. It seems unlikely that Shakespeare ever took on an apprentice, because choice or necessity kept him in theatrical lodgings in London rather than in the comfortable domesticity which he seems to have confined to Stratford; but Phillips had several, of whom he mentions Samuel Gilburne and James Sands in his will, Heminges was master of the more successful Alexander Cooke and John Rice, and

Richard Burbage of the talented Nicholas Tooley and the 'ingenious youth'[5] Richard Robinson. After Burbage's death, Robinson did the decent thing and married his widow. Heminges had probably done the same for the widow of his master, William Knell, and Philip Henslowe did himself no harm at all by marrying the wealthy widow of his non-theatrical employer. It was a custom honoured in the observance, preserving a nice domestic economy at the same time as it allowed a widow to maintain a hold on life.

It is worth trying to piece together an outline of the background and the individual qualities of the people who together formulated and carried through the extraordinary scheme that shuttled Shakespeare from Shoreditch to the Bankside in the thirty-fifth year of his life. We can begin somewhere between 1590 and 1592, with a performance by Lord Strange's Men, probably at the Rose, of Part Two of *The Seven Deadly Sins*. The play, by the greatest of all Elizabethan clowns, Richard Tarlton, has been lost, but a quirk of book-binding has preserved a playhouse synopsis clearly intended to help with backstage organisation. Almost all the actors are mentioned by name, and several of them have a part in the subsequent history of the Globe. Richard Burbage played Gorboduc, Augustine Phillips Sardanapalus. Thomas Pope, William Sly, John Sincler, Richard Cowley, and perhaps Nicholas Tooley played several smaller roles. The ascendancy of Strange's Men at this time is attested by their popularity at court. They were commanded for nine of the fourteen performances recorded in the Revels accounts during the two winters of 1591–2 and 1592–3. How long the supremacy and cohesion of Strange's Men might have continued, but for the major outbreak of bubonic plague that reached its peak in London in 1593, is necessarily unknowable. Forced to tour until deep into the winter of 1593, since London performance was banned until 30 December, the *Seven Deadly Sins* company split up. In the meanwhile, their patron had become Earl of Derby, on the death of his father in September 1593.

It is as well that we should understand the characteristics of bubonic plague, since its effect on professional theatre was so severe throughout the Elizabethan and Jacobean age. Major outbreaks in London, causing the banning of public performances, occurred in 1563, 1574, 1577, 1578, 1581, 1593, 1603, 1625, and 1636, and the stutter of a secondary outbreak often led to a restraint on plays in the years immediately following major epidemics, as in 1580, 1583, 1586 'in respect of the heat of the year now drawing on', 1587, 1594, 1604, and 1605. To the Elizabethans, it was a medical mystery, and it is not surprising that each visitation provided a text for the morally manipulative sermons of the theatre-haters. It became an established custom to order the closing of the theatres when London deaths reached forty in any one week. The effect on the morale of the professional actor is acknowledged by Smallshanks in Lording Barry's

7

Ram Alley (1607–1608), when he confesses that he dwindles at the sight of a sergeant 'almost as much as a new Player does at a plague bill certified forty.'[6]

What then was mystery is now understood. Bubonic plague reached England in 1348, and remained, sometimes dormant sometimes virulent, at least until the Great Fire of London in 1666. It was spread from rats to humans by rat-fleas. When a flea bit an affected rat, its digestion was blocked, and no blood could reach its stomach. The blocked flea continued to bite in quest of more blood, and when the rat died, the ravenous flea sought a human alternative. It was the bite of the rat-flea that spread the plague. Since the thatched roofs of English houses welcomed rats, the epidemics spread with savage, though measurable, speed. Plague killed over a quarter of the population of Stratford in 1564, the year of Shakespeare's birth. Roger Green, who lived in Henley Street, almost next door to Shakespeare's birthplace, lost four children to it that summer. The stone-built town of Aberdeen, on the other hand, was not affected. The mystery of preservation was as great as the mystery of doom. The parish register of St Peter's upon Cornhill contains an indicative verse:

> In a thousand five hundred ninety and three,
> The lord preserved my house and mee.
> When of the pestilence theare died,
> Full manie a thousand els beeside.

Explanations of the dwindling of an epidemic were as fanciful as those of its origin. Salvation was, in fact, owed to the hibernating habit of the rat-flea. We can be fairly certain that, under normal climatic conditions, winter epidemics were not of the bubonic plague. Typhus, spread by unhibernating body-lice, was a likelier cause, or measles. The English plague months were April to November, and the usual peak from July to October. Although the cause was never identified, there is evidence of intelligent deduction in the 1587 restraint on plays because the summer is growing 'hotter and hotter'; but the attempts to improve hygiene had less effect than is fondly supposed. Rats dislike strong smells.

The epidemic did not die out in London until 1595, and continued virulent elsewhere in England until 1598.[7] It was an inauspicious time to form a new company of players, but what is extraordinary about the group that assembled in 1594 under the patronage of the Lord Chamberlain, Henry Carey, Lord Hunsdon, is the familiarity of its names. This was not a random collection of individuals, but a re-union of friends. Loyalty and genuine affection play a part in the subsequent history of the Chamberlain's Men in a way that we can neither ignore nor adequately measure. Even among some of the hired men, there is evidence of a commitment beyond the normal limits of a working relationship.

It has been plausibly argued[8] that the Chamberlain's Men at this time, and perhaps until 1616, had twelve adult members and four boys. We know very little about them. That needs to be stressed. T. W. Baldwin has done all that can be done – and then a great deal more – with the information at our disposal.[9] Against his assumption that each actor developed a consistent line (irascible old man; low and high comedian; strong-minded lady; pert maid; benevolent old man, etc.) must be set the stronger alternative of the necessary versatility of a small number of actors in a company familiar with large cast-lists and the prudent paring down of pay-rolls. The playing of four, three, or two parts was much more a rule than an exception. John Sincler (Sincklo or Sinklo) played five in *The Seven Deadly Sins*, and may well have done the same for the Chamberlain's Men, whom he joined as a hired man in 1594. If he was notable for anything, it may have been his thinness.[10] He appears under his own name in the Induction to the rewritten version of *The Malcontent*, which was performed at the Globe in 1603 or 1604. That is the last we hear of him. It suggests little more precise than that he was socially at ease with the sharers, an equal rather than a servant. Richard Cowley is down for six parts in *The Seven Deadly Sins*. We know that he toured with Strange's Men in 1593, and we know, more interestingly, that he played Verges to Kempe's Dogberry in *Much Ado About Nothing*, probably in 1598. That suggests that he was stylistically or physically – or perhaps vocally – a foil to Kempe; but it is no more than a suggestion. We do not know when Cowley became a full member and sharer; not, certainly, until after 1599. But he is remembered in the will of Augustine Phillips in 1605, named two of his sons after the Burbage brothers, and had his own will witnessed by John Heminges and Cuthbert Burbage. His progress illustrates the upward mobility of the Chamberlain's Men.

Thomas Pope was a senior sharer in the Chamberlain's Men from 1594 until his retirement, and retained shares in the Globe and the Curtain until his death in 1604. Samuel Rowlands refers to him as 'Pope the Clowne' in a poetic satire published in 1600,[11] coupling him with John Singer of the Admiral's Men, who certainly *was* a clown, identifiably in the tradition of Tarlton and Kempe. Pope may, then, have been a stopgap after the defection of Kempe, and before Armin had proved himself. There seems no reason to question his usefulness to the Chamberlain's Men. He earned and preserved enough to leave £100 and considerable property to a mysterious Suzan Gasquine 'whom I have brought up ever since she was born', and he was, like Shakespeare, granted a coat of arms.

Augustine Phillips was another to receive, or at least to apply for, a coat of arms. He may well have been the social leader of the company. It was to him that Sir Gelly Meyrick came in February 1601, with the dangerous invitation to revive *Richard II* as a harbinger of the Earl of Essex's street revolution, and his will is an eloquent expression of a theatre-man's priorities. Having left £5 to be shared between the hired men of the company and 20-shilling gold pieces to five of his fellow-shareholders, he made a special gift of 30-shilling gold pieces to Shakespeare and Condell, and silver bowls worth £5 to Heminges, Richard Burbage, and Sly, his executors. To one apprentice he left his best clothes, to another his musical instruments – both very valuable bequests to young men embarking on a theatrical career. There seems no doubt that the Chamberlain's Men were Phillips's family. We know nothing for certain about his Shakespearean roles, but we can be sure of his versatility as a performer. The musical instruments bequeathed to James Sands included 'a citterne, a bandore, and a lute'. We must assume that they were intended for use, not ornament, and that he himself could play them. We know that he was the author/performer of a jig – one of the short song-and-dance afterpieces that were a popular feature of the public theatres – entered in the Stationers' Register on 26 May 1595 as 'Phillips his gigg of the slyppers'. There is some excuse for picturing him as the exemplary extrovert Elizabethan actor-athlete-entertainer; a man who would follow a part in a comedy with 'other feates of activitye and tumblinge',[12] and cap the occasion by dancing, playing, and singing in a jig of his own invention.

If the John Heminges who was granted a coat of arms in 1629, was, as seems probable, the actor, it was a fair reward for a lifetime of co-operative work on and off the stage. There is strong presumptive evidence that he was an unexceptional actor, though his immortality is assured by his initiative towards the publication of the Shakespeare Folio in 1623. In about 1611, he abandoned performance to become, in all but name, the financial controller of the Chamberlain's Men. It was a job at which he excelled, and in which he was trusted by his own colleagues, respected by rival companies, and taken seriously by the officers of the Lord Chamberlain. By the time he died in 1630, Heminges had accumulated property and wealth, despite costly problems with at least two of his fourteen children. The esteem in which he was held is attested by his appointment as churchwarden and sidesman in the parish of St Mary's Aldermanbury (between St Paul's and Moorgate), where he lived for about thirty years. There was nothing of the rogue and vagabond about John Heminges.

Much the same could be said of Henry Condell, a near neighbour in Aldermanbury, where he also was a churchwarden. Baldwin suggests that Condell was Heminges's apprentice before 1589, and whilst there is no evidence to support this, it has a human plausibility whose appeal is increased by the collaboration of the two men on the Shakespeare Folio. We know that Condell played the Cardinal in The Duchess of Malfi, which argues for a voice and presence sufficient to command, rather than merely to deserve, attention. However, there is reason to believe that he, like Heminges, turned increasingly to management, at least after 1619. He ran his own affairs with notable success, acquiring property in Blackfriars and on the Bankside as well as in Aldermanbury, and the reputation of being 'of great lyveinge, wealth, and power'. He became a sharer some time after 1599, like Cowley an example of the way in which the Chamberlain's Men rewarded loyalty.

We know that William Sly performed in *Sejanus*, *The Malcontent*, and *Volpone*, but we do not know what he played. He was probably with the Chamberlain's Men from the start, perhaps an actor-athlete after the fashion of Augustine Phillips, who named him overseer, residuary executor, and legatee in his will. He may have been Phillips's apprentice, and the inheritor of the essential accomplishments of the actor as itemised in *The Rich Cabinet of Rare Gems* in 1616: 'dancing, activity,[13] music, song, elocution, ability of body, memory, vigilancy, skill of weapon, pregnancy of wit'. Sly had to wait until after Phillips was dead before being admitted to a share in the company. It may be that his ways were considered a little wild by his colleagues. His son John, baptised in St Giles's, Cripplegate, on 24 September 1606, was 'base-born on the body of Margaret Chambers', and there is no record of Sly's ever marrying. The Dulwich portrait is of a dark, strong face, turned slightly sinister by the curl of the lips. The aura is curiously dangerous.

Four other people are known to have taken a leading part in the establishment of the Lord Chamberlain's Men in 1594–5. George Bryan left the stage in or shortly after 1596, and need not concern us, but the other three are of outstanding interest.

That William Kempe was recognised as England's most notable stage clown after the death of Richard Tarlton in 1588 is generally accepted. We have, for example, in Thomas Heywood's *Apology for Actors* (1612) a reference to the popularity of Tarlton 'whom succeeded Wil. Kemp, as wel in the favour of her majesty, as in the opinion and good thoughts of the generall audience'. We have also a quite surprising number of allusions, and two plays into which he enters *in propria persona*. In the anonymous Cambridge piece generally known as *2 Return from Parnassus* (c. 1603), Kempe instructs an undergraduate in the playing of 'a foolish mayor or a foolish justice of peace'. Since we know that Kempe created the role of Dogberry, it is tempting to believe that he specialised in such parts. The speech he gives as an example is characterised by the grinding of grammar we too readily associate with the attempts of social climbers to address public meetings. A modern English actor who was a master of the style was the late Arthur Lowe. It was Lowe's peculiar talent to endear himself to the mass television audience in the impersonation of people who unjustifiably consider themselves superior to the mass television audience. Had Kempe a similar sleight-of-hand? In John Day's *The Travels of the Three English Brothers* (1607), it is Kempe's speed at an impromptu, his bawdiness, and his rapport with an audience that are illustrated. The style is closer to Max Miller's than to Arthur Lowe's. It may represent a genuine contrast between Kempe the actor, finding other men's words a little too big for his mouth, and Kempe the solo performer, supremely at ease with his audience. 'I am somewhat hard of study,' Day has Kempe say, 'but if they will invent any extemporal merriment I'll put out the small smack of wit I ha' left in venture with them.'

The only Shakespearean roles we can confidently assign to Kempe are Dogberry and the insignificant Peter in *Romeo and Juliet*. We can be sure that he would have made the most of Peter's illiterate attempts to deliver invitations to the Capulets' ball, but even so, the part has little to commend it to a popular idol. If Kempe had had nothing to do when *Romeo and Juliet* was scheduled, he would probably have left Peter to a hired man. But, of course, he had something else to do. He had the jig to perform as an afterpiece. In Tarlton's hands, the jig had developed from popular song-with-dance of the kind that enlivened village greens during maying festivals, through comic and satiric song, to short musical farces that maintained an impromptu air, but were as carefully scripted as the plays to which they served as afterpieces. The German Paul Hentzner, writing in 1598, noted the 'excessive applause' that accompanied these jigs. We can be fairly certain that he saw Kempe in full swing. In the following year, the Swiss traveller Thomas Platter noted in his diary:

> After dinner on the 21st of September, at about two o'clock, I went with my companions over the water, and in the strewn roof-house saw the tragedy of the first Emperor Julius with at least fifteen characters very well acted. At the end of the comedy they danced according to their custom, with extreme elegance. Two in men's clothes and two in women's gave this performance, in wonderful combination with each other.

Platter is here giving a precious contemporary account of what was almost certainly a performance of *Julius Caesar* at the Globe, but we might take greater note of the apparently disproportionate attention he pays to the jig. He was not alone in that. On 1 October 1612, at the General Session of the Peace in Westminster, 'An order for suppressinge of Jigges att the ende of Playes' was issued, to meet protests about the disorderly crowds that rushed to the Fortune for the jig at the end of the performance. We have seen that Augustine Phillips had his 'Jig of the Slippers', but the star of the jigs that helped establish the popularity of the Chamberlain's Men was Will Kempe. He joined them in 1594, remained with them through the perilous years of 1597 and 1598, and then, with the Globe newly built or under construction, he left. We do not know why. It may have been the culmination of a series of disputes over the relative merits of plays and jigs. Whatever the reason, Kempe sold his share in the Globe, and took his genius for self-advertisement elsewhere, most famously to Norwich, on the nine-day morris dance from London in 1600. This extravagant marathon was the result of a wager. It is the last we hear of Will Kempe. Even his death is obscure.

Richard Burbage, who joined the Chamberlain's Men in 1594 and quickly established himself as the company's leading actor, was brought up in the professional theatre. He was probably less than twenty in 1590, when he performed the job of bouncer for his father at the Theatre. The dispute between James Burbage and the widow of his former business partner had reached flashpoint, and the widow brought Robert Myles and Nicholas Bishop along to see that she got her rights. Young Richard Burbage, having beaten Myles with a broom-handle, threatened to do the same to Bishop, while 'scornfully and disdainfully playing with [his] nose'. The evidence from the resultant law-suit is quoted for the possible guidance it offers about Burbage's stage-presence. He was not built like a contemplative aesthete, and he had inherited his father's aggressive temperament. The word 'attack' is sometimes used in the modern theatre to describe an actor's determination to dictate the pace and tone of his performance. Burbage, we can guess, was an attacking actor. He was also a painter. There are records of his scene-painting for the Earl of Rutland's tilts in 1613 and 1616, and it is probably a self-portrait at Dulwich that shows a keen-eyed, serious man, with a large nose and a tailored beard. We know too little about playhouse practice to do more than speculate about the uses to which his scene-painting talent might have been put there. He made his reputation in heroic parts. There are allusions to his playing Hamlet, Othello, Lear, and Richard III for Shakespeare, Ferdinand in *The Duchess of Malfi*, Malevole in *The Malcontent*, and 'Jeronimo', possibly in a revival of *The Spanish Tragedy*. He was a big enough actor also to play Volpone, though we cannot be sure that he did. Baldwin, predictably, assigns to him every major Shakespearean role from Richard III to Prospero. Later research has done nothing to prove or to disprove his claims. Surmise remains the basis of much of Martin Holmes's *Shakespeare and Burbage* (1978). We will do better to take stock of the peculiar relationship between Burbage and the other members of the Chamberlain's Men. In 1594, when he joined the new company, he was the son of the manager of the theatre which that company was keen to occupy. He could hope to profit from both sides of the enterprise. When his father died in 1597, Richard inherited his interest in the Blackfriars – and trouble, whilst his brother Cuthbert inherited his interest in the Theatre – and more trouble. The brothers were confident enough of each other to become business partners. Together they took on their father's old adversary, Giles Allen, and together they took half the shares in the new project which would be known to history as the Globe. But Cuthbert Burbage limited himself to the role of theatre manager, whilst Richard remained a full member of the Chamberlain's Men. If, as it seems, he maintained his close friendship with several of his fellow actors, it says much for the strength of feeling that united this remarkable company.[14] The unequal division of money between partners is normally a cause of friction, and the fact is that, if the sharers of the Chamberlain's Men were equals, Burbage was more equal than the others.

There remains William Shakespeare, whose decision to purchase a share in the Chamberlain's Men proved decisive, and whose ability to purchase it is surprising.[15] We do not know whether he was ever formally appointed 'ordinary' playwright to the company, or whether he was acceptable purely on the strength of his acting. The tradition that he played Adam in *As You Like It* and the Ghost of Hamlet's father is not very firmly based. We know that Shakespeare acted, but we do not know what he acted, nor how long he continued acting. We know that he had built himself a sufficient reputation as a dramatist to goad Greene into abuse in 1592, and Chettle into apology in 1593. Even so, his purchase of a share in the Chamberlain's Men in 1594 was his clearest declaration of professional commitment so far. He was thirty years old, the author of *The Comedy of Errors*, *The Two Gentlemen of Verona*, *The Taming of the Shrew*, *Titus Andronicus*, a large share of the *Henry VI* plays, and – the most encouraging sign that he had the popular touch – *Richard III*.[16] He had also reached a fashionable audience with his two narrative poems, 'Venus and Adonis', and 'The Rape of Lucrece'. From now on, his career was that of a professional playwright, but his evident aspiration was to be a gentleman.

These were the men who, in 1597, mulled over the implications of the Privy Council's order. It is unlikely that they consulted their apprentices, but the decisions to be taken in 1597 and 1598 were so weighty that they may well have discussed them with the senior hired men, like Condell, Sly, Sincler, and Cowley. The immediate response to the order was the seeking – and granting – of permission to tour, but that merely shelved the problem of where, if anywhere near London, they could play when the tour was over. As early as August 1597, there were hopeful signs. Philip Henslowe, with the Admiral's Men still on tour, was signing on new actors for November, and he would scarcely have done that without some intimation of the Privy Council's intention to soften the blow. If he had inside information, we can assume that Shakespeare and his colleagues had it too. There was, though, a crucial difference. Henslowe, and through him the Admiral's Men, had a theatre, the Rose. The Chamberlain's Men did not. They had been playing, in the main, at James Burbage's Theatre, which stood on land owned by a certain Giles Allen, a vigorous man of broadly Puritan sympathies. Burbage's lease on the land ran for twenty-one years, and unless renewed would expire on 13 April 1597. Relations between Allen and Burbage were not good, and nothing had been resolved when Burbage died in February 1597, leaving the Theatre and its problems to his elder son, Cuthbert. We can fairly assume that Cuthbert would have done his best to help the company to which his brother Richard belonged, but what *could* he do? It would have been madness, at such a time, to perform illegally in the Theatre. A makeshift answer offered itself. Cuthbert had, we presume, inherited his father's financial interest in the neighbouring Curtain, and it was in this rough-and-ready theatre that the Lord Chamberlain's Men most probably performed on their return to London in October/November 1597.

It is important to realise that this was an experienced and highly practical group. What they had now to decide, in a context of considerable legal peril and no job security, was whether to make a long-term investment or to settle for quick results and short-term benefits. The immediate prospects were much better than they had looked in July. Anticipating the burden of the Privy Council letter of 19 February 1598, the Office of the Revels had invited the Chamberlain's Men and the Admiral's Men to provide the entertainment at court during the 1597–8 winter. We know that the Chamberlain's Men played on 26 December, 1 January, Twelfth Night, and Shrove Sunday, and that the Admiral's Men played on 27 December and Shrove Tuesday. No other companies were invited. We do not know the names of any of the plays, though the two parts of *Henry IV* are likely to have figured in the repertoire of the Chamberlain's Men. We can, though, guess some of the subjects of their business deliberations.

There was, first of all, the matter of the Blackfriars. On 4 February 1596, James Burbage completed the purchase of the Parliament Chamber of the Blackfriars at a cost of £600. He had in mind, not only the imminent expiry of his lease on the Theatre, but also, if Professor Wickham is right, the marked preference of Elizabethan actors for indoor performance.[17] He began work on converting the building at once, relying on the support of the Lord Chamberlain, Lord Hunsdon. But Hunsdon died in July 1596, and it was not long before Burbage discovered that it was not enough simply to trust in the fact that Blackfriars was outside the jurisdiction of the City of London, though inside its walls. Lord Hunsdon's son, who had accepted the patronage of his father's company of players, was among the signatories of a petition, presented to the Privy Council in November 1596, requesting a ban on the opening of a *public* playhouse in the Black-friars precinct, whose complaining residents evidently considered themselves to be too nice a class of people to be put at risk. The use of the converted building was still unresolved when James Burbage died in February 1597, leaving the property to his younger son, Richard. That same Richard was, at the end of the troubled year of 1597, asking Shakespeare and the others what he should do with it; and the advice he seems to have received was to leave it alone. Not until 1600, when he leased it to Henry Evans for use by the Children of the Queen's Chapel, did Burbage begin to get a return on a considerable family outlay. The residents of the Blackfriars would accept a *private* theatre, whose boy-actors were fast becoming fashionable rivals to the adult players. It is not unusual for a professional theatre company to set itself a new problem by solving an old one.

With plenty of friends in high places through 1597 and 1598, the Chamberlain's Men still lacked a suitable theatre in which to exploit their advantages. It cannot have pleased them that, while they were restricted to playing in the Curtain through the spring, Oliver Woodliffe was converting the Boar's Head in Whitechapel into an attractive theatre. For what company? The Privy Council had declared an intention to restrict public performance to two companies, but it was a third, an amalgam of Worcester's and Derby's Men, that established itself at the Boar's Head in 1599, and was even invited to perform at court on Shrove Tuesday 1600 and 1 January 1601. As Muriel Bradbrook has noted, 'the Acts of the Privy Council often seem to indicate a target which they hope will be approached, rather than an order which they fully expect to be carried out.'[18] The infuriating possibility that they might be squeezed out at the eleventh hour must have kept the Chamberlain's Men on edge throughout 1598. Shakespeare had bought New Place, the second largest house in Stratford, in May 1597. He made a small investment in malt (malting was Stratford's principal industry) early in 1598. There is a real possibility that he was contemplating the life of a country gentleman. His loss would have been a perilous gash to the Chamberlain's Men. In addition to being a shareholder and minor actor, he was their 'ordinary' poet – a writer, that is, either formally or informally enrolled as part of the 'order'. His national status would be declared with the publication in September 1598 of Francis Meres's *Palladis Tamia*. But, in a litigious age, Shakespeare was untypically shy of public controversy; and 1598 was a year for taking shelter. Among actors, the *Isle of Dogs* affair died slowly. Nor was it a year of religious and political ease. Moderate English Catholics risked an appeal to Rome, and inevitably kindled the flame of religious dispute. On 2 July, Queen Elizabeth boxed the ears of the ambitious Earl of Essex. Lord Burghley's steadying influence was lost with his death on 4 August, and on 9 November a certain Edward Squire tried to kill the queen by poisoning the saddle of her horse.

The threat to the future of the Chamberlain's Men was made more galling by the obvious fact that their affairs had prospered so vigorously between 1594 and 1597. Of the eight court commands in the winter of 1594–5, five went to the Admiral's Men and three to the Chamberlain's. The following year, the position was reversed, and the Chamberlain's Men took four to the Admiral's Men's two. But the winter of 1596–7 was a wonder. All six of the royal commands went to the Chamberlain's Men. Shakespeare provided them over this period with three of his greatest popular successes, *A Midsummer Night's Dream*, *Romeo and Juliet*, and *The Merchant of Venice*, as well as *Love's Labour's Lost* and *Richard II*. England was experiencing an economic recession, and Shakespeare's formerly prosperous father was feeling the effects in Stratford. It was from the ample playhouse profits that the family found the money to pay the heavy fees charged by the Heralds' College for the grant of a coat of arms in 1596. When it became clear in the winter of 1597–8, that the Privy Council held the Chamberlain's Men in special favour, the wish somehow or other to keep the leading ship afloat must have been overwhelming. The events of 1598, however, threatened the company's morale. The solution that presented itself towards the end of 1598 was simple, but not straightforward. A clause in James Burbage's lease of the Theatre authorised the tenant to dismantle and remove the building, but the legality of doing so after the lease had run out was questionable.[19] The main risk would be Cuthbert Burbage's – he was the leaseholder, and he was *not* a member of the Chamberlain's Men. But something had to be done, or the advantages of a strong position would be squandered. The Burbages were Elizabethan businessmen – Cuthbert with a threatened property, and Richard with a threatened company of players – and Elizabethan businessmen loved the whiff of a good project. When Giles Allen refused to accept Richard Burbage as security on a renewal of Cuthbert Burbage's lease of the Theatre – this was in the autumn of 1598, and the desperation of the Chamberlain's Men probably lay behind Cuthbert's initial preparedness to accept Allen's exorbitant terms – the plot was hatched. With their performance of Jonson's trend-setting *Every Man in His Humour* the talk of the town, the Chamberlain's Men could confidently expect invitations to court. It was a desperately cold winter. On 18 December, the Thames was frozen. On 26 December, Richard Burbage was one of the performers at Court. On 28 December, under cover of darkness, he was with his mother, his brother, a financial backer and friend called William Smith, a carpenter-architect called Peter Street, and about a dozen labourers, outside the empty Theatre. That night, despite attempts to interrupt and prevent them, they began to dismantle it. They carried the timbers, the best preserved of them anyway, down Bishopsgate Street and into the walled city. The Thames was still frozen on 28 December, and it may be that the timbers were slid across. It would have saved the toll on London Bridge, or the considerable cost of several trips in a Thames ferry. They had the promise of a plot of land not much more than a hundred yards from Henslowe's Rose theatre, and the measured sections of timber from the Theatre were on their way there as 1 January, the date of a second royal command, approached. The Burbages had probably made sure that Giles Allen was out of town. By the time he reached Shoreditch, it was too late. He was the angry owner of a vacant lot.

On 21 February 1599 an agreement was formally signed. It was tripartite. Nicholas Brend, as the owner of the Bankside land, assigned half the lease to Richard and Cuthbert Burbage, and the other half to five of the Lord Chamberlain's company of players – Pope, Phillips, Heminges,

Kempe, and Shakespeare. The die was cast. Shakespeare was a shareholder in a theatre company and a theatre building of which he himself was a major asset. Richard Burbage was part of an oligarchy which promised to maintain unusually open access, but which preserved for him a family interest. As for Cuthbert Burbage, silenced by history but vocal in his own time, he had become a Chamberlain's Man in all but name when he accepted the plan to transport the timbers of the Theatre from Shoreditch to the South Bank. It must have been with his agreement that a unique system of ownership was worked out. For the first time in England, and perhaps anywhere in the world, a theatre was to be designed by actors, run by actors and built on land leased and paid for by actors. Once built, the Globe would become, in Glynne Wickham's words, 'from a dramatist's and actor's viewpoint ... outstandingly the most attractive playhouse in London'.[20]

2

BALANCING THE BOOKS

A successful theatre company is not going to change its methods simply because it changes its home. It is, however, going to adapt where adaptation seems sensible, and it may take the opportunity offered by a new start to put into practice some of the innovations that have been talked about but not yet risked. The Chamberlain's Men had just taken a bone-shaking risk; it is reasonable to suppose that, when the building and furnishing of the Globe were completed, probably in the autumn of 1599, the company chose to play safe.

The theatrical year was by now established. Performances would begin in London as early as possible in September, or even in late August if circumstances were auspicious.[1] The period up to Christmas was critical. In most years, it was the longest uninterrupted playing spell, and it provided the Office of the Revels with the evidence from which the choice for court performance during the Christmas celebrations would be made. To be commanded to court was a double pleasure. It brought a separate and generous payment, and it offered the warmth of indoor performance at the height of the English winter. We do not know what attempts were made to provide heating in the open-air theatres, but we have evidence that post-Christmas performances continued in them throughout the one or two months prior to the variable commencement of the Lenten break. It seems extraordinary that so many scholars have accepted this information without comment. The putting on of plays in the open air in England in December, January, and February is an uncommercial prospect today. No management would see the point of risking defeat by rain, snow, or temperatures near freezing-point. With the weather at its worst, even football crowds dwindle – but they do not vanish, and that is of some significance. It is always misleading to transport modern theatrical expectations back into history. Muriel Bradbrook has suggested that the social atmosphere of the Globe or Rose was 'less like the modern theatre than it was like a funfair', and Glynne Wickham that 'the physical conditions of performance came much nearer to resembling those of a modern public meeting' than those in any theatre where an audience expects to be segregated from the actors.[2] What is certain is that it was no love of literature that took people into the arena on a winter's afternoon. A football crowd is held by its undiscriminating loyalty, and by a passionate uncertainty about the outcome. An unknown story vividly told can grip in parallel ways. The Chamberlain's Men would surely have preferred an indoor playhouse just the same.

The restraint on performance during the forty days of Lent was inconsistently observed, but could not confidently be flouted, so that full-scale playing had to be delayed until the spring. Even then there were limitations. Year after year, as high summer approached, plague deaths rose. It became commonplace for London companies to cut their losses and take to the road in July and August – the very months best suited to open air performance. Since the exodus from the city included all the citizens who could afford it, the actors would have lost their wealthier audience anyway. It was not simply a matter of reducing the risk of disease. As the historian of bubonic plague in England reminds us, 'The summation of fleas, lice, bugs, and body-odours must have made church attendance, especially in hot weather, a true test of Christian endurance.'[3] An outdoor theatre would, of course, test endurance less severely, and the players must have regretted the loss of their regular home during the hottest months of the year, but it is not surprising that those with sufficient resources took to the country during perspiration peaks. We know too little in detail to build up a satisfactory picture of a player's summer tour. All we can say is that the theatrical year of the Chamberlain's Men was probably completed by a series of performances in provincial centres of population. The drumming up of audiences on such occasions was a literal undertaking. Henslowe's records make that clear: 'Lent unto the company the 6 of February 1599 for to buy a drum when to go into the country 11s 6d.'[4] The two trumpets bought the following day by the actor Robert Shaw were for the same purpose. The touring players announced themselves in each new town with two trumpets and a drum.

It is clearly implied by the lists in Henslowe's *Diary* that performances in London took place daily, sometimes even on Sunday, despite various attempts at legislative limitation. The law against Sunday performance dates from at the latest 1583, but it would not have been so frequently re-affirmed if it had not been even more frequently ignored. A Privy Council order of 1591, for example, invites the Lord Mayor not only to remember the Sabbath Day, but also to ban plays on Thursdays, because that was the day for bear-baiting, and the playhouses were attracting too many of the potential audience. The Thursday ban was ineffective, but the outstanding failure was the order of 22 June 1600, which reiterated the Privy Council's view that there should be only *two* companies and only *two* theatres, and added that these companies should perform on only *two* days each week, never on Sundays, never in Lent, and never at times of 'extraordinary sickness'. What evidence we have suggests that this order was ignored in all three respects. More than two companies continued to perform in more than two theatres, and they continued to perform daily (though only exceptionally on Sunday), weather and the plague permitting.

Our best evidence of the precise time of performance comes in a request from Lord Hunsdon to the Lord Mayor of London, dated 8 October 1594, that his Men be allowed to play at the Cross Keys in Gracious (Gracechurch) Street:

> the which I praie you the rather to doe for that they have undertaken to me that where heretofore they began not their plaies till towardes fower a clock, they will now begin at two and have done betwene fower and five, and will nott use anie drumes or trumpettes att all for the callinge of peopell together, and shall be contributories to the poor of the parishe.

A two o'clock start was sensible. Dinner, the main meal of the day for all classes of society, was taken between ten o'clock and noon; and it was important that the audience should be able to get home before dark. The four o'clock start to which Hunsdon refers can only have been a summer expedient.

The move from Shoreditch to the Bankside involved, for the Chamberlain's Men, the loss of a local section of audience before a compensating gain could be anticipated. The clutch of houses around the site of the Globe in the lucid foreground of Hollar's Long View of London (published in 1647, but sketched a few years earlier) may already have been there in 1599, and there were populous areas east of London Bridge too. But the suburbs south of the river carried the stigma (or the promise) of brothels, rowdy taverns, and the uneasy high spirits of those who had just attended the violent ceremonies of bull- or bear-baiting. The walled City of London was all north of the River Thames, with the Tower at its eastern extremity. An anachronistic Circle Line, at its most efficient, could have completed the journey round the wall from the Tower, stopping at the seven gates of Aldgate, Bishopsgate, Moorgate, Cripplegate, Aldersgate, Newgate and Ludgate, and perhaps on a return along the river from the western extremity of Blackfriars, at Paul's Wharf and London Bridge, in about twenty minutes. Tudor centralisation had raised London from being England's largest city to being its capital, but it remained geographically compact. By 1600, the population within the walls may have been as much as 160,000. 200,000 is a reasonable approximation if the suburbs are included, and such villages as Kentish Town, Charing Cross, Islington, and Hoxton (Hogsden) excluded. Under both Elizabeth and James, there was alarm at the city's dangerous growth. An act of 1580 banned both new building and the conversion of existing houses into tenements. Both went on, as is evident from the reinforcing legislation of 1590 and 1593. It is easier to get away with tenement conversion than with new building, and we have to take account of a city whose tall houses became rapidly overstocked with people as the century progressed, and as London's importance became established.

That importance was embodied in the court. Increasingly Elizabeth and particularly James I made the palaces around London their habitual residences. Whitehall, St James's, and the Tower were familiar to all Londoners: Hampton Court, Richmond, and Greenwich were easy to reach by water: and the palace and city of Westminster, upstream from the Globe, were a gentle ferry-trip away from it. The proximity of the court was of such importance to the Chamberlain's Men that we can neither overstate nor comprehend it. We can take as typical the position on 18 November 1581. A severe plague epidemic in London had led to the banning of all plays through the summer, but now the Privy Council, 'as the sickness was almost ceased, and not likely to increase at this time of year', asked the Lord Mayor *immediately* to 'suffer the players to practise such plays, in such sort, and in the usual places, as they had been accustomed.' Why? 'In order to relieve the poor players, and to encourage their being in readiness with convenient matters for her highness's solace this next Christmas.'[5] The story remained much the same until the closing of the theatres in 1642. It was the rabbit the players pulled out of the hat when threatened by the city Puritans. Some scepticism is inevitable. The claim that a March performance at the Globe was, in fact, a practice for Christmas at Whitehall might have seemed far-fetched – November was plausible enough – but the players could always claim that they must hold themselves in readiness for sudden invitations to entertain the queen. It would be a serious mistake to neglect the influence of the royal command on repertoire and on styles of performance. The fixed fee of £10, payable to the company for acting at court, was more than could be guaranteed from an afternoon at the Globe. What is more, there was always a chance of its being augmented, and of the benefits that might result from the catching of a noble eye. We can assume that the Chamberlain's Men were good at adapting performances to suit new spaces, but we must also recognise that, since playing at court was a major feature of their year, they would not plan a production too elaborate to be scaled down, nor build theatres vastly more sophisticated than the cockpits, banqueting halls, or assembly rooms of the London palaces.[6] Just discernible among the guesses and glimpses of their business practice is the attempt of the Chamberlain's Men to reconcile a traditional 'nomadic economy'[7] with the new capitalism.

While they were performing at the Theatre or the Curtain (and, perhaps, the Cross Keys Inn in Gracechurch Street) Shakespeare and his colleagues would have been largely independent of the magnificent waterway that brought London its trade; but they had all, or nearly all, some experience of playing south of the river. It was at Newington Butts that they established themselves in the immediate post-plague days of 1594. The marked increase in Henslowe's share of the takings between 13 and 15 June (14 June was a Sunday) suggests that they might have moved to the renovated Rose to complete the short summer season's sharing with the Admiral's Men.[8] As Strange's Men, some of them would anyway have played at the Rose in 1592. It is important to note this kind of detail. The Chamberlain's Men were about to establish themselves within a stone's throw of their major competitors, the Admiral's Men. They would need to know some of the tricks of the Bankside trade. The lease of a wharf would be essential – Henslowe paid 8 shillings for the Rose's in 1592–3[9] – and it would surely be cheaper to own a theatre boat than to depend on the Thames watermen. The 70 shillings Henslowe paid 'for a barge' in 1592–3 may have been a precedent. Apart from its service as a transporter of timber, canvas, costumes, paint, and properties, a theatre barge would provide magnificent advertising possibilities. It would have taxed no one's ingenuity to publicise *Antony and Cleopatra* with the Thames as the main approach road to his theatre. If 'the barge she sat in' did not appear on the Thames when *Antony and Cleopatra* was scheduled for performance at either the Globe or the Blackfriars, it was a missed opportunity. The Bankside theatres were a blessing to the Thames waterman, of whom John Webster (?) wrote, 'The play-houses only keep him sober; and, as it doth many other gallants, make him an afternoon's man.' 'London Bridge,' Webster added, 'is the most terriblest eye-sore to him that can be.'[10] It had twenty arches, was lined with shops and houses, and was noted for the display of traitors' heads outside the gate-house that guarded its middle drawbridge. Unless you had your own boat, you would pay a toll on the bridge, or a fee to the waterman. The artisan from Shoreditch, unless he were abnormally keen, would have been deterred from attending the Globe, and there is a distinct possibility that the Chamberlain's Men attracted a more sophisticated, more free-thinking audience to their new house than they had to the Theatre. Such, at least, is the argument Andrew Gurr propounds in *Playgoing in Shakespeare's London*, the most recent substantial contribution to our understanding of the subject.

The first thing to say about Elizabethan playgoers is that they were used to listening. Much important information reached the Elizabethan citizen by way of public proclamation, and if he went to law, as Elizabethans so tirelessly did, he might *hear* but never *see* a judgment. The second thing to say about it is that we can *know* only a little compared with the amount we have to infer. Let us take the simplest assumption first. There is some evidence that the charging of a penny for admission was common playhouse practice, and that a further penny (presumably paid to a gatherer inside the theatre) bought access to a seat in the gallery. Beyond that, we must speculate. Alfred Harbage argues interestingly for a three-price system,[11] with the 'orchestra' of the de Witt sketch housing the most expensive seats. It is an arrangement that encourages a clear class-distinction. The groundlings in the open yard, standing and jostling for their pennysworth, would be artisans, craftsmen, soldiers returning from the wars. In the twopenny galleries would be the middle-class merchant, perhaps with his family, together with the less showy and perhaps less wealthy lawyers and students from the Inns of Court. The costliest seats would then belong to those members of society who went to the theatre to be seen – courtiers, younger sons of the nobility, friends and relations of the resident company's patron. This is, of course, too tidy. We need to explore the composition of the audience in a little more detail. A theatre company that misjudges its appeal rarely lasts long or lives well.

We owe Shakespeare one portrait of the groundlings, 'who for the most part are capable of nothing but inexplicable dumb-shows and noise' (*Hamlet*, III.ii.13–15). This is Hamlet's snobbish assault on the intelligence of the penny-payers. Casca in *Julius Caesar* is more graphic, and more olfactory, concealing the theatrical sting of his outburst until he reaches its tail:

> the rabblement shouted and clapped their chopp'd hands, and threw up their sweaty night-caps and uttered such a deal of stinking breath because Caesar refused the crown, that it had almost choked Caesar; for he swounded and fell down at it: and for mine own part, I durst not laugh, for fear of opening my lips and receiving the bad air. . . . If the tag-rag people did not clap him and hiss him, according as he pleased and displeased them, as they use to do the players in the theatre, I am no true man.

> (I.ii.243–50 and 259–63)

This is Casca's allusion to auditorium odours, and to the playhouse combat between a lively audience and an unpopular (or popular!) actor. But we will profoundly misjudge the position if we do not recognise that, whilst this is Hamlet talking *about* the groundlings, it is also Burbage talking *to* the groundlings, or that Casca would not have these words if Shakespeare had had less confidence in the ability of the 'tag-rag people', to take a joke. It is quite inconceivable that the great plays of the Elizabethan and Jacobean eras had to reach the discerning audience across an intervening mob of noisy, ignorant yobbos. Harbage has calculated a capacity of 818 for the yard of the Fortune Theatre, with room for a further 1,526 in the galleries.[12] The proximity of the groundlings to the actors would have given them a disproportionate power to dictate the terms of performance, and we should give due weight to the fact that it was not until after the seventeenth century that the written drama of England showed a significant decline in ambition. The conclusion must be that, if the groundlings were a dominant feature of the Elizabethan public playhouses they were not unruly, or that, if they were unruly they were not dominant. Given their position, immediately below and around the actors, the first alternative is the likelier. It is born out by the findings of A. J. Cook, who argues that it was not only in the private theatres that elite spectators dominated the audience, but also in such public theatres as the Globe.[13] An Elizabethan artisan could have afforded the penny admission, but he would have paid it only if his interest was genuine. Given the Elizabethan mistrust of crowds, it is surprising how rare the recorded disorders in theatres are. Where trouble was caused, it was most likely by an apprentice who had drunk beyond his capacity, and was in the mood to draw attention to himself. There is no evidence worth the name that it was socially demeaning to stand among the groundlings.

One good reason for paying the extra penny for gallery admission was to get a seat. It can reasonably be assumed that the women in the audience preferred it. It must also have happened that, if the yard was almost empty at a performance, the groundlings would have improvised seats or sat on the ground, particularly during lulls in the performance. In the indoor theatres, the whole audience could be seated. In spaces adapted for theatrical indoor performance, it was evidently the custom to provide benches. It is, perhaps, to these that Dekker alludes in *Satiromastix*, when he writes of 'pennie-bench Theatres' (IV.ii.53), though the possibility that he is there recording an occasional practice, weather and sightlines permitting, at the Globe cannot be utterly discounted. The merchant would certainly have preferred to sit. Unless the type has changed, he would have believed that his enterprise and effort had earned the reward of comfort, and paid his extra penny as of right. London was the business centre of a largely unrecognised economic revolution, in which money was replacing goods and property as the measure of wealth. 'Good morning to the day,' says Volpone at the opening of his play, 'and, next, my gold!' Usury thrived in the new world of credit and capital, and the lively response to the spirit of the age was to set all upon a venture. The sharers of the Chamberlain's Men were in business. Shakespeare, for instance, had risked more than was prudent in buying his way into the Globe in 1599. The alchemical dream fired more than the gullible. It is the recognition of a common urge that leads Martin Holmes to the assertion that 'practically every playgoer of consequence was a business man.'[14] The merchant would have been likely to bring a small (family) group, but the players would have been more wary of the larger groups from among the residents of the Inns of Court. There were just over a thousand of these in 1600,[15] the majority of them being sons of the landed gentry, and they formed the largest colony of cultured men in the immediate vicinity of the city.[16] Their preferences could be ignored only at peril, so that Philip Finkel-pearl's observation of a 'group tendency toward physical violence and untimely exhibition of wit' may explain some of the decisions taken by practical dramatists.[17]

The top-price patrons of Harbage's scheme remain something of a mystery. Despite his suggestion about the de Witt 'orchestra', there is no certainty about where they sat, nor any certainty about whether a third price existed. Harbage has taken into account de Witt's comparison of the Swan with the Roman theatres about which he knew much more. The Roman orchestra was the area immediately in front of the stage, reserved for distinguished spectators only. Harbarge has translated this with perilous literalism, putting together de Witt's classical scholarship and his own independent knowledge that there was an area in the Elizabethan theatre for particularly privileged spectators, and giving it a price-range to suit certain financial calculations. His proposal is not disreputable, but neither is it particularly persuasive. Mention of an orchestra is peculiar to de Witt. The bottom gallery may, or more likely may not, have been more expensive than the upper two of the Swan. There is no real evidence that it was ever reserved for privileged spectators. A likelier area is the gallery over the stage, peopled in the de Witt drawing by a line of eight onlookers. Anyone sitting there would certainly be seen, and there could be no complaints about sightlines or distance from the action. Henslowe's record of an income of 10 shillings for 'selling the Room over the tirehouse' would be more useful corroborative evidence if it were not qualified by an associated reference to an income of 14 shillings for 'selling my lord's room'.[18] What we can be sure of is that there was an area in the Rose familiarly known as the Lord's Room. It does not *sound* like a stretch of the gallery. Later tradition would have commended a secluded space, in which the 'lord' could meet his assignations in secret; but that was not a known priority of the Elizabethan theatre. The privilege lay in being seen, rather than in being unseen, and the gallery over the stage answers more of the questions raised by contemporary allusions than any alternative location. In the indoor theatres, the wish to be seen was gratified by the sale of seats on the stage, but this is a practice that seems to have been resisted at the Globe – a fact which suggests that the groundlings' right to see the stage was respected there. The rights of the patron, though, would have to be respected as well. What would happen if the Lord Chamberlain himself announced his intention to attend a performance? He would expect the freedom of the Lord's Room for himself or for his guests. Such privileged patrons demanded, and would have received, special treatment from the company. Ben Jonson expected the audience of *Every Man out of His Humour* to be familiar with playhouse custom in the matter. In claiming acquaintance with Count Frugale, Signior Illustre, and Signior Luculento, the social-climbing gallant, Fastidius Brisk, earns this rebuke from Carlo Buffone:

There's n'er a one of these, but might lie a week on the rack, ere
they could bring forth his name; and yet he pours them out as
familiarly, as if he had seen 'hem stand by the fire i' the presence,
or ta'en tobacco with them over the stage, i' the lord's room.

(II.iii.189–93)

The play was written for the Chamberlain's Men at the newly opened
Globe in 1599. It hints persuasively at a location and an atmosphere for
the place of real privilege in that theatre. It would need brilliance, high
birth, or both to achieve access to the Lord's Room at the Globe. We do
not know how often, or in what numbers, the nobility chose to attend
the public theatres, but their possible attendance would always be a consideration for an alert company.

The chapter has sketched in some of the background against which the
Chamberlain's Men had to draw their plans in 1599. No account books
have been discovered, nor any systematic listing of membership, repertoire,
and possessions. Even John Payne Collier (1789–1883), who was wont to
turn to forgery when scholarship fell short, forged or found nothing of
major significance. The one crucial document to have survived is the
gathering of papers loosely known as Henslowe's *Diary*. Philip Henslowe
was the son of the master of the game in Ashdown Forest. He was born
in about 1550, and was certainly living in the Liberty of the Clink, close
to the eventual site of the Rose Theatre, by 1577. Having been apprenticed
to a dyer named Woodward, he made himself wealthy by the simple
expedient of marrying his master's widow. He acquired a step-daughter
by the match, and, in 1592, a son-in-law through her marriage to the most
famous actor of the day, Edward Alleyn. Henslowe's interest in theatrical
property was established by then. The Rose, built in 1587 or 1588, was
the result of a speculation developed in partnership with a certain John
Cholmley. A later partnership, with Alleyn, brought him the joint patent
as Master of the Royal Game of Bears, Bulls, and Mastiff Dogs. That was
in 1604, but it probably crowned a decade or so of commercial interest
in animal baiting, for Henslowe was the most consistently successful of
all the Elizabethan speculators in entertainment. The financial wizards of
the Globe, Heminges, Condell, and the Burbage brothers, seem stick-in-
the mud by comparison. Henslowe went where the money was. In 1600,
when the Rose looked like losing in its competition with the Globe, he
built the Fortune north of the river, just along Golden Lane from Cripplegate, specifying in the building contract those features of the Globe he
was keenest to have copied. He may well have had some share in the
management of the Swan as well as of the theatre in Newington Butts.
Finally, in 1614, he brought together his interests in animal-baiting and
drama in the building of the Hope on Bankside. This was to be an

adaptable arena, with 'a stage to be carryed or taken awaie' when the business of the day was not drama.

Henslowe's interest in theatre is irrefutable evidence of its profitability as commerce. He was a businessman, and not an over-scrupulous one. Apart from maintaining some interest in his brother's mining in Ashdown Forest, he was involved also in the manufacture of starch, in real estate, in pawnbroking, and in money-lending. Before adding to the dirt thrown at Henslowe by some scholars, we should take note of the view of the *Diary*'s most recent editors that there was 'a friendly and, on the whole, harmonious relationship between Henslowe and the players'. Their reading is that Henslowe was not a grasping usurer, whose manner of exploiting actors was a shameful contrast to the actor-centred policy initiated by James Burbage and inherited by his sons: 'there is little justification for drawing a contrast between Henslowe, as a mercenary capitalist, and the Burbages; the evidence suggests that they were all capitalists.'[19]

Henslowe's *Diary* is a precious document, but it is also an eccentric one. It is not the systematic record of a fanatical book-keeper. Rather is it evidence of the fitful attempts of a wealthy man to keep his affairs in better order. Anyone who has been shaken by an unexpected bank statement and resolved to keep a closer check on his income and expenditure from now on will find something familiar about its pages. The manuscript includes his brother's mining accounts,[20] records of Henslowe's private affairs, three sets of pawn accounts, a fascinating list of unlikely cures for ailments, and various theatrical records. Additional manuscripts associated with the *Diary* include a petition from Strange's Men and an accompanying petition from several Thames watermen for the re-opening of the Rose, possibly dating from 1594 – just before several of Strange's Men regrouped as the Lord Chamberlain's Men, the responsive warrant from the Privy Council licensing the re-opening of the Rose, a long wardrobe inventory in Edward Alleyn's handwriting, the deed of partnership in the Rose between Henslowe and Cholmley, and the contract for the building of the Fortune Theatre. The *Diary* itself gives us certain kinds of information which we can relate directly to the financial expectations, and probably to the financial practices, of the Chamberlain's Men at the Globe. To make the most of this information, we need somehow or other to find a foothold in the shifting sands of comparative economics, bearing in mind that, throughout Shakespeare's life, the purchasing power of money was declining, but at a rate that would be scarcely discernible to anyone used to the skidding inflation of the second half of the twentieth century.

Admission to the yard of the Globe cost one penny. An orange, probably purchasable there, might cost a farthing. In the early 1560s, a pig for roasting could be bought for sixpence.[21] Two decades later, the cheapest tobacco could be bought for 12 shillings a pound, and the cheapest beer for a penny a quart. You could pay a lot more for either. The pig-woman

Ursula, in Jonson's *Bartholomew Fair* (1614), has a 'sixpenny bottle of ale' for anyone rash enough to ask for the 'best' (II.ii.138). Food prices were, of course, subject to fluctuation, but eggs rarely cost more than a halfpenny each, beef averaged about twopence per pound, and clothing material was cheap and durable. Prudent housekeeping, which included the making of bread and of clothes, allowed people to survive, despite the manifest failure of wages to keep pace with prices. Outside London, an income of £2 a year was on the low side of tolerable, and the schoolmaster appointed to the school Shakespeare attended in Stratford was doing well with a salary of £20. Half of that was a commoner income for a schoolmaster. A London artisan would earn from 6 to 8 shillings, for a seventy-hour week (approximately £17 in a year, if his health held). Against that, a competent barrister in this litigious age could hope to make £600 in an average year, and a junior judge £1,000. He would have been one of very few Elizabethans in the four-figure bracket. The queen's annual revenue was less than £250,000 – a figure that puts into context James I's extravagant expenditure of £4,000 on the Christmas masque at court in 1618.

Henslowe lists his own receipts from admission charges in a number of different ways. It is fair to assume that, until 29 July 1598 when he states, 'Here I Begyne to Receue the wholle gallereys', he took half the income from the twopenny (and threepenny, if there ever was one) gallery at the Rose. This amounted, on a sequence of days chosen at random in January 1596, to:

26 shillings on 5 January
60 shillings on 6 January
20 shillings on 7 January
18 shillings on 8 January
56 shillings on 9 January
18 shillings on 10 January
50 shillings on 12 January
15 shillings on 13 January
23 shillings on 14 January
27 shillings on 15 January
61 shillings on 16 January

The typical income is over 20 but less than 30 shillings. The four 'good' days in the list above are exceptional. They came, respectively, from *Hercules Part One*, for whose popularity since its first performance in May 1595 I know of no explanation, from *The Jew of Malta* at the theatre where Marlowe had become – posthumously – almost a house-playwright, *Chinon of England* at its second ever performance, and *Pythagoras* at its first. The popularity of new plays, together with the important matters of repertoire and the treatment of playwrights, will be discussed in Chapter Four. Our concern at present is with the bare bones of theatrical income.

On a day when Henslowe took 25 shillings from a twopenny gallery, the actors of the Admiral's Men would have taken the same plus the income from those spectators who got no higher than the yard. With a total gallery income of 50 shillings, the maximum paying audience in the galleries would be 300. We simply do not know whether there was likely to be a greater number in the yard. If the numbers were equal, the total takings for the actors that day would amount to 50 shillings, and the total attendance to 600. That is less than half the number that Harbage puts forward as the average at the Rose in 1595.[22]

We need to distinguish between what is average and what is characteristic. There is a high probability that an audience of 600 or less was a more regular occurrence than an audience in excess of 1,000. But the love of novelty, together with the unembarrassed quest for entertainment, boosted the numbers attending any performance that had a special promise. Calculated in the same rough-and-ready way, the gallery audience for *Hercules* on 6 January 1596 amounted to 1,440 and even half that number of groundlings would have raised the total attendance to 2,160. Later evidence strongly suggests that the theatre became more popular as the sixteenth century drew to its end. Using Henslowe's *Diary* as his primary source, Harbage concludes that 15,000 people attended London's theatres each week in 1595, and that this had risen to 18,000 by 1601, and to 21,000 by 1605. His calculations, however defensible, give a misleadingly comfortable view. They find 13 per cent of London's population attending the theatre each week; but the theatre companies could not depend on statistics. The impresario Sol Hurok's caution that, 'If people don't want to come, nothing will stop them' is quite as relevant to Elizabethan England as to post-war America. Henslowe's figures are equivocal, if not downright depressing. If the weekly sums of his takings after he began to receive 'the whole gallery' are genuinely that, they suggest no increase in the theatrical public since 1595. To be sure, he records an income of over £16 in the week of 3 June 1599 and over £15 in the week of 24 February 1599, but he broke £10 in only twelve of the remaining seventy-eight playing weeks between 29 July 1598 and 13 July 1600. Since we have no information on the number of performances in any of those weeks, it is impossible to draw hard-and-fast conclusions. We know that Henslowe was planning the move north of the river from at least January 1600, the date of the Fortune contract, and it may be that the diminishing gallery returns from the Rose illustrate the way in which the Lord Chamberlain's Men were eating the Lord Admiral's Men's audience. Even so, we should view Harbage's count of Rose-coloured spectators with some scepticism, accepting only that, in a good week, in 1601 for example, as many as 18,000 people may have attended London's theatres, and being careful to add that the company that took that number for granted would not have lasted long in the commercial world of the capital city.

A close reading of Henslowe leaves no doubt of the importance of costume in the theatre. Entries vary from the quaintly informative:[23]

Lent at the appointment of the company unto the little tailor to taffeta sarsenet to make a pair of hose for Nick to tumble in before the queen the 25 of December 1601, sum of 14 shillings.

to the frankly astonishing. Of the latter kind is the listed cost of £9 for taffeta to make two women's gowns for *The Two Angry Women of Abington*, and the preparedness of the actor Richard Jones to pay £3 for 'A man's gown of Peachcolour in grain'.[24] Set the first sum against a likely average company take of less than £3 per performance, and the second against a likely annual income of approximately £30, and the conclusion is an excessive concern for costume. That is in line with the extravagance of Elizabethan fashion, whose determination to disguise natural lines, to stiffen, to pad, and to distort, has never been surpassed. Given the fondness for men's cloaks, it is no surprise to find Henslowe's constant references to their purchase or improvement. It cost the Admiral's Men £12–10s to get two cloaks out of pawn in September 1598,[25] and Alleyn's inventory lists fourteen, many of them richly adorned.[26] The inventory suggests a tolerably stocked wardrobe, but leading actors, like Richard Jones and all the sharers of the Chamberlain's Men, would have dressed themselves. Only hired men and boys would expect to be costumed out of stock.

Expenditure on the making of properties and the decoration of the stage is less easily identified. Malone found an inventory of 'all the properties for my Lord Admeralles men', dating from 1598 or 1599, in a bundle of loose papers at Dulwich College.[27] It has subsequently disappeared, together with other inventories printed in his 1790 edition of Shakespeare's *Plays and Poems*. Since we can expect the holdings of the Lord Chamberlain's Men to have been similar, it is here printed as Appendix A. There is negative evidence that properties were a lower priority for the Admiral's Men than costume – whereas the company certainly had a wardrobe master (or 'tireman')[28] there is no parallel reference to a property master, nor to any equivalent of the modern stage designer. Henslowe certainly purchased timber and nails in considerable quantities. We must assume, either that the regular members of the company were competent to make their own properties, or that it was acceptable practice to farm out specialist work to specialist craftsmen. For the difficult job of making the throne, and ensuring its effective rise and fall from the roof over the stage, Henslowe paid an unnamed carpenter the considerable sum of £7–2s. As a master carpenter, James Burbage might have been able to do that job at the Globe had he survived the winter of 1597. His son Richard could certainly have saved his company the money Henslowe paid out for 'payntinge my stage'.[29]

One set of payments, sporadically recorded by Henslowe, would certainly have been echoed in the accounts of the Lord Chamberlain's Men. These are the sums paid to the Revels Office, or directly to the Master of the Revels. The progress of this arbiter of entertainment from minor court official to powerful holder of a rich monopoly has been fully recorded elsewhere.[30] The *Diary* shows payments of two kinds. The first, and lesser, are the fees paid to the Master of the Revels for reading and licensing new plays. By the end of the century, the cost was 7 shillings per text. The second are the regular charges for licensing the building. They went up from 10 shillings per week to £3 per month in 1599. As regular as a rental, this £3 was at worst protection money, at best an insurance against the attacks of the Puritans. From the point of view of the Master of the Revels, it signalled the end of a successful campaign to make himself the real power behind the theatres of London. To ignore or to displease him would put the guilty company in peril.

Henslowe was the lessee of a theatre before he was the associate of any particular company. James Burbage had an exactly contrary career, beginning his theatrical life as a member of Leicester's Men and becoming the lessee of a theatre for the last twenty years of his life. But there are strong similarities as well. At the time of his death, James Burbage was being drawn into close involvement with a single company, the Chamberlain's Men, just as Henslowe was drawn into the Admiral's Men. When Henslowe moved from the Rose to the Fortune, the Admiral's Men went with him. The Chamberlain's Men would have gone with James Burbage to the Globe. As it was, they went with his sons. It was probably the commitment of Richard Burbage that engaged his father's special interest in the company. It was almost certainly his son-in-law's commitment to the Admiral's Men that brought Henslowe into a participation more active than he had envisaged. There must have been differences in the ways the two companies ran their affairs, but there were sufficient similarities to justify a consideration here of Henslowe's way with actors.

There is a famous entry in the *Diary* which has shocked and intrigued many readers: 'Bought my boy James Bristow of William Augustin player the 18 of December 1597 for £8.' That purchase price is slightly greater than the yearly wage of £7–16s at 3 shillings a week which James Bristow earned in 1600.[31] There is no evidence that the Chamberlain's Men ever bought a boy, nor any certainty that they did not. How many Elizabethan fathers would have despatched their sons to act except for gain? And how many theatre companies could have resisted the lure of a talented boy? James Bristow's wage was probably standard, as might have been the terms of contract for the hired man, Thomas Hearne:[32]

Memorandum that the 27 of July 1597 I hired Thomas Hearne with twopence for to serve me two years in the quality of playing for five shillings a week for one year & six shillings and eightpence for the other year which he hath covenanted himself to serve me & not to depart from my company till this two years be ended.

Henslowe was worried about losing actors to rival companies, and he had good cause in 1597. The *Isle of Dogs* scandal at the Swan had involved several defectors from the Admiral's Men, and Henslowe was as careful to bind them to the company as he was to bind Hearne when they returned to him in search of work after the dissolution of Pembroke's Men. The Chamberlain's Men maintained a more stable company than the Admiral's Men, but they may well have bound their hired men in the same way.

Henslowe, initially in partnership with Cholmley, was the lessee of the Rose. With Edward Alleyn he became lessee of the Fortune in 1600, acquiring the freehold there in 1610. The Admiral's Men may have felt friendly towards him, but their friendship had to take account of the fact that he could throw them out at any time. The position of the Chamberlain's Men at the Globe was significantly different. When the urgent need to find a new playhouse hit the Burbage brothers, they had to call up money in a hurry. They might have borrowed at the heavy interest rates that Elizabethan speculators were too often forced to accept. Instead, they invited the five senior (or the five richest) members of the Chamberlain's Men to form a sort of joint stock company, each to contribute his portion to the £600 or so that it cost to build the Globe. As we have seen, the Burbage brothers shared half the ten holdings, and Phillips, Pope, Kempe, Heminges, and Shakespeare took one each of the remaining five. This group of seven stood towards the Globe as Henslowe alone (after the unrecorded death of the neglected Cholmley) stood towards the Rose. They were its 'housekeepers', with the first claim on the takings to cover rent and upkeep. Perhaps, like James Burbage and Henslowe, they took the receipts from half the gallery seats in their role as housekeepers. As sharers, all except Cuthbert Burbage would then take their share of the receipts from the other half of the gallery and the whole of the yard. This double function was, in good times, a double asset, at all times a double risk. In the long run, it worked to the advantage of every housekeeper/sharer; which is to say that the Chamberlain's Men were successful and well run. The crucial relationship was probably that between Cuthbert Burbage, a businessman without pretensions as an actor, and John Heminges, an actor with a flair for business. It would have been Heminges's dexterity in bridging the roles of housekeeper and sharer that persuaded him finally to abandon acting in about 1611. The hiring, firing, and paying of actors, musicians, stage-hands, door-keepers (who took the money at the galleries as well as at the outside doors) was the responsibility of the sharers. Too much bungling would be costly.

We have no certain information about the value of shares at the First

Globe, and nothing for the Second Globe before 1635, when a one-sixteenth interest was worth £25,[33] but there is no reason to doubt that every actor aspired to become a sharer. When Shakespeare bought his first share in 1594, he thrust his foot firmly on to the ladder. When he became a housekeeper at the Globe in 1599, he was thirty-five and a highly successful professional. His annual income from the Globe alone, between 1599 and 1608, may be conservatively estimated at £55. That makes no allowance for any special payment for the plays he provided, nor for the stronger possibility that he was allowed all the takings on a second-day benefit performance of each of his new plays. We do not know exactly what he did at the Globe. We do know that, by 1602, he could afford to pay £320 for 107 acres of arable land in Old Stratford, and that three years later £440 bought him an interest in the lease of tithes in and around Stratford. The housekeeper share in the Blackfriars, which he bought in 1608, was more profitable than the Globe share. It probably raised his annual theatrical earnings to over £200. Shakespeare's last investment was in the gate-house of the Blackfriars precinct, which he bought in 1613 and immediately mortgaged. Such solid achievement argues solidly acceptable labour. He had made for himself a career as an actor, since that was, by 1594, an established profession, with a promise of power and profit, but he was one of the creators of the profession of playwright. Even if we are right to assume that he had abandoned acting by the time James I transformed the Chamberlain's into the King's Men in 1603,[34] he would have been thought of as a 'player' in London, whatever he claimed to be in Stratford. It is likely that he took a major part in the staging of his own plays. He was a shrewd judge of an audience's taste, confident enough to take risks with language and dramaturgy without, for example, Jonson's self-consciousness. His plays reveal a feeling for stage groupings and the interaction of figures in three dimensions. Such a sensitivity distinguishes the effective director in the modern theatre, but there was no director in the Elizabethan theatre. A house playwright might well have laid claim to aspects of the directorial function. If Shakespeare continued to pull his weight without acting, he must have had other responsibilities. Did he, perhaps, use his sense of an audience to improve the publicity of the Chamberlain's Men?

One crisis struck early in the Globe's history, perhaps even before its opening. Kempe left. Perhaps there had been a quarrel. Hamlet's advice to the Players has been read as Shakespeare's revenge:

> let those that play your clowns speak no more than is set down for them; for there be of them that will themselves laugh, to set on some quantity of barren spectators to laugh too, though in the mean time some necessary question of the play be then to be considered;

that's villainous, and shows a most pitiful ambition in the fool that
uses it.

(III.ii.43–51)

Robert Armin, who took Kempe's place, was very different. The critical
contrast is between Dogberry and Feste. The first was written with Kempe
in mind, the second for Armin. Touchstone might just have been played
by both, but with divergent emphases. Dogberry, like Kempe, demands
attention and the centre of the stage. Feste is content in the corners. An
over-simple distinction between a stand-up comic and a character-actor
helps to point up the tonal shift in the constitution of the Chamberlain's
Men. The effect on the social balance was also considerable. Armin was
easier company than Kempe, temperamentally closer to his colleagues; but
the loss of Kempe would have required, in compensation, a strenuous
publicity drive. The Chamberlain's Men were not proof against the
unease of the years between 1599 and 1608. Their achievement of cost-
effectiveness has to be seen in its nervous context, with the new capitalism
silently overcoming the resistance of feudal traditions. Both they and the
Admiral's Men were beneficiaries of the Tudor drift towards monopolies,
but the popular theatre, which was approaching a new peak in 1599, was
also approaching its end.

However stable its membership, we cannot isolate Shakespeare's company from the unavoidable hassles of theatrical production. The sharers,
though they may have worked to reduce risks, had to take them. Every
new play was a risk, every break in the weather a threat. The upkeep of
a theatre and the gratification of its patrons cannot be left to chance,
though chance will always intrude. The building of the Globe, although
it came at a time when the company seemed firmly established, was a
make-or-break venture. But no theatre company in British history has
ever firmly 'made' it. The successful history of the Chamberlain's/King's
Men at the first Globe is also a history of small disasters smothered. It
was not only the business acumen and artistry of the company that raised
it to supremacy; it was also the stamina of its members.

3

'THIS LUXURIOUS CIRCLE':[1] THE GLOBE THEATRE

Reconstructions of the Globe theatre have always betrayed the prejudices of their notional architects. It will be as well if I declare mine at the outset. The structure we are trying to resurrect is one in which plays were performed with a minimum of scenic and mechanical aids, in costumes whose lavishness would surprise us more than it surprised the first audiences. It is a theatre in which Lear's descent on Fortune's wheel will be visibly emphasised, not by changes of scenery, but by changes of costume. Disguise flourishes on such a stage, because it stands out, and because the audience is interested in clothes.

When James Burbage built the Theatre in 1576, he had the ambiguous precedent of the Red Lion behind him. The Red Lion project was undertaken by Burbage's brother-in-law, John Brayne, a grocer from Bucklersbury. Documents newly discovered in 1983 have corrected earlier assumptions that Brayne's Red Lion venture involved nothing more than the modest conversion of an inn-yard for occasional use by players. The Red Lion was, in fact, a farmhouse, situated outside the city walls in the village of Whitechapel, and Brayne's architectural plans, drawn up in 1567, were for a much more ambitious and specialised structure than scholars had realised. In addition to galleries surrounding the courtyard, probably on three sides, there was to be a 'Skaffolde or stage for enterludes or playes', 5 feet high and some 40 feet × 30 feet in dimension. There were specific plans for a trapdoor 'in such convenyent place of the same stage as the said John Braynes shall thynk convenyent' and a turret, 30 feet high and 'sett upon plates', presumably to stabilise it. We can further presume that the turret was secured to the scaffold, thus providing a backing unit which could serve as a dressing room and access from or onto the stage. The turret was not connected to the galleries. It was part of the stage unit. Very possibly, it was designed for easy dismantling, along with the scaffold. Two features of the Red Lion are of particular interest. The records of the lawsuit from which our information is derived contain the only known reference to the height of an Elizabethan stage, and the dimensions of that stage are astonishingly close to those of the

Globe and the Fortune, built over thirty years later. John Brayne had anticipated the needs of the emergent professional theatre with remarkable accuracy. What we do not know is whether the Red Lion was ever completed or who, if anyone, used it.

Whatever the hidden history of the Red Lion may have been, it was not so disastrous as to deter Brayne from trying again. He was James Burbage's business partner in the building of the Theatre. We may, on the assumption that the Red Lion failed, see in this new project a commercial leap in the dark, but, even without the precedent of the Red Lion, it was not an architectural breakthrough. Plays had been performed in public places for centuries. The raised stage, boards supported on barrels or trestles, was a practical refinement. It was easier to lift into visibility a small number of actors than a large number of spectators. The curtained booth at the back of that raised stage was a further refinement, extending the players' range of shifts and surprises. An amateur troupe, looking to recoup expenses, would rely on the collecting of coins from a satisfied audience; but the custom of 'bottling' is tedious and unreliable. Spectators can evade a bottler by drifting off. The enclosed space of an inn-yard had commercial advantages for both the players and the publican. Guildhalls or any available indoor space facilitated the move towards charging for admission. The popular pleasure in watching animals kill each other had also an influence on the development of the playhouse. Twenty people could stand around a yard to watch cocks fighting, but of two hundred the majority would see little more than the back of a human neck. The tiered auditoria of the cockpits were a practical response. Bear- and bull-baiting required more room and greater safety precautions. Between 1546 and 1576 there were six baiting rings, most of them short-lived, on the Bankside. They pointed the way towards the establishment of such an ambitious, specialist structure as the Theatre, without themselves suiting Burbage's purpose.[2] It is probable that Burbage, as a hard-headed but not particularly wealthy man, would have settled for the leasing and converting of an existing structure had such a structure been available. The fact that he and John Brayne risked up to £683 on building their playhouse invites us to be cautious in applying too readily the arguments that the 'typical Elizabethan playhouse' – if such a thing can be clearly seen to have existed – was *like* an inn-yard, or *like* a baiting arena. On the other hand, we should be cautious about assuming that Burbage had the nerve to erect a building suitable for the staging of plays and for nothing else. It is more after the style of a bad grocer than a thrifty master-carpenter to put all his eggs into one basket. The likelihood is that, when he built the Theatre, Burbage gave it a stage that could be removed. There would have been precious little point in fixing it permanently, and no precedent either. The wiser innovations would have been in the provision of facilities for the audience, ensuring both their comfort and an efficient way of collecting their money, and of 'back-stage' space for dressing, for storage, and for the effective preparation of all kinds of entertainment.

The Theatre probably had three galleries, surrounding an open yard. Its basic frame may have looked 'round', but was almost certainly polygonal. Practical carpentry, given the implausibility of circular timbers and round trees, would have demanded as much. Richard Hosley, taking his starting-point in building rather than in architecture, proposes 'a large number of sides such as sixteen, eighteen, twenty, or twenty-four'.[3] Remembering the comparative ease with which the Theatre was dismantled in 1598–9, Herbert Berry makes the sensible suggestion that many of the main members of the frame were held together 'not in the usual way, with neatly fitted joints, mortices, tenons, and dowels, but with ironmongery which could be easily unscrewed or bolted.'[4] As the original lease makes clear, Burbage thought of his new building as something closer to a tent than to a castle. He was empowered to 'take down and Carrie awaie ... all such buildings and other thinges as should be builded erected or sett vpp.' The fact that the timbers of the Theatre were incorporated in the Globe has tempted Irwin Smith and Richard Hosley to the assertion that the basic frame of the Theatre and the Globe 'must have been, piece-for-piece and timber-for-timber, the same'.[5] Since it is based on carpentry rather than sentiment, the argument is appealing, but it assumes that almost all the original timbers were immediately redeployed, and that can only be a guess. The Burbages later talked of 'usinge and Disposinge of the woodde and tymber of the saide Playe house'. It is quite as feasible that few of the timbers were found suitable for the Globe as that most of them were.

The frame of the Theatre is of less immediate interest than its stage. We can safely assume that it was a simple platform, probably on trestles, backed by a tiring house that stood against the frame but separate from it. When Henslowe planned his adaptable Hope thirty-seven years later, he instructed the builders to provide a 'fitt and convenient Tyre house and a stage to be carryed or taken awaie, and to stande uppon tressells'. There is no evidence and not much likelihood that there was a roof over the Theatre's stage, though Burbage might have added one early in 1592, when building and repairs cost him £30 or £40. Henslowe was paying for extensive work at the Rose at exactly the same time, so that there is a strong possibility of theatrical competition along the lines of 'anything you can do I can do better.' The idea of a free-standing stage, complete with dressing rooms, plonked at one end of an arena has appealed to few scholars before Glynne Wickham; but it makes excellent sense if that arena is to be genuinely adaptable. Clear the stage and tiring house, and the audience can fill the complete circle of the galleries to look down on the popular displays of fencing or, with adequate safety precautions, animal-baiting. Access from the simple tiring house to the stage would be through either of the two doors which seem to have been a common feature of

Elizabethan stages. The basis is the booth stage, and Burbage would have added few refinements. There was, in 1576, no great store of plays, and those that existed were not written for technically complex performance.

Between 1576 and 1599, there were significant developments, not the least of them the building of the Rose in 1587 and the Swan in 1595. The first thing to notice about the Rose is its location. Henslowe chose to build it near his home in the old borough of Southwark. Although the City of London had assumed formal jurisdiction of Southwark in 1550, the citizens on the Surrey side of the Thames continued to display a defiance of metropolitan authority that had its origin in the notorious lawlessness of Southwark's earlier history. Furthermore, the Bankside was largely partitioned into 'liberties' and 'manors', areas previously or currently in the possession of a Lord and therefore outside London's direct jurisdiction. The Rose was built in the Liberty of the Clink, among the lines of fashionable and not-so-fashionable brothels that increased the Bankside's drawing power. The very name 'rose' was a street euphemism for a prostitute, and it is very probable that Henslowe augmented his playhouse profits by retaining the old Rose brothel as well. There was no shortage of distinguished company in the business. The first Lord Hunsdon, cousin to Elizabeth I and, as Lord Chamberlain, soon to become patron of Shakespeare's company of players, was enriched by the brothel trade in the Paris Garden Manor, of which he was Lord. But this is not to imply that the Rose was a squalid structure. On the contrary, it was considered 'magnificent' by Johannes de Witt in 1596, and there is every indication that Henslowe intended it to look lavish. Most probably, its stucco was given a green, mock-marble finish, designed to be as eye-catching as possible. But it is the inside of the Rose that has been brought into new prominence by the excavations of the site in 1989, and it is to the new discoveries made then that we should pay particular attention.

The unearthing of the Rose's foundations has provided our first visible evidence of the shape, structure and dimensions of an Elizabethan theatre. Further excavations on the nearby site of the Globe are in prospect, although it appears that only a very small portion of the foundations of Shakespeare's theatre will be available for scrutiny. The Rose discoveries, then, are of the utmost importance; but there is a need for caution in assessing them. We must not, for example, assume that all Elizabethan theatres were the same. Available evidence suggests that Henslowe and his partner Cholmley invested in the original building only about half as much as Burbage and Brayne had invested in the Theatre a decade earlier, and it may be that their thrift is a sufficient explanation of the unexpected smallness of the Rose. John Orrell's detailed work on the Globe has led him to the belief that that theatre had a diameter of about 100 feet and its inner yard a diameter of 70 feet, a figure not supported by the findings of the 1989 Globe excavations.[6] The Rose, by contrast, has an inner diameter of about 66 feet and its inner yard a diameter of about 49 feet. Inevitably, the stage is proportionately smaller than that of the later Fortune and, by inference, the Globe, on which the Fortune stage was modelled. But, if the surviving substructure of the Rose stage can be relied on as evidence, there are two features that are more surprising. Firstly, the platform tapered from back to front, so that its upstage width of about 37 feet may have dwindled to 27 feet at the front; and secondly, it was only about 17 feet deep, which means that it jutted only about two-fifths of the way into the yard rather than to the middle, as was specified in the Fortune contract. This proposes a rather different actor–audience relationship, with the actors in flatter lines playing *in front of* a greater proportion of the audience than has been generally assumed in recent years. It could well be argued that such an arrangement suited the rhetorical style of Edward Alleyn, leading actor of the Admiral's Men at the Rose, better than it would have suited Shakespeare's more robust colleague, Richard Burbage. It is certainly of significance that, when Henslowe ordered major alterations to the Rose in 1592, the stage dimensions remained much the same.

It is probable that the 1592 alterations were largely dictated by a determination to increase the capacity of the galleries. It seems likely that the original Rose had a free-standing 'turret' of the same kind as the Red Lion had housed. Possibly, in 1592, when he had the stage moved backwards, Henslowe dispensed with the turret, reconstructing the tiring house within the existing galleries. With the turret removed, the sight-lines of spectators in galleries behind the stage would no longer be obstructed. Again, there are implications for the actor–audience relationship. It has long been argued, though never proved, that there was a 'Lord's Room (or Rooms)' over and behind the stage, set aside for those privileged spectators who were as happy to be seen as to see. The forward impetus of actors on a thrust stage would have had to be tempered by an awareness of the audience behind, and account has to be taken of the possibility that Elizabethan performance was always 'in the round'. I do not believe that stage grouping would have been radically affected by this, though the individual actor would have been at liberty, and perhaps expected, to address those in the Lord's Room on occasion.

One thing is confirmed by the foundations of the Rose. The building was polygonal, probably fourteen-sided, with each 'side' about 15 feet long. But if speculation on that issue can now be put to rest, the discovery that the front half of the yard sloped down towards the stage is utterly unexpected. In terms of sight-lines, this raking makes excellent sense, of course, as it may also in terms of drainage in a playhouse exposed to the weather. But if the Rose, built in 1587, exhibited such concern for the groundlings standing in the back half of the yard, could the Globe and the Fortune have afforded to disregard them? It is evident from the famous drawing of the Swan – misleadingly known as the de Witt drawing – that there was no rake in that playhouse. The words 'planities sive arena' (flatness or arena) are clearly written along the empty space of the yard. We may conclude that the Swan, unlike the Rose, Globe and Fortune, was designed to house spectacles other than plays, or we may conclude that the raked yard of the Rose was an eccentricity which proved mysteriously unattractive. Speculation on this issue is in its infancy.

Before the Rose excavations, by far the most important surviving visual record of the interior of an Elizabethan theatre was a sketch of the Swan. This playhouse, built in 1595, was a first theatrical venture by the successful goldsmith, Francis Langley. A Dutch visitor to London, Johannes de Witt, found London's four theatres 'of notable beauty' when he visited them in 1596, but 'Of all the theatres . . . the largest and most distinguished is that of which the sign is a swan'. He made a sketch of it from a vantage-point in an upper gallery, and the sketch was copied by his friend Arend Van Buchell. It is that copy that has survived, and its ambiguous evidence can never be discounted. The Burbages would have looked at the Swan's example in building the Globe as surely as Henslowe looked to the example of the Globe in building the Fortune. Before turning to those features which the sketch makes clear, let us consider one which remains uncertain. If the tiring house of the Swan was built into the frame, de Witt has drawn it badly (or Van Buchell has copied it badly). It is true that my holiday sketch of the Sydney Opera House, adorning a letter to a friend in England and copied by him for the attention of somebody else, would be a flimsy source for a reconstruction of the stage and auditorium four centuries from now, and we do well to bear that caution in mind. Even so, the de Witt sketch is enough to make us wonder whether the Swan's stage and tiring house formed a separate unit, set inside a polygonal frame, after the fashion of the Red Lion. Plays had sufficiently proved their attractiveness by 1595 to justify the building of a public arena devoted solely to their presentation, but Langley might well have preferred to hedge his bets. The Elizabethans built their theatres to suit needs that were not already *known* but were being discovered through practice. The Globe was almost as much a present excitement as the plays it housed. It is likely that it marked an advance on the Swan in much the same degree as the Swan marked an advance on the Rose.

All serious attempts to reconstruct the Globe have been based primarily on the de Witt sketch of the Swan, and the findings at the Rose, however fascinating in themselves, seem unlikely to change that. Internal evidence from the Globe plays and inferences drawn from the Fortune contract may modify our conclusions, but anything that contradicts or flouts de Witt invites our question. (Those who argue for the existence and extensive use of an inner stage – and some still do, though with a weakening voice – will find no support in de Witt.) What he saw was a curved building, close enough to being circular to encourage him to indicate lightly its complete circumference. The three galleries are clearly drawn, with entrances on either side of the stage. There would have been door-keepers to gather pennies at these if they were the 'ingressus' to the galleries, a probability not contradicted by their possible use in reverse by actors as an 'ingressus' to the yard.[7] The galleries are variously titled. A plausible interpretation sees the top one, marked 'porticus', as a walkway, perhaps with standing room only, but used more disreputably as a place of assignation for gallants, apprentices, prostitutes, or country wives. The middle gallery is distinctly a seating area, 'sedilia' allowing of no other interpretation, whilst de Witt has exploited his knowledge of the Roman theatre in describing the lowest gallery as an 'orchestra'.[8] The orchestra of the Roman theatres was left empty unless distinguished spectators were in attendance. It is not easy to know what to make of de Witt's use of the word. The section of the gallery on which he writes it would be fine for those who came to be seen, inadequate for those who came to see. Audibility would be a major problem only if the actors were standing on the opposite side of the stage and speaking away, and there would always be some sense of intimate contact with the stage. But if the whole bottom gallery is being described by de Witt as the 'orchestra', some questions are raised. If the groundlings gathered in front of the stage, would they not impede the view for some of the occupants of the bottom gallery? Or was the gallery raised well above ground level? Or was de Witt writing in ignorance, having himself watched a performance from the upper gallery and sketched the theatre from the same vantage-point? Or is there an explanation in the claim that the Swan was essentially an aural theatre rather than a visual one?[9] From the point of view of the actors, the remotest section of the whole audience would have been those facing the stage in the bottom gallery. The conclusion has to be that we do not know which would have been considered the prime seats by an Elizabethan theatregoer, and that de Witt does not really help us to find out. His claim that the Swan had seating accommodation for 3,000 must be, however understandably, an exaggeration. It suggests that, where certainty was out of reach, he was prepared to approximate – a further cause for prudence in the assessing of the evidence provided by his drawing.

Two further features of de Witt's sketch will repay brief consideration before we turn to the stage itself. The first is the description of the yard as 'planities sive arena'. Familiar with the terraced seating of the Roman theatres, de Witt was obviously struck by the level ground in front of and around the stage. He describes it simply as 'flatness' (*planities*). But he evidently found the single word inadequate, and added the alternative 'arena'. *Planities* is a neutral word, without theatrical reference in the Roman world, whereas *arena* is associated with the most violent and the most acrobatic of Roman entertainments. There is just a hint in the pairing of the two words that the flatness of the yard was, during de Witt's visit, used by the actors as well as by the spectators. We do not know that the yard was ever used during the performances, but the possibility that it was is strong. The temptation, particularly during the high jinks of the post-play jig, must have been hard to resist. A standing audience is easily moved and readily re-grouped round an outstanding focus of activity. The second, and more insistent, feature of the drawing is the human figures it reproduces. There are three actors, but no audience. Is it a rehearsal? Perhaps, but there is a man in the roof-top hut, blowing a trumpet to announce the imminence of a performance. The sketch is too general to be a depiction of anything so particular as the last-minute rush to perfect a tricky scene. And what of the row of people in the gallery above the stage doors? Are they musicians? Or are they the privileged spectators for whom the Lord's Room is reserved? We have to conclude that the sketch is a composite of impressions, recording some of the memorable elements of an occasion that excited de Witt's intelligence. The human figures help to establish a sense of scale, but they tell us nothing very certain. Yet no study of Elizabethan acting can afford to neglect the placing and the gesture of this oddly contrasting trio of players. What the sketch boldly presents to us is a platform thrusting out into the yard. It is big. We know that the Fortune stage was 43 feet wide, and that it thrust out about 27 feet 'to the middle of the yarde'. The stage dimensions of both the Swan and the Globe were similar. Timid acting has no chance in such a setting. The Elizabethan actor, if he was to be effective, must have determined to dominate both the platform and the surrounding audience. Nor is it simply a matter of underfoot dimensions. Acting in the open air reduces the apparent size of an actor as surely as a low ceiling increases it. It is not a setting for inward acting. Passion cannot be contained. It has to be shown.

There remain for consideration the outstanding features of the Swan stage as de Witt reveals them. The first three are negatives. There is no concealment of the understage area. It seems unlikely that this was normal practice. A tipsy apprentice could have caused quite a disturbance by getting underneath and acting the mole – something which the ghost of old Hamlet presumably did at the Globe. However the Swan stage was supported, and de Witt's props are remarkably crude, the probability is that some attempt was made to mask it. There is, secondly, no sign whatsoever of a trap-door in the platform. That may simply be an oversight. De Witt may have seen a performance in which there was no call for a trap. He has, anyway, not concerned himself with the surface of the stage. The third negative, the absence of an inner stage or, indeed, of any discovery space at all, is less ambiguous. The inner stage is an invention of later scholars, who could envisage drama in performance only if it had a proscenium arch to frame it. There is no evidence at all of the existence of an acting space between and behind the stage doors. Nor should we expect any. Elizabethan actors came out on to the platform to present their story. They would have been defying convention and the common sense of visibility and audibility if they had retreated behind it, carrying the story with them.

De Witt gives us only two wooden double-doors, with heavy hinges that clearly indicate that the doors opened outwards on to the stage. The lack of curtains or drapes of any kind is not decisive. We would not expect these to be permanent, but neither would they be difficult to set if and when required. The doors, set square into the tiring house facade, provide the actors with a strong upstage entrance, and with a lot of ground to cover before they reach a commanding speaking position. The move downstage into contact with the full audience is not made easier by the surprisingly bulky Corinthian columns, standing perhaps 12 feet from the tiring house. They are there to satisfy the demands of a theatre more technically advanced than James Burbage could have anticipated in 1576. The canopy they support, often supposed to have been decorated with symbolic representations of heavenly bodies from which it derived the shorthand name of 'Heavens', was roomy enough to accommodate a throne and any actor who was required to 'fly' down to the platform. Suspension gear for these 'flyings' was probably housed in the hut behind de Witt's trumpeter. The evidence for this is not, of course, in the drawing; but we know that, before the Swan was built, Henslowe had paid £7–2s for 'mackinge the throne in the hevenes' at the Rose. Langley would not have allowed his proud theatre to drop behind the times. By the time Jonson wrote his prologue for the 1612 revival of *Every Man in His Humour*, boasting that this was to be a play:

> Where neither Chorus wafts you o'er the seas,
> Nor creaking throne comes down, the boys to please ...

the elaborate Heavens, throne and flying-effects were commonplace. Elizabethan theatre companies had a professional ability to make virtue of necessity, and the stage pillars were habitually incorporated in the action. Even so, it is difficult to deny that performance would have been easier without them. It is something of a relief to find Henslowe instructing the builder of the Hope to 'builde the Heavens all over the saide stage, to be borne or carryed without any postes or supporters to be fixed or settvpon the saide stage'. It was the essential purpose of the canopy to protect the actors from rain, and to provide mechanical effects. The science of timber roofing in Tudor England was sufficiently advanced for the roofing of the stage at the Swan or the Globe to have been contrived without supporting pillars. The problem was one of cost. Henslowe could afford it in 1613. C. Walter Hodges has argued fascinatingly that the Burbages also could afford it when they rebuilt the Globe in 1614.[10] But Langley may not have thought of it in 1595, and the Chamberlain's Men had insufficient resources in 1599. The pillars, then, were a feature of the later Elizabethan public theatres – but no one liked them enough to erect unnecessary imitations on the indoor stages.

We come, finally, to the gallery above the stage doors. De Witt depicts it in six sections and filled with people. Seen in isolation from its surroundings, the tiring house facade with its two doors and superior gallery is irresistibly reminiscent of the halls in great Tudor houses and palaces, or of Oxbridge refectories, and these were, of course, familiar venues for touring actors. The similarity adds weight to the view that this gallery was primarily intended for musicians. The only surviving play that was certainly performed at the Swan, Middleton's *A Chaste Maid in Cheapside*, calls for 'a sad song in the Musicke-Room'. Against that, we have seen Jonson referring to the Lord's Room 'over the stage' at the Globe. The probability is that the gallery served both purposes, and that it was available for actors appearing 'above' as well.

However impressionistic it was, de Witt's drawing gives us a strong feel for the varied style of Elizabethan performance. Downstage centre is a piece of substantial stage furniture, a bench much plainer than the richly gowned actor sitting on it. Behind and just far enough to the right of the seated actor to be visible to most of the audience is a 'lady'. Her gesture is formal and balanced. The third figure, extravagantly bearded and within poking distance of the groundlings, could be about to do the splits. It is a characteristically Elizabethan conjunction of the stately and the grotesque. Behind the actors, the stage doors are shut, indicating, perhaps, that an indoor scene is in progress. When one of the stage doors opens, anything could happen.

Because of the chance survival of de Witt's sketch we have invaluable external evidence of the facilities at the Swan, but we have only one play to give dramatic life to that evidence. The position at the Globe is exactly reversed. We have no really valuable external evidence, but several plays from which to draw conclusions. Stage directions, either explicit or implicit, reveal a certain amount, but we must be prepared, in reaching for certainty, often to settle for probability. Some of the characteristic features of performance on the Swan/Globe stage can be explored, in an atmosphere of reduced critical anxiety, in some of the non-Shakespearean plays that were presented at the Globe by the Chamberlain's Men.

ENTRANCES AND EXITS

Most exits in Elizabethan drama are announced in words before they are carried through in action. A selection from *Volpone* makes the point no better than any other selection would:

> I will go see her, though but at her window. (I.v.127)
> Lead, I follow thee. (III.ii.70)
> Patron, go in, and pray for our success. (III.ix.62)
> Will you go, madam? (IV.iii.17)

There is nothing surprising about this. An unobtrusive exit from an open stage is almost a contradiction, and there was no conventional equivalent for the device of dropping a curtain on a conversation that can be supposed to continue in the same place after the audience has ceased to listen. In order to enable the actor to make the turn and take the steps towards the stage door, the dramatist usually provided him with a cue to leave. A concluding couplet was an aural equivalent.

The entrance on to the platform in mid-scene is almost always prepared for, too. The shocking arrival or the untimely return, dear to the writers of farce and melodrama, were not part of the Elizabethan dramatist's stock-in-trade. Bonario's interruption of the attempted rape of Celia by Volpone may surprise Volpone, but the audience has already learned that Bonario is in the house. And how differently a nineteenth-century dramatist might have treated the ghosts of old Hamlet and Banquo, or Sebastian's sudden incarnation in Illyria and Orlando's violation of Duke Senior's feast. The sudden bursting open of the stage door at the Globe to reveal, with the accompaniment of a triumphant or menacing drum-beat, the hero or the villain is notably absent. A later taste would have preferred to *see* the scene of Cordelia's death in *King Lear*, probably with the arrival in the nick of time of the saving message from Edmund. Tragic time, of course, has no nick, but the interesting fact would seem to be that the stage doors did not invite this kind of dramatic thrill. It is not a matter of superior dramatists refusing to stoop to low tricks. Elizabethan dramatists would have tried anything. The lack of such entrances is strong presumptive evidence that the positioning of the stage doors discouraged them. The doors were too far upstage, too remote from the focus of attention, and too distant for easy audibility. (Lingering adherents of the 'inner stage' might note that it would have been worse still in each respect, had it existed.) It is precisely because the audience is attending to the action downstage that the upstage entrances have to be prepared for. Mosca always announces Volpone's visitors, not only to give Volpone time to prepare himself, but also to give the audience the signal. If an actor has a good entrance, he does not want any of his audience to miss it.

Since there was no way of pre-setting a scene, all Elizabethan plays began with an entrance. The roof-top trumpet and the traditional knocking of the stage were attempts to settle the audience into preparedness for that first entrance. Even so, actors probably liked a prologue to do more of the work for them. Volpone's opening lines are too important to be risked.

Jonson provides a prologue to involve the audience and stir it up. It was said of Sir Henry Irving, during his occupation of the Lyceum at the end of the nineteenth century, that he would never stage a play that gave him the opening scene. He liked a build-up. Elizabethan actors were less self-protective, their art less removed from the world of their audience. Even so, Burbage (if it was he) would have been glad of an attentive house for the first lines of *Volpone*. This is not, of course, a 'typical' entrance. Volpone's passage downstage is conditioned by the placing of the enclosure containing his gold. We know from a later stage direction, 'Volpone peeps from behind a traverse' (V.iii.8), that curtains were used in this play. A traverse is the likeliest concealment for the gold, too. When we read the opening two lines of *Volpone*:

> Good morning to the day; and next, my gold!
> Open the shrine, that I may see my saint.

we have to picture the entrance, through the same stage door of Volpone and Mosca, their immediate moving apart, Mosca to the traverse, Volpone to a point that will give him a view of his money without blocking the audience's, the opening line spoken out only after Volpone has walked at least 20 feet downstage,[11] and a silent turn in contemplation before the subsequent outburst into blasphemous apostrophe.

The primary aim of Elizabethan staging was to maximise the presence of the actor. To allow him the diminution of a dragging exit or an unannounced and unobtrusive entrance would be to threaten his presence. The 'ability of body', which was the actor's pride and the playwright's resource, could not be so carelessly treated.

STAGE DOORS

Elizabethan plays are written in scenes. Act divisions are often editorial afterthoughts, and rarely if ever essential to the shaping of the story. Because so many of the scenes are short, and because the flow of the action is therefore dependent on the smoothness of entrances and exits, stagecraft was dominated by the need to maintain access to and from the stage doors. After analysing 276 plays from the period 1599–1642, T. J. King concluded that 'playwrights of the period thought of the stage as having two entrances'.[12] There is nothing in the surviving Globe plays that demands a third door, though resourceful actors would have made good use of any touring venue that provided three. That *some* explicit use of the doors occurs in these plays is less surprising than that *so little* explicit use occurs. I have already suggested that this was a result of their remoteness from the centre of attention. That they were conventionally used for simultaneous entries by characters about to meet is sugggested by common sense, and also by such stage directions as this from Marston's *The*

Malcontent: 'Enter Malevole at one door; Biancha, Emilia, and Maquerelle at the other door.'[13] Slightly more adventurous theatrically is the use implied in the dispute between Mosca and Lady Politic Would-Be in *Volpone*. The Lady is determined to see Volpone, Mosca equally determined that she shall not:

> LADY: No, I'll go see your patron.
> MOSCA: That you shall not:
> I'll tell you why. My purpose is, to urge
> My patron to reform his will ...
>
> (IV.vi.95–7)

Implicit in the dialogue here is the urge of one actor towards one stage door, and the stronger pull of the second actor towards the other stage door. Such confrontation of alternative exit routes is a common feature in scene-closes in Elizabethan drama. But there are livelier possibilities. Jonson, typically, is alert to them. A wonderfully inventive scene in the Globe play, *Every Man out of His Humour*, shows Fallace in furious dispute with her husband Deliro and with Macilente. 'I'll not bide here for all the gold and silver in Heaven,' she says, and storms out through one of the doors. 'O good Macilente, let's follow and appease her, or the peace of my life is at an end,' says Deliro, and they go out through the same door. With all the aplomb of a twentieth-century farceur, Jonson lets Fallace turn the tables on the men by immediately bursting back through that now-important door and 'locking' it. The stage direction reads: 'Re-enter Fallace running, and claps to the door.' She then shouts a warning to her husband that she will 'do myself a mischief' if he comes in, and his protests are heard from within the tiring house 'offstage'.[14] Jonson is here turning convention into reality. It is an example of his fascination with the material paraphernalia of his stage. But such direct use of the stage doors, unprotected by convention, is exceptional. Their normal neutrality is vital to the smooth conduct of a story. Whilst they may sometimes represent real doors, they may equally provide access to a seashore in Illyria or to a plain in Syria.

THE FREEDOM OF THE STAGE

From the moment when Fallace 'claps to the door', about a minute of stage time elapses before, in the words of the stage direction, 'Deliro and Macilente pass over the stage'. We do not know what precisely was meant by this frequently encountered direction. In the context of this particular scene, Allardyce Nicoll's suggestion that the actors came into the yard through one 'ingressus', climbed up on to the stage, crossed it, descended into the yard at the other side, and made their exit through the opposite 'ingressus' is attractive.[15] What the scene certainly illustrates – Professor

Nicoll's proposal is less widely accepted than the alternative view that the passing over of the stage involved nothing more than an entrance at one door and an exit at the other – is the speed with which location could be changed on the Globe platform. The space available to an actor at the Globe is roughly comparable to half of a tennis court (with the tramlines included, as in doubles play),[16] nor is that space cluttered with attempts to transform it into something resembling a quite different space. When an Elizabethan actor came out on to the platform, he came with or to other people much more often and more importantly than to a place. The characters take precedence over the location. Whatever its precise provenance, the surviving text of *A Yorkshire Tragedy* illustrates stagecraft at its most functional, even at its most perfunctory. An account of what happens over a sequence of 130 lines (lines 500–631) will show the variety of location and the rapidity of its shifts.

The unnamed Husband, having lost his fortune gambling, determines to murder his three sons to save them from beggary. 'Enters his little sonne with a top and a scourge', and with the fascinating complaint – on an open and empty stage – that 'I cannot scourge my top as long as you stand so: you take up all the room with your wide legs.' The Husband 'takes up the childe by the skirts of his long coate in one hand and drawes his dagger with th' other.' He then stabs his son to death and carries him off. His exit at one stage door is matched by an entry – probably simultaneous – at the other: 'Enter a maide with a childe in her armes, the mother by her asleepe.' Presumably the thrusting out of a mobile platform is envisaged here, since an entry asleep would be inappropriately comic otherwise. Almost at once the Husband follows them in, still carrying his bleeding elder son, kills the child-in-arms, and wounds his Wife and a Servant. The dead children and the injured adults are left lying in one section of the stage – perhaps upstage of the pillars – and the Husband moves down to address himself and the audience:

> My horse stands ready saddled. Away, away,
> Now to my brat at nurse, my sucking beggar.
> Fates, I'll not leave you one to trample on.

It is downstage of the pillars that he is met by the Master of the College attended by his younger brother. The audience must accept that he is now 'outside the house', and that the Master cannot see the carnage inside. 'Please you walk in Sir,' the Husband invites, and leads the Master out through one of the stage doors. The wounded Servant, having remained 'invisible' on stage throughout the brief Master/Husband dialogue, starts speaking as soon as the stage is clear, and the Master enters the house through the other stage door to discover the dead and wounded. Two minutes or so later, the stage is again briefly cleared, as Wife and Servant are led off to where 'a surgeon waits within', and there follows the challenging stage direction: 'Enter Husband as being thrown off his horse, and falls.' He tells the audience both what has happened and where he is:

> To throw me now within a flight o' th' Town,
> In such plain even ground, sot, a man may dice upon 't.

The entrance is remarkable, and it risks bathos, but the practice of supplying the audience with necessary information about the location is familiar. Where words are felt to be sufficient, scenic aids are superfluous.

It should be possible, after a careful study of these 130 lines from *A Yorkshire Tragedy*, to apply simple Elizabethan stagecraft to almost any scene from Shakespeare and his contemporaries. Two vital conventions are illustrated in them – the first of inaudibility, the second of invisibility. The audience accepts that actors on one part of the platform may not be heard by actors on another part of the platform, and it accepts also that actors who are visible to spectators may not be seen by other actors. If we add the convention of the impenetrability of disguise, we have the basis for intrigues quite as complex as need be.

The long opening scene of *Sejanus* is a fine example of Jonson's exploitation of the convention of inaudibility, as well as demonstrating the scope for significant groups on the open stage. Sabinus and Silius, having entered through different stage doors, establish themselves in a dominant downstage position, though not at the centre. They lead the group of disaffected patriots, commenting scathingly on Natta and Satrius, who are in unheard conversation upstage of them. When the audience is to hear what Natta and Satrius say, formal movement would permit but not necessitate a downstage travel. The passing over the stage of the Emperor's son Drusus and his retinue is another formal convention. It causes an adjustment of the on-stage groupings. When Sejanus and his sycophants also pass over the stage, it is in meaningful echo of a royal prerogative, telling us more of Sejanus's ambition than his own words do. Patterned movement of this kind on the Globe stage can carry its own significance. The entry of the Emperor Tiberius is, presumably, to the centrally positioned throne, his emblem of office. Around that throne takes place the dramatic confrontation of Drusus and Sejanus at the close of the scene. Drusus is standing near the throne when Sejanus enters 'followed with clients' to whom he distributes official documents:

SEJANUS: There is your bill, and yours; bring you your man:
        I have moved for you, too, Latiaris.
DRUSUS: What?
        Is your vast greatness grown so blindly, bold,
        That you will over us?
SEJANUS: Why, then give way.

DRUSUS: Give way, Colossus? Do you lift? Advance you?
Take that. (*Drusus strikes him.*)

(I.i.560–5)

At a theatrical level, it is a fight for the centre of the stage. The competing clusters of friends and enemies have been able, throughout the scene, to conduct their conversations confident of their inaudibility, despite their on-stage proximity. Towards the end of the scene, battle is joined, and joined audibly.

The convention of invisibility is so frequently employed in Elizabethan drama that it scarcely needs illustration. Its acceptance by the audience does not preclude concealment if there was dramatic advantage to be taken of it, but it removes its necessity. The eavesdropping Duke of *Measure for Measure* need not hide from the audience in order to be unseen by Claudio and Isabella in III.i., nor *need* Claudius and Polonius 'bestow' themselves out of our sight when they witness Ophelia's encounter with Hamlet in III.i. They have the freedom either to leave the stage altogether, to take shelter beside a pillar or behind a curtain, or to remain in view. An actor is invisible to other actors if he says he is.

DISCOVERY SPACES AND STAGE FURNITURE

To say that the Globe stage did not provide hiding places for every fugitive from sight is not to say that it never did. The Chamberlain's Men were a pragmatic group, with a willing eye for a good effect and no reason to be slaves to convention. If the store contained a property box-tree, that would be a reason for Shakespeare's choosing to conceal Sir Toby Belch, Sir Andrew Aguecheek, and Fabian in a box-tree. Or perhaps an all-purpose shrubbery 'ground-row' could be used for *Twelfth Night* as well as for *The Merry Devil of Edmonton*, where Young Clare instructs the escaping Millicent to 'Shadow yourself behind this brake of fern.' A few strokes of Richard Burbage's brush could have turned a box-tree into a fernbrake. The list of properties compiled by Henslowe in 1598 suggests that the Admiral's Men at least were not so restrictive. He mentions a bay tree, a tree of golden apples, a Tantalus tree, and two moss banks.[17] Butler, whose creation is the brightest achievement of George Wilkins's *The Miseries of Enforced Marriage*, is required to ascend a tree at the beginning of Act Four. He may, of course, have used one of the stage pillars, but a free-standing climbable tree was not beyond the ingenuity of the Chamberlain's Men. They had also in their repertoire *A Warning for Fair Women* (1598 or 1599), one of whose Dumb Shows calls for the sudden rising up and the abrupt chopping down of a great tree – an image of the rise and fall of Sanders. Certain large properties had always to be available. The throne is the outstanding one. We know, from both

Henslowe and Ben Jonson, that a mechanism installed in the Heavens could raise and lower this vital piece of furniture on demand. It may be that the throne was the only flyable property in the Globe. It was something more than an ornate chair. Glynne Wickham has described it as 'an open pavilion containing a chair mounted on a dais and capped with the invariable cloth of estate'.[18] It must have commanded the centre of the stage, creating a pecking order of downstage activity, and denying much upstage activity. Volpone's bed, or Desdemona's, would command a similar centrality. But a bed is not a flying piece. It would be brought on to the Globe stage on the kind of moveable platform we have already seen deployed in *A Yorkshire Tragedy*. The Greeks had a similar piece of equipment, so that it is misapplied primitivism that denies to the Elizabethans the necessary mechanical know-how. The building of stage 'mansions', for instance, was a skill inherited from mediaeval performers. Noah builds his ark in full view of the spectators in a Mystery Cycle. Volpone's entourage constructs for him a mountebank's scaffold with equal economy and confidence. It may well be that Cleopatra's monument, still a staging mystery despite countless attempts at scholarly reconstruction, was constructed on stage with the same craftsmanlike efficiency.

The enclosure, or discovery-space, translated by the proscenium-arch generations into an 'inner stage', was an available feature of the Globe stage; but it is required in only nine of the surviving twenty-nine Globe plays – more specifically in sixteen out of 519 scenes.[19] A technical competence that can thrust out a mobile platform on demand can certainly provide a study for Peter Fabel in *The Merry Devil of Edmonton* or for Horace in *Satiromastix*, and a vault for Volpone's gold. The stage doors were probably 7 or 8 feet wide. To anyone who has worked in the often cramped conditions of the twentieth-century theatre, such room for manoeuvre is a luxury. Swift and easy access for stage-hands – together with an audience's recognition and acceptance of their work as part of the process of performance – makes simple the construction on the open stage of battlefield tents, for example. And traverse curtains were always in stock, to be draped across the stage doors, on the mobile platforms, or even slung between the pillars for climactic scenes such as the masque of *The Revenger's Tragedy*, or the play-within-the-play in *Hamlet*. We should be cautious about the idea, generally proposed by scholars whose reluctance to abandon the inner stage is undeclared, that a wide-open stage door might serve as a discovery-space, or even a tent. To play a scene of any kind, or even to make a significant disclosure, behind the platform would have run counter to the natural inclination of the Globe actors to bring all action out into the open.

It is a mistake, when trying to reconstruct performance conditions at the Globe, to presuppose that the Chamberlain's Men had fixed methods of production, which they applied unvaryingly. Professional craftsmen

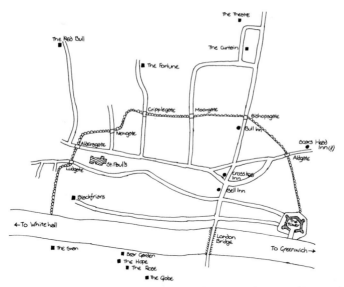

1 The walled city of London and its theatres, from 1576 (the Theatre) to 1613 (the Hope). It is less than one mile and a half from the Tower to Ludgate, and three-quarters of a mile from London Bridge to Bishopsgate *(Drawing by Kate Thomson)*

2 Southwark Bridge and the south bank of the Thames *(Photograph reproduced by permission of Aerofilms Ltd)*

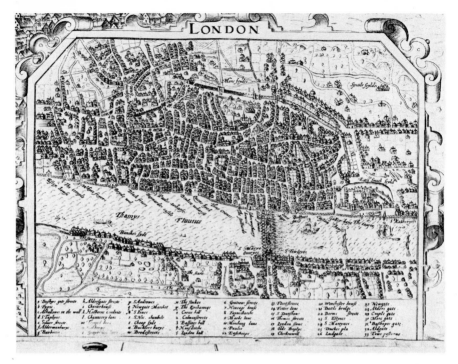

3a Norden's 1600 revision of his Civitas Londini map. It gives a vivid impression of a busy waterfront, and some indication of the sprawl of Southwark *(Royal Library Stockholm)*

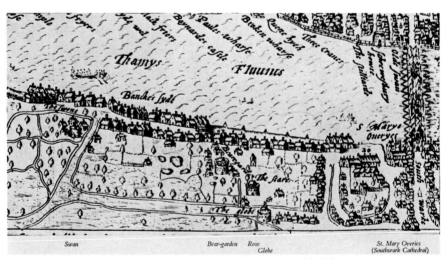

3b Section of the Norden Civitas Londini map *(Royal Library, Stockholm)*

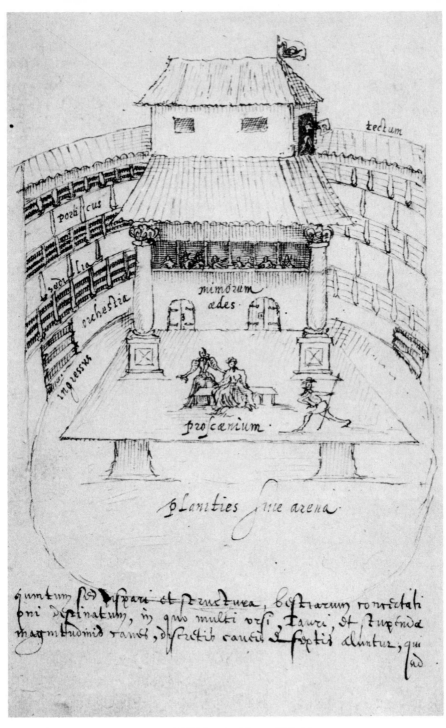

4 De Witt's drawing of the Swan, *c.* 1596 (*University Library, Utrecht*)

5 Detail from a model of the Swan (after de Witt). 'If the groundlings gathered in front of the stage, would they not impede the view for some of the occupants of the bottom gallery?' (p. 39) *(Model built by Jenny Bell and Tony Addicott at the University of Exeter)*

6 View of the yard and stage from the same model. 'Timid acting has no chance in such a setting' (p. 41)

7 Air view of the same model, showing the Heavens, 'roomy enough to accommodate a throne and any actor who was required to 'fly' down to the platform' (p. 41)

8 The height of this mountebank stage is typical (the drawing dates from about 1600). So is the simplicity of its construction. Volpone's would not have been so high, but well might have been as substantial (*British Museum*)

9 Detail from the Sir Henry Unton Memorial picture, showing a broken consort playing at his wedding masque. Unton was a friend of the Earl of Essex. The picture is an assembly of scenes from his life (*National Portrait Gallery*)

10 The hall screen at the Middle Temple, in front of which *Twelfth Night* was played in February 1602. The demands and the possibilities of the stage doors are very clear

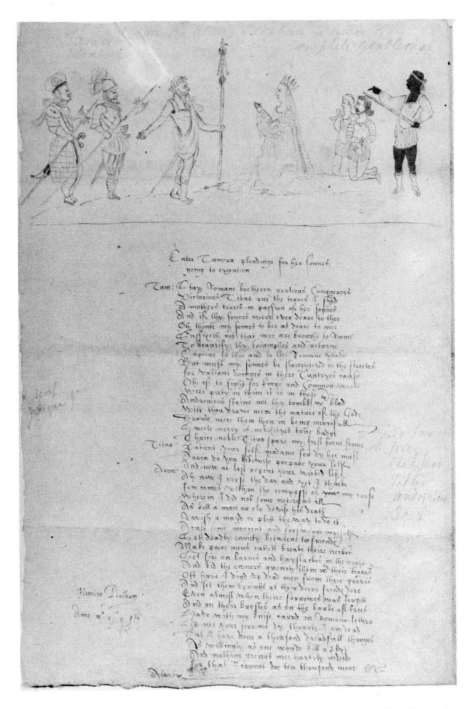

11 A scene from *Titus Andronicus*, probably drawn by Henry Peacham in 1594 or 1595. The drawing, and the lines of verse beneath it, has survived in a single folded sheet, and is in the library of the Marquess of Bath (*courtesy of the Marquess of Bath*)

12 Drawing illustrating the technique of changing rapiers, from Henri de Saint-Didier's treatise on sword-play (1573) (*British Museum*)

13 Woodcut from the pamphlet, *The Wonderful Discoverie of the Witchcrafts of Margaret and Philippa Flower*, 1619. It is not so far from Banquo's description of the Witches in *Macbeth* (*British Museum*)

have always a favoured system, and also the ability to adapt. For a company so familiar with the demands of touring, adaptability was an essential. It is equally true that the practical playwrights of the period would not present them with texts whose requirements were beyond them. Compared with the mechanical wonders of the court masques of Inigo Jones, or with the spectacular nineteenth-century stage, Globe performances were simple. But we should not suppose that they were unadventurous. How else can we explain the demand, from that most professional of contemporary playwrights Thomas Heywood, that Hercules should enter 'from a rock above tearing down trees'? *The Brazen Age*, in which this direction occurs, was written for Queen Anne's Men, playing probably at the not very reputable Red Bull, and probably in 1613, but it would be surprising if the King's Men could not by then, have matched the effect at the Globe, and presumptuous to claim to know just how they would have done it.

BELOW AND ABOVE

The space under de Witt's Swan stage is generous enough to allow for the effective use of a trap-door. The Globe probably had one, but, if so, used it sparingly. Bernard Beckerman, who confidently asserts the existence of a downstage trap, has found only seven instances of its use in the extant Globe plays, four of them in *The Devil's Charter*.[20] And, whilst an available trap would have been useful in each of his instances, it would be a denial of theatrical resourcefulness to call it necessary. *Hamlet* provides the best-known case, but once the practicality of mobile platforms has been recognised, it has to be said that the grave-diggers and even Hamlet himself, *can* function without a sunken grave. Nor can the stage direction for *Macbeth* IV.i., informing the reader that each apparition 'descends', be confidently used as evidence. *Macbeth* was not published until 1623, by which time performance practice at the indoor Blackfriars had had its effect. That there was practical space below the stage is certainly implied by the activity of the Ghost in *Hamlet* I.v. After the first 'Swear' (l.149), Hamlet refers to 'this fellow in the cellarage', and guides Horatio and Marcellus to another part of the platform. After the second 'Swear' (l.155), he moves them again, this time, according to the dictates of formal logic, into closer proximity with the audience. The understage actor moves to the prearranged spot, and, for the third time, urges those immediately above him to 'Swear' (l.161). 'Well said, old mole! canst work i' the earth so fast?' comments Hamlet, at once establishing the nervous jocularity of his relationship with the Ghost and congratulating the Chamberlain's Men on a resourceful piece of stage business. The 'Music of hautboys under the stage' in *Antony and Cleopatra* (IV.iii.11) is less conclusive. The probability that the understage area was practical does not mean that it was pleasant. The *Hamlet* scene is an isolated example of its significant use, something which may argue a reluctance on the part of the actors to soil their costumes. Playing an oboe down there sounds like a musician's nightmare.

No such doubt surrounds the existence of a practical upper level at the Globe. There are instances where a raised unit constructed on stage seems to be implied, but the gallery above the stage doors is the likeliest regular resource. Celia could certainly appear here to throw down her handkerchief to Volpone in his mountebank disguise (II.ii.222). But the view from the third gallery would be poor, and audibility a problem throughout the theatre. The conclusion must be that the gallery in the tiring-house facade was ideal for the accommodation of a silent observer, but inadequate in every respect for any scene of prolonged dialogue. Beckerman has found only twelve scenes in the Globe plays that require the use of the 'above', much the most complex being scene ten of *The Miseries of Enforced Marriage*.[21] This is, in fact, an untidy piece of writing, showing evidence of hasty plotting and a bludgeoning of the audience into accepting shifts of focus. The outstanding special case is *Antony and Cleopatra* IV.xiii. It begins with the entry 'aloft' of Cleopatra, Charmian, and Iras, includes the stage direction 'They heave Anthony aloft to Cleopatra' (l.37), and contains the important last conversation of Cleopatra and the dying Antony. The mechanics of this scene invite, and have received, speculation in abundance. To take a recent example, Richard Hosley has suggested the use of suspension gear to raise Antony, seated on a chair, to the gallery over the stage. He calculates that the suspension line from the Heavens would have passed within 3 to 4 feet of the tiring-house facade, enabling Cleopatra or her maids to haul Antony in without difficulty.[22] There is no doubt that the enterprise of the company could have measured up to such a challenge, however serious the demand it may have made on the three boy actors in the gallery. The problem comes with the dialogue that follows the raising of Antony. To set one of the play's climactic moments at the back of the stage, behind at least a railing or bannister if not something more solid, seems to me to be lunacy. 'O! see my women,' says Cleopatra as Antony dies, 'The crown o' the earth doth melt' (ll.62–3). It is a feed-line, if spoken from the gallery at the back of the stage, for a groundling wag: 'Never mind the women seeing. What about us?' The preference, whatever the associated problems, must be for some structure erected on the platform proper, with upstage treads concealed from most of the audience. Access to the Monument for Cleopatra and her attendants would be through the stage door and up these treads. Diomedes then enters through the other stage door, and stands against the tiring-house facade to answer Cleopatra's question by telling her of Antony:

> His death's upon him, but not dead.
> Look out o' the other side your monument;
> His guard have brought him thither.
>
> (ll.7–9)

The instruction can be obeyed quite literally. Cleopatra turns to look downstage as Antony is carried in. He dies, as any actor of the part would choose, in full view of the audience – and his body is carried out by way of the upstage treads and the stage door.

MUSIC

If the gallery above the stage doors was used by the musicians, as seems likely, they would, on occasion, make way for the actors, as well as for the privileged guests in the Lord's Room. The exact composition of the Globe 'orchestra' is not known. Drums and trumpets, hautboys (harsher and louder than the modern oboe), strings, and plucked instruments like lutes and citherns were available, together with the plebeian pipes. Robert Armin and Augustine Phillips were accomplished musicians, and there were almost certainly other actors with instrumental skills. The boy actors were expected to sing, and it may be possible to trace the genius of Armin through the singing roles of Amiens, Feste, Pandarus, and Lear's Fool to its apotheosis in Autolycus. The boy actor of Desdemona had to be good enough to sing the willow-song unaccompanied, but his voice had probably broken before he had a chance to test himself against the supreme challenge of Ariel in *The Tempest*. Music, then, had an important part to play in Globe performances. Yet the Induction to Marston's *The Malcontent*, specially written by John Webster for its re-staging at the Globe by the King's Men, emphasises how much more important was the music in its original staging by the boys' company at the Blackfriars. 'What are your additions?' asks Sly in his assumed role as a would-be spectator, and Burbage answers:

> Sooth, not greatly needful: only as your sallet to your great feast, to entertain a little more time, and to abridge the not-received custom of music in our theatre.
>
> (ll.79–82)

It is a comparative matter. We know that, when the Duke of Stettin-Pomerania watched the boys at the Blackfriars in 1602, the play was preceded by an hour of music, and that there was entr'acte music too. This is the 'not-received custom' at the Globe, and the extra 594 lines together with the part of Passarello, written in for Armin, are there to lengthen the play in compensation. But the opening of *The Malcontent* is a brilliant reversal of the audience's aural expectations. *Twelfth Night* begins with music, performed to suit a love-sick duke, and we can be confident that the Globe audience, whilst it would not have *expected* an overture at any performance, would not have been astonished by one either. It is against familiar responses that Marston opens *The Malcontent* with 'The vilest out-of-tune music', an audibly startling emblem of the malcontent, Malevole, who ' 'gainst his fate/Repines and quarrels' (III.ii.11–12). It would seem that the Globe musicians were either well paid or good-humoured – or both. They played where they were sent – on stage, in the gallery over the stage, inside the tiring house, even, if the *Antony and Cleopatra* instruction is an honest guide, under the stage. It may be that their greatest pleasure came with the post-play jig, of which Jonson provides such a monstrous parody when Volpone's dwarf, hermaphrodite, and eunuch 'make sport' (I.ii.1–62).

UPSTAGE AND DOWNSTAGE

Experienced actors, working behind a proscenium arch, will often, consciously or unconsciously, 'upstage' their fellows. They have an instinctive sense of focus. Louis Parker remembers seeing the famous Lyceum performances of *Othello*, when Irving 'generously' alternated Othello and Iago with the great American actor, Edwin Booth:[23]

> We were quite ready to be polite to our American guest; but I think I can honestly say we never saw him. There was, to be sure, a pleasant gentleman representing Othello, but he was timid, he acted in corners; he seemed to beg us not to look at him. And, indeed, it was difficult to see him as all the time our Henry was doing clever bits of by-play, eating grapes and spitting out the pips in a significant manner, which rendered Booth invisible.

Such bad behaviour is a product of the star-system and of the picture-frame of the proscenium arch. Focus on the Elizabethan open stage was determined as much by the voice of the actor as by his gesture or position. But the terms 'upstage' and 'downstage' remain useful in visualising Globe performances. It is only a theatre-in-the-round that eliminates them completely. Upstage at the Globe, even with the audience on three sides, was the tiring-house facade. A straight move downstage to the edge of the platform took the actor very close to the building's architectural centre. It also took him very close to the audience in the yard. To achieve his greatest proximity to the gallery spectators, he would need to take up a position at either side or any corner of the platform, but he could not remain there without doing a disservice to half the audience. A passing over the stage that began and ended in the yard would have given an opportunity to a high proportion of the spectators to experience a pleasing sense of proximity to the actors, as well as gratifying the contemporary love of processions and ceremonial splendour. The distinction between downstage and upstage at the Globe defines the relationship of the actor and his audience. Whilst King Lear remains regal, he will keep his distance, but the experience of the heath can carry him down to the edges and corners of the platform, where the Fool and Clown will always be at ease. Upstage of the pillars, beneath the shadow of the Heavens, is an area best suited to silent groups and to observers of an active scene. That is not to dub it a dead area. Its liveliness would depend on the nature of the story, and the dynamics that relate the various sections of the stage during a performance. A movement away from this shadowed area might be sufficient to suggest a change of location, given the further support of appropriate words, and could certainly detach the individual actor from his group, permitting the easy delivery of an aside or a soliloquy. The platform at the Globe belonged, not to a designer, but to the actors. It was they who changed the location, and who picked out the significance of the stage's permanent features to suit each story.

4

THE GLOBE PLAYS

When James Burbage built the Theatre in 1576, there was no great store of plays in English, and no self-styled 'playwright' to provide them. The success of Burbage's enterprise encouraged the building of new theatres, each calling for new plays. With the additional demand from the Children of Paul's and the Children of the Chapel Royal, the field was wide open for opportunist writers. By 1617, Fynes Moryson could fairly claim:[1]

> The city of London alone hath four or five companies of players with their peculiar theatres capable of many thousands, wherein they all play every day in the week except Sunday . . . as there be in my opinion more plays in London than in all the world I have seen.

A rapid creation of a national repertoire is among the most astonishing achievements of the period. G. E. Bentley has conservatively estimated that 'two thousand or so plays . . . were probably written in England between 1590 and 1642.'[2] A handful of them may have been the product of gentlemanly leisure, but the rest were written for money, and generally as fast as possible. Present literary fame and posthumous glory were not a playwright's legitimate aspirations. In 1612, Sir Thomas Bodley grouped plays with almanacs and proclamations among the 'idle books, and riff-raffs' which he reproached the keeper of his library for cataloguing, admitting that 'Haply some plays may be worth the keeping: but hardly one in forty.'[3] The need was to satisfy an audience, and that involved the regular provision of new plays. The first performance of a new work almost invariably increased the take; which means either that the price of admission was increased, or that more people attended – or both. It was clearly a special occasion, advertised with flair and thoroughness. We know something of the incidence of new plays in the repertoire of the Admiral's Men at the Rose, and the practice at the Globe cannot have been very different. Dispersed through the disorderly pages of Henslowe's *Diary* is what looks like a complete list of performances from 5 June 1594 to 28 July 1597. In that period, fifty-four new plays were produced, an average of seventeen or so in a year. Successes as durable as *The Seven Days of the Week* (twenty-two performances in this period) and *The Wise Man of Westchester* (thirty-two performances) were exceptional. Nine or ten revivals over a year and then oblivion was a more likely fate. The pursuit of novelty was a commercial necessity. The demand on the actors, which is a by-product of this pursuit, must have affected the standard of performance. The companies were not large enough to allow rest periods for individual members, so that a leading actor, Thomas Downton of the Admiral's Men for example, might have had fifty sizeable parts in new plays between 1594 and 1597, as well as twenty in revivals of such old favourites as *Doctor Faustus* and *Tamburlaine*. The blood and sweat of even 'weekly rep' in the first half of the twentieth century is an inadequate parallel, since it was not the custom in Elizabethan London to present the same play on successive afternoons. There is nothing special about the Rose programme for the first week of September in 1595, as recorded by Henslowe: it is listed here simply as an example of the kind of pressure under which the Admiral's Men worked:

1 September – *Hercules Part I* (first performed 2 May 1595)
2 September – *Hercules Part II* (first performed 23 May 1595)
3 September – *The Seven Days of the Week* (first performed 3 June 1595)
4 September – *Olympio and Eugenio* (? first performed 5 March 1595)
5 September – *Crack Me This Nut* (first performance)
6 September – *Antony and Vallia* (date of first performance unknown)

Only two of these were repeated in the following week, alongside four different pieces, so that, within a period of two weeks, the actors performed in ten plays. A theatre company will only risk a run of any length if it can be confident of a virtually total change of audience each day. The fact that successive performances were avoided at the Rose suggests that there was no ground for such confidence, and perhaps that a sufficient number of people attended the theatre more than once a week to have their wish for a change of bill respected. Such circumstances do unquestionable damage to the notion of 'polished performances' in the Elizabethan public theatres, and may help to explain the attraction of the once-a-week boy-players at the private theatres. This is not to say that everything in a Rose or Globe production was the rough-and-ready outcome of an unwilling response to outrageous demand. A professional company does not regularly undertake the impossible. We must assume, for example, that Elizabethan actors had a fine memory for lines, whilst being prepared to admit, despite the surprising lack of evidence, that a system of prompting was well established.[4] The safety factor was the relationship of actor and audience. Because this did not apply at court, particular care was taken in the rehearsal of plays that were to be shown there. We can only guess at rehearsal practice in the Elizabethan theatre, but we know that time was short. Henslowe's *Diary* allows us to draw certain conclusions about the policy adopted by the Admiral's Men at the Rose. We may take as exemplary the case of a play bluntly called *Civil Wars: Part One*. Its authors, Thomas Dekker and Michael Drayton, delivered the completed manuscript to the company on 29 September 1598. Five weeks later, on 4 November, it was staged at the Rose; but those five weeks were not all available for rehearsal of the new text. The manuscript had first to be copied at least twice – once to provide a reliable promptbook for the company and once to be cut up and divided into individual parts for the actors. There was then the intricate job of pasting each 'part', probably onto parchment, so that it could be delivered, complete with cues, to the actor who would play it. At least a week, more likely two, would be needed for the completion of all the necessary preparation of a manuscript for playhouse use. That, we might suppose, would have allowed a tight but plausible three weeks for rehearsal of *Civil Wars: Part One*. But another of Dekker's new plays, *Pierce of Winchester*, was given its first performance on 21 October, and it must clearly have taken precedence over *Civil Wars* in the previous week. We are left, then, with thirteen clear days before the opening on 4 November. How clear? There were performances each afternoon and it was probably too cold and certainly too dark to rehearse on the Rose stage in the evenings. Nor, I believe, would it have been acceptable practice to rehearse openly in the playhouse on Sundays. That leaves eleven or twelve mornings for the rehearsal of a five-act play, together with necessary costuming, property and scenery making *and learning*. It is not easy to see how there could have been much more than twenty-four hours of rehearsal, from which it is possible to argue high efficiency, low expectations – or both. My own view is that what the modern theatre would recognise as rehearsal was scarcely practised at all, that leading actors worked hard in personal preparation, that conventional stage-groupings, not only of attendant lords and servants but also of characters in dialogue, reduced the need for 'blocking' the disposition of actors on the platform and that only 'unconventional' or technically demanding scenes were tested through rehearsal. I am not suggesting that stage management at the Rose or at the Globe was left to chance, but that every performance was more hazardous than would be acceptable in today's theatre. The idolatrous proposition that the text never suffered is absurd.

Henslowe's playwrights were employees of the actors. It was often, perhaps normally, left to a particular member of the Admiral's Men to negotiate with a particular writer. The going rate for a full-length play was £6. (Among many unexplained exceptions is the £7 paid to Samuel Rowley in 1602 for *Joshua*.) If more than one writer was involved, the money was shared. Smaller pickings were regularly available. Ben Jonson, for example, received £2 in 1601 for 'additions in *Jeronimo*', and Dekker £2 for 'his pains in *Phaeton* ... for the Court'.[5] Henslowe's business relations with Dekker provide a fascinating sub-current in the *Diary*. Between 24 July and 10 August 1599, Dekker received separate payments for three plays, one completed and two promised. On 3 September, he received a down-payment for yet another promised play. Altogether during the year, work for the Admiral's Men brought him £28–7s–6d, a drop of nearly £9 on the previous year, when he wrote or worked on sixteen plays for the company. We know nothing about his other earnings, but we do know that he was imprisoned in the Poultry Counter in February 1599. This was a prison that normally housed debtors, or offenders against the London by-laws. It may be that Dekker was involved in a brawl, but debt is a likelier explanation. If he was in debt in early 1599, after receiving nearly £40 from the Admiral's Men in 1598, he must have had extravagant habits, or a recent financial disaster of major proportions. An income of £40 was much more than a competence. It was also much more than could be expected from any other kind of writing. But such money was hard-earned. Jonson's admission in 1619, after twenty active years, that his plays had brought him £200 in total, was probably accurate. He was a much slower worker than Dekker. We do not know exactly when the custom of authors' benefits was first established. The benefit was a grant to the writer of all or part of the taking at the second (or third) performance of his play. Jonson's calculation of his dramatic income might include his benefit money. The calculation of Dekker's income from the Admiral's Men does not.

There was more prestige in being an actor – provided that you were a successful actor – than in being a playwright; and a more reliable profit in being one of the shareholders in a good theatrical company. This is not to suggest that writers were despised. Their craftsmanship was respected, as well as their ability to deliver work on time. The prevalence of collaboration[6] indicates the importance of speed. Two, three, four, or even five writers would agree on the plot and its leading characters, and compile their assigned episodes more or less to order. The down-payment served as a kind of contract, and final payment was made on the delivery of a satisfactory complete version. In hailing Anthony Munday as 'our best plotter',[7] Francis Meres is recording the usefulness of a skill in dividing a given story into appropriate dramatic episodes. The possession of good stories was more important to an Elizabethan theatre company than the spreading of fine literature. The fact that Shakespeare and so many of his contemporaries provided both cannot be used to defend a claim that the Chamberlain's Men *demanded* both. The more immediate reason was the tempting profitability of dramatic writing, sufficient to attract men who might otherwise have applied their genius only to epic, lyric, or satiric poetry. If you were writing for money, plays brought quicker rewards.

Jonson was probably an actor with the Admiral's Men in December 1597 when he came up with an idea, wrote it down as a 'plot', and showed it to his colleagues. On the strength of it, Henslowe paid him £1, noting the transaction in his *Diary*:[8]

> Lent unto Bengemen Johnsone the 23 of desember 1597 upon a Bocke which he was to writte for us befor crysmas next after the date herof which he showed the plotte unto the company.

The transaction reveals a characteristic anxiety on the part of an Elizabethan company to secure a good story. It was no disrespect to a play to see it as a commodity, worth £6 new, and perhaps £2 second-hand.[9] Like many other artefacts, it could be altered and 'improved'. It was normal practice for a company to ask a dramatist to revise his own work or that of other dramatists before a revival. Some surviving texts are the end-product of revisions over one or two decades, but all plays, in whatever form they have come down to us, were liable to the same process. There is good reason for supposing that Shakespeare's were changed less than most, but none for claiming that they were, on principle, untouched. The Admiral's Men paid Dekker £2 for changing the end of *Old Fortunatus* for its performance at court in 1599. That the Chamberlain's Men asked similar things of Shakespeare is certain.

Ben Jonson's preparedness to publish his plays in Folio in 1616 must have appeared vainglorious. The publication of individual plays in Quarto editions was not unusual by then, though the reasons and methods were not always reputable. Pirated versions, like the 'bad' Quarto of *Hamlet* (1603), represented unscrupulous attempts to cash in on a theatrical success. They forced the hand of the rightful owners of the playbook, so that corrective 'good' Quartos generally followed bad. But professional companies did not relish the publication of their plays. It made them available to other actors, and might well reduce their drawing power in the theatre. Playwrights who 'belonged' to a particular company seem generally to have refrained from publication, perhaps by agreement with their colleagues, perhaps because performance was more personally profitable. Marston, who did not 'belong', published his twelve plays with all convenient haste. Shakespeare, with his record of loyalty to the Chamberlain's/King's Men, did not. Jonson, whose eyes were equally on Henslowe and posterity, made up his own mind. The choice of folio, a dignified format in any age, was notable. Whatever the contemporary gossip, it can be seen in retrospect as an elevation of the status of playwrights as a whole. The Shakespeare Folio of 1623 and the Beaumont and Fletcher Folio of 1647 were remarkable publishing ventures, but it was Jonson who set the precedent. It is particularly in him that we can see the occasional outburst of resentment about the undervaluing of the playwright by actors and promoters; but it should be born in mind that almost half the money paid out by Henslowe on behalf of the Admiral's Men between 1597 and 1603 went to writers. It is reasonable to suppose that those who wrote for the Burbages did at least as well, and possibly better.

Of the plays which can be said, with reasonable confidence, to have had their earliest performance at the Globe, twenty-nine are extant. They are, in approximate chronological order:

	Author	Title	Additional information
1599	Shakespeare	As You Like It	
	Shakespeare	Julius Caesar	Platter saw it on 21 September
	Jonson	Every Man out of His Humour	
1600	Anon.	A Larum for London	Entered in Stationers' Register on 27 May
	Shakespeare	The Merry Wives of Windsor	Some argue for a date as early as 1597 for this play
	Shakespeare	Twelfth Night	The performance in the Middle Temple on 2 February 1602 was a notable revival
1601	Dekker	Satiromastix	Later than March and before 11 November
	Shakespeare	Hamlet	

On 7 February, the eve of the Earl of Essex's inept street rebellion, the Chamberlain's Men revived *Richard II*.

1602	Anon.	The Merry Devil of Edmonton	
	Anon.	Thomas Lord Cromwell	Entered in the Stationers' Register in August
	Shakespeare	Troilus and Cressida	

This year probably saw one of the many revivals of the immensely popular *Mucedorus* (1598).

1603	Shakespeare	All's Well that Ends Well	
	Jonson	Sejanus	

For much of this year the theatres were closed – from 19 March as a token of respect for the dying queen, and subsequently because of the plague epidemic. By letters patent dated 19 May, James I appointed the company to be the King's Men.

1604	Anon.	*The Fair Maid of Bristow*	
	Anon.	*The London Prodigal*	
	Shakespeare	*Measure for Measure*	Played at court on 26 December
	Marston	*The Malcontent*	This play had already been performed, perhaps in 1603, by a boys' company
	Shakespeare	*Othello*	Played at court on 1 November

In December, the company gave offence with a play about the Earl of Gowry's plot against Scotland's James VI, now England's James I. The authorship is unknown.

1605	Anon. (? Middleton)	*A Yorkshire Tragedy*	
	Wilkins	*The Miseries of Enforced Marriage*	
	Shakespeare	*King Lear*	Played at court on 26 December 1606
1606	Jonson	*Volpone*	
	Tourneur (or Middleton)	*The Revenger's Tragedy*	
	Shakespeare	*Macbeth*	
1607	Barnes	*The Devil's Charter*	Played at court on 2 February
	Shakespeare	*Antony and Cleopatra*	
	Shakespeare	*Timon of Athens*	
1608	Shakespeare	*Coriolanus*	
	Shakespeare	*Pericles*	

I have listed above only a selection of the plays known to have been revived by the Chamberlain's/King's Men at the Globe. Title pages of Quartos published during the Globe decade claim recent performances for *Love's Labour's Lost*, *The Merchant of Venice*, *A Midsummer Night's Dream*, *Richard III*, *Romeo and Juliet*, and *Titus Andronicus*. It was possible at any time to plug a gap in the repertoire with a Shakespeare revival or with such popular stand-bys as Jonson's *Every Man in His Humour* or the anonymous *Mucedorus*. The Admiral's Men made similar use of Marlowe, who had the comparative disadvantage of being less productive than Shakespeare and dead. A year-by-year exploration of the decisions and concerns of the company during its first decade at the Globe will be necessarily sketchy, but even a sketchy survey should tell us something about the realities of survival in an always time-pressed, always opportunistic profession.

1599

The Chamberlain's Men performed at court on 26 December 1598 and again on 1 January 1599. It would be surprising if the immensely successful *Every Man in His Humour* was not one of the chosen plays. Established favourites would have been vital to the company's well-being during this frantic period, when negotiations with the Office of the Revels over court performances were running alongside plans for the dismantling of the Theatre, and for the erection of the Globe on its South Bank site. Formal agreement for the leasing of the land was signed on 21 February 1599, but building continued into the early summer. In need of a temporary home, the Chamberlain's Men may have settled at the Curtain, to the shortcomings of which the apologetic Chorus of *Henry V* may be alluding. The play was certainly revived that year, with an inserted addition to the Act Five Chorus that boldly hints at the company's adherence to the Earl of Essex. The queen had dispatched the Earl to Ireland in March 1599, to tame the rebellious Earl of Tyrone. News of his inglorious campaign there had probably not reached London when Shakespeare added his telltale comparison of Henry V's triumphant return from Agincourt with the welcome that would surely greet Essex's victorious return from Ireland:

> But now behold
> In the quick forge and working-house of thought,
> How London doth pour out her citizens,
> The mayor and all his brethren in best sort,
> Like to the senators of the antique Rome,
> With the plebeians swarming at their heels,
> Go forth and fetch their conquering Caesar in:
> As, by a lower but loving likelihood,
> Were now the general of our gracious empress –
> As in good time he may – from Ireland coming,
> Bringing rebellion broached on his sword,
> How many would the peaceful city quit
> To welcome him! much more, and much more cause,
> Did they this Harry.

It is most unlikely that Shakespeare knew the extent of the queen's displeasure with the Earl of Essex, but if he was so naive as to suppose that all was well between monarch and former favourite, the supposition would have been rudely shattered by the events that followed the Earl's headlong return from Ireland in September and his year-long house arrest. However you look at them, the inserted Chorus lines for the 1599 revival of

Henry V are a rallying cry for supporters of the Earl of Essex. The company's confidence that the audience would approve is noteworthy in the context of Elizabethan politics in general and of theatrical politics in particular.

If, as seems likely, the Chamberlain's Men were broadly sympathetic to the aristocratic Puritan faction of which the Earl of Essex was the volatile leader, their South Bank neighbours, the Admiral's Men at the Rose, were in the opposite 'establishment' camp. The Lord Admiral, Charles Howard (created Earl of Nottingham in 1597), cordially loathed the Earl of Essex, who had been his Vice-Admiral in the naval campaigns of 1596. Howard was brother-in-law to the patron of Shakespeare's company, Lord Hunsdon, and they were both influential members of the Privy Council. There is no evidence that Hunsdon was a supporter of the Essex faction. If his players were, they would have found it prudent to keep their patron in ignorance of the fact. But Hunsdon was, however indirectly, involved in one dispute that came to a head in 1599. He had hoped to succeed as Lord Chamberlain when his father died in 1596, but the office went instead to Lord Cobham, among whose ancestors was a certain Sir John Oldcastle. This was the name first given by Shakespeare to the fat and fraudulent knight whose presence dominates the two parts of *Henry IV*, and it was because of objections from the Cobham family that the name was changed to Falstaff. Cobham died in 1598 and Lord Hunsdon succeeded to the office he had coveted, but the row simmered on. It cannot have been an accidental decision of the Admiral's Men in 1599 to commission from a team of writers a play called *The true and honourable historie, of the life of Sir John Old-castle, the good Lord Cobham*. On the contrary, it was a deliberate bid for status among the elder statesmen who had the ear of the ageing queen and a vivid example of the two leading Elizabethan companies in open rivalry. It would not be long before the Chamberlain's Men were drawn into the political fray again.

Competition between the two companies was made inevitable by the building of the Globe almost within a stone's throw of the Rose. The signs are that the Chamberlain's Men were the immediate winners. Before the end of 1599, Henslowe was laying plans for a playhouse north of the river (the Fortune was ready for use in 1600). But the Chamberlain's Men had trouble to fend off, too. In the spring of 1599, Giles Allen sued the Burbages' builder, Peter Street, in the Court of the King's Bench – for trespass and damage. The case was ably defended and remained open. No one made any money, except the lawyers. There was internal dissension as well. At some time in 1599, Will Kempe left the company. We do not know the reason. He had been one of the signatories of the February lease and must, then, have been contemplating a long association. His sudden defection threatened the popularity of the new venture. If, as seems likely, he was (or felt) driven out by professional differences, the arguments may have centred on the status of the jig. Kempe had been the supreme jig-maker at the Theatre and the Curtain, but the Chamberlain's Men may well have wished to downgrade jigs in their new playhouse. Whatever the cause, Kempe's going removed a people's favourite from the company and deprived it of one of the sharers in financial liability. Financial success was urgent. The choice for opening the season at the new playhouse may have fallen on *As You Like It*, a festive comedy whose very title is an advertising promise, and whose uncharacteristically flirtatious epilogue is an appropriate wooing of a new audience. If so, Shakespeare probably did some hasty re-writing, introducing the first of his wordly-wise fools, Touchstone, and reducing the role of the Kempe-style clown, appropriately named William. Touchstone is a part for Kempe's successor, Robert Armin. David Wiles's interpretation is sensitive to the intimacy of Elizabethan theatre practice:

> When Armin/Touchstone declares: 'It is meat and drink to me to see a clown' (V.i.10), he reminds the audience that it is his – Armin's – livelihood. The other clown's name – 'William' – is repeated three times, so that the audience will not miss the contrast between the departed company clown, William Kemp, and the new fool/clown. The traditional simple-minded rustic clown is symbolically dismissed from the new Globe stage.[10]

Even the touch of malice was probably intentional. Kempe had deserted the ship in stormy weather.

Shakespeare may have spent the summer of 1599 writing *Julius Caesar*. It was in September that the Swiss visitor, Thomas Platter, saw it at the Globe – with the post-play jig still prominent. The other surviving play from the 1599 repertoire was an altogether riskier affair. The background is a little tangled. It brings us, initially, into contact with Elizabethan censorship. The last decade of the sixteenth century saw the growth of poetic satire, in conscious but often misguided imitation of Juvenal, and of prose satire that shared its propensity for indiscriminate railing. In the summer of 1599, the Archbishop of Canterbury, Whitgift, and Bancroft, the Bishop of London, published an edict 'That no Satyres or Epigrams be printed hereafter'. Like so much Elizabethan legislation, the Bishops' Ban was not particularly effective, but it may have diverted John Marston towards the theatre. The bishops had ordered the burning of his satires, and Marston's response activated a dispute with Jonson that has come to be known as the war of the theatres, or the *poetomachia*. His poetry threatened by censorship, Marston wrote, or perhaps refurbished, his first play, *Histriomastix*, an incoherent allegory about the workings of the law in a decadent society. It included a portrait of Jonson (as Chrisoganus) which Marston may genuinely have intended to be complimentary. That was not how Jonson saw it. *Every Man out of His Humour*, the play he sold to the Chamberlain's Men at the end of 1599, includes a wicked portrait of Marston as Clove, together with one of Dekker as Clove's unimpressive sidekick, Orange. Clove is a flasher of turgid polysyllables, many of them submerged quotations from Marston. He finds his place in a sprawling, Aristophanic comedy, whose sole intention is to expose the pretensions of a clutch of vacuous time-servers. *Every Man out of His Humour* was an extraordinarily bold choice for a company striving to establish its image in new surroundings. It tells no story, but purports to be a random happening before the very eyes of its audience. Just how much attention that audience paid to the bruising of Marston and Dekker cannot be known, but the Chamberlain's Men would not have been surprised that Marston and Dekker themselves smarted. Controversy, they must have calculated, is good publicity.

1600

Early in 1600, Richard Burbage sublet the large rooms in the Blackfriars to a scrivener, Henry Evans. Evans succeeded in mollifying the inhabitants of the precinct sufficiently to establish regular performances there – but by a Boys' Company, the Children of the Chapel Royal. The Children of St Paul's had, by then, been active for at least a year, and boy actors retained a challenging hold on the theatrical public until well into James I's reign. The 'praise-and-abuse' style of drama, to which the *poetomachia* gave such impetus, had evidently its peculiar appeal when delivered in the ingenuous voices of pubescent boys. It is a subject on which Shakespeare makes his own opinion unusually clear, most famously but not uniquely in *Hamlet*. Unlike adults, the boys were able to perform within the city walls, and their productions were invested with an aura of privilege. Henslowe, after nearly fifteen years in the business, had still to build his new playhouse outside the Cripplegate.

We do not know how Shakespeare's company reacted when their patron was 'seized with an apoplexy' in March. It would have been singularly tactless to do nothing. Lord Hunsdon was cousin-german to the queen, who wrote to promise him that 'you shall find in us a mother and wife to minister unto you'.[11] She visited him three times during his long convalescence (he died a few months after her), much of which was spent in his house in the Blackfriars. On one of these visits (29 December 1601), the Chamberlain's Men performed a play. That would seem to be characteristic of the relationship between patron and acting company. However distant the contact, Hunsdon enjoyed the prestige of his players. But he, like the rest of the Privy Council, was embroiled in the succession crisis. In such a fraught atmosphere, faction was unavoidable. The Earl of Essex remained under house arrest until 26 August and was banned from court thereafter, but any courtier with a grievance had natural access to his company. Impoverished and neurotic, Essex easily persuaded himself that his mission was not to *attack* but to *save* the queen: to save her, that is, from evil counsellors like Robert Cecil, the Earl of Nottingham and the ageing Lord Buckhurst. Richard II had surrounded himself with parasitic flatterers (Bushy, Bagot, Green), and the cant phrase for such Elizabethan caterpillars remained 'King Richard's men'. Elizabeth I was well aware of Essex's jaundiced view of her and of her advisers, her 'King Richard's men'. It was this knowledge that informed her famous observation to William Lambarde after the collapse of Essex's rebellion: 'I am Richard II, know ye not that?' Any allusions to Richard II were highly charged, as can clearly be seen in the fate of John Hayward. In February 1599, Hayward had published *The First part of the life and reign of King Henry the IIII*. The book carried a fulsome dedication to the Earl of Essex. Despite its treatment of the deposition and death of Richard, the volume escaped censure in February 1599, but the combination of topic, dedication and succession crisis led to Hayward's imprisonment in the Tower of London in the summer of 1600. His printer, John Wolfe, suffered too. He spent two weeks in prison for bringing out a second edition and had his attempt to build a playhouse in Smithfield thwarted by the justices of he peace. This was one of several Elizabethan theatre projects that never reached completion.

There is no evidence that Shakespeare's *Richard II* was still in the regular repertoire of the Chamberlain's Men, although the two parts of *Henry IV* almost certainly were. It is part of the Shakespearean legend that *The Merry Wives of Windsor* was written to please the queen, who had enjoyed the antics of Falstaff. The dating of the play is uncertain. If it was written in 1600, it would have been one of many 'local' plays belonging to that year, but it is determinedly unpolitical. This was no time to advertise a sympathy for the Earl of Essex. If I am right that the Chamberlain's Men were of the radical Protestant persuasion, *A Larum for London* was a prudently camouflaged vehicle for the carriage of the message. This anonymous play is an episodic dramatisation of the Siege of Antwerp by the Spaniards, and it stands as an overt piece of anti-Catholic scaremongering. Its address to Londoners is securely patriotic. Unless the city can settle its differences and purge itself of disloyal profiteering, it will be vulnerable to the Spanish threat. Shakespeare's hand is not visible in the writing. We do not know with certainty what he wrote in 1600, though *Twelfth Night* probably belongs to that year. The part of Feste was tailored for Kempe's successor, Robert Armin – a worldly-wise Illyrian fool/clown skilled in English folk-song.

1601

On 22 January 1601, John Hayward was again questioned about the writing of his book on Henry IV. The queen was pressing Francis Bacon to uncover Hayward's treasonable intentions. Something of her displeasure must surely have been known to the Chamberlain's Men. It was certainly known to the Earl of Essex, living in self-pitying exile and sporadic anger in Essex House. Through January, in conversation with other impoverished malcontents, Essex allowed his dotty scheme to save the queen from her 'King Richard's men' to take shape. On Thursday or Friday, 5 or 6 February, Sir Gelly Meyrick and other adherents of the Essex faction crossed the Thames by wherry and visited the Globe, where they 'spoke to some of the players in the presence of this Examinate[12] to have the play of the deposing and killing of King Richard the Second to be played the Saturday next, promising to get them xls. more than their ordinary to play it'. Augustine Phillips claims to have objected that the play was 'so old and so long out of use that they should have small or no company at it', but this protest, if it was ever made, was overruled. It must, anyway, have been disingenuous. Even the Chamberlain's Men could not have cast, memorised and performed a forgotten play in time for performance one or two afternoons later; nor can it be believed that the company was acting in total ignorance of political implications when they staged *Richard II* on 7 February. The following morning, the Earl of Essex, with about two hundred followers on horseback, left Essex House. He might, at this point, have turned right and ridden against the ill-guarded Palace of Whitehall. Instead, buoyed up by an irrational belief in the vehemence of popular support, he turned left and rode into the City of London, shouting slogans like 'For the Queen! For the Queen! The crown of England is sold to the Spaniard! A plot is laid for my life!'.[13] To the gaping citizens, it must have seemed like a street carnival rather than a call to arms. The earl had expected to gather an army – on a Sunday morning in February! All he gathered was a patchwork audience. When Ludgate was closed against him, he had to sneak back to Essex House by water. His position there was hopeless, and it would have galled him that the man to whom he had finally to surrender was his old enemy, Charles Howard, Lord Admiral and Earl of Nottingham. It is not the least extraordinary aspect of this extraordinary episode that the Lord Chamberlain's Men should have allowed themselves to become embroiled in it. What, beyond £2, were they hoping to get out of it? As the author of the dangerous play, Shakespeare was lucky to escape imprisonment. There is no record of his being questioned, and it may well be that he prudently skipped town, but that would not have protected him from a charge of treason, had the queen so chosen. For the company as a whole, it was a crazy risk, and it was their good fortune that the canny queen, perhaps advised by the equally canny Robert Cecil, chose to make an example of the Chamberlain's Men by pardoning them. The invitation to perform at court on 24 February was not withdrawn. They had played *Richard II* on the eve of Essex's rebellion. Let them now perform at court on the eve of his execution. It was through such theatrical timing that Elizabeth I sometimes bit her biters.

Chastened, but still solvent, the Chamberlain's Men may have found the petulant war of the theatres almost light relief. Marston had tried to revenge himself on Jonson in *Jack Drum's Entertainment* (1600) and *What You Will* (?1601), both written for the Children of St Paul's, and Jonson responded by providing the Children of the Chapel Royal with the vitriolic *Poetaster* (1601). Perhaps riled by Jonson's allusions to their poor winter season, the Chamberlain's Men chose to revive Dekker's cumbersome *Satiromastix*, performed by the Paul's Boys earlier in 1601. Dead quarrels are not easy to revive in the modern theatre, and *Satiromastix* is unattractively splenetic out of its historical context, its archaic plot (virgin takes poison rather than lose her honour to the lustful king) tucked away behind undisciplined abuse of Horace/Ben Jonson. It would not be surprising if the Chamberlain's Men floundered a little in the aftermath of the Essex fiasco. The saving grace was *Hamlet*. It says much for Shakespeare and the company that *Hamlet* was not written on the retreat from *Richard II*. It is, after all, a story of regicide and civil unrest. It might, of course, also be argued that it conveys a powerful warning against the dangers of an elective monarchy. It was clear, at the end of 1601, that Elizabeth I could not live long. The Essex uprising had been coloured by the issue of elective succession, and there were deep schisms at court over the 'rightful' or 'best' heir. If *Hamlet* points anywhere, it points to James VI of Scotland, whose wife was a princess of Denmark – but the pointing is equivocal. If Shakespeare was not primarily concerned to protect himself and the Chamberlain's Men in 1601, he was not hell-bent on exposing himself either.

1602

The Chamberlain's Men performed three times at court over the Christmas of 1601–2, which seems to imply that they had been forgiven for their complicity in the Earl of Essex's rebellion. There must, even so, have been a need to consolidate. Fortunately, *The Merry Devil of Edmonton*, despite narrative inconsistencies that probably reflect inefficient collaboration, was a success at the Globe. The title is a trick, a shameless catchpenny, reliant on the audience's acquaintance with the story of Peter Fabel's pact with the devil. Norden, the mapmaker, tells us that Fabel's tomb was in the church at Edmonton, and that the date of his death (early in the sixteenth century) is not recorded on it. The play begins with conscious echoes of

Doctor Faustus, a theatrical in-joke seeming to promise that Fabel will be the central character. It is a gentle trick, played *with* rather than *on* an audience that knew the repertoire of the Admiral's Men as well as that of the Chamberlain's Men. We might reasonably infer that the Fortune had just staged yet another revival of *Doctor Faustus*, and that the Globe audience was being invited to snigger. As the story unfolds, Fabel dwindles into a beneficent minor character, about as far from Faustus as the Lincoln Imp is from Marlowe's Mephostopheles. The real purpose of *The Merry Devil of Edmonton* is to tell a sentimental tale of constancy rewarded. Its popularity rewarded the company's awareness that an audience may be theatrically sophisticated whilst remaining emotionally naive. It was on this same conjunction of sophistication and naivety that the regularly revived *Mucedorus* (1598) relied.

There is some indication that 1602 was a year of indecision for Shakespeare. It is notoriously difficult to assign precise dates to his plays in the early years of the seventeenth century, but neither *Troilus and Cressida* nor *All's Well that Ends Well*, which may have been written or in the making in 1602, flowed easily. An anonymous preface to the 1609 Quarto of *Troilus and Cressida* claims that this was 'a new play, never stal'd with the Stage, never clapper-clawd with the palmes of the vulgar'. The statement should be read with caution. The play was not new (it was entered in the Stationers' Register in 1603), and there is no reason to rely on the greater accuracy of the second claim – that it had not been publicly performed. It may, as some scholars have claimed, have been first written for performance at one of the Inns of Court. Like any professional writer, Shakespeare was open to commissions, but there is no reason to suppose that he would have treated *Troilus and Cressida* as a private play. A likelier explanation is that this play was, unusually, a failure with the theatrical public and quickly withdrawn. In preparing the First Folio edition of Shakespeare's plays in 1623, Heminges and Condell had evident difficulty in finding a satisfactory copy of *Troilus and Cressida*. Was there, perhaps, some adjustment in Shakespeare's relationship with the Chamberlain's Men? It was probably in 1602 that he moved from his lodgings close to the Globe into the house of Christopher Mountjoy, up in the north-west of the walled City of London. It would not have been sensible for a working actor to live so far from his playhouse. Quite possibly, Shakespeare virtually abandoned acting in 1602, perhaps with a view to dividing his time between writing and regular periods of residence in Stratford, where his elder daughter was now of a marriageable age. He may also, of course, have taken on some of the more inglorious writing chores as a way of recompensing the Chamberlain's Men for allowing him to abandon acting. It is, at last, being recognised that even Shakespeare was capable of slipshod writing, only rarely that he may also have shouldered a house playwright's editorial responsibilities. It would seem to me odd if he were never asked to emend, cut or augment the work of other writers. He may have been fastidious, but that is no reason for supposing him downright selfish. I would not, however, argue that he had a hand in the undistinguished *Thomas Lord Cromwell*. The title-page of the 1602 Quarto ascribes the play to 'W.S.', which wins it a place among the Shakespeare apocrypha, but there were probably writers other than William Stanley, sixth Earl of Derby, with whom Shakespeare shared his initials.

1603

Despite her failing health, the queen commanded a full round of Christmas entertainments in 1602–3. The Chamberlain's Men were called to perform on St Stephen's Day and again on 2 February, during the last Shrovetide festivities of the old reign. On 7 February, perhaps at the Globe, certainly in one of the Bankside theatres, there was a fencing match between two master-swordsmen, Turner and Dun. It came to a sudden end when Turner ran Dun 'so far in the brain at the eye'[14] that he died instantly. Such accidents did no damage to the income of the shareholders who rented out their playhouse, but the death of Elizabeth I the following month was a commercial disaster. The theatres were closed on 19 March, when it became clear that the queen was dying, remained closed for a period of national mourning after her death on 24 March, and had scarcely reopened when an increase in plague-deaths caused a further closure on 26 May. The actors were not to know that the ban on playing would continue until April 1604. By then, approximately 30,000 Londoners had died of the plague.

Prudently, the new king delayed his arrival in the stricken capital. He was, however, quick to declare his interest in the theatre. On 19 May 1603, letters patent announced that the former Lord Chamberlain's Men would be henceforward known as the King's Men:

> Knowe yee that Wee of our speciall grace, certeine knowledge, & mere motion have licenced and aucthorized and by theise presentes doe licence and aucthorize theise our Servauntes Lawrence Fletcher, William Shakespeare, Richard Burbage, Augustyne Phillippes, Iohn Heninges, Henrie Condell, William Sly, Robert Armyn, Richard Cowly, and the rest of theire Assosiates freely to vse and exercise the Arte and faculty of playinge Comedies, Tragedies, histories, Enterludes, moralls, pastoralls, Stage-plaies, and Suche others like as theie haue alreadie studied or hereafter shall vse or studie, aswell for the recreation of our lovinge Subjectes, as for our Solace and pleasure when wee shall thincke good to see them, duringe our pleasure.

The sovereign's insistence on the right of his players to perform for his subjects as well as for himself was a significant strengthening of the professional theatre's position, and the letters patent go on to spell out the right of the newly appointed King's Men:

> to shewe and exercise publiquely to their best Commoditie, when the infection of the plague shall decrease, aswell within theire nowe vsual howse called the Globe within our County of Surrey, as alsoe within anie towne halls or Moute halls or other conveniente places within the liberties and freedome of anie other Cittie, vniversitie, towne, or Boroughe whatsoever within our said Realmes and domynions.

The king's protection was a powerful asset, and his interest was not an idle one. When he heard that his players were feeling the pinch during their enforced provincial tour, James I summoned them to perform at Wilton House, where he had taken refuge. We do not know which play they presented on 2 December – their first appearance before their new patron – but we do know that they received the rich reward of £30 in payment. The king had already 'given' them his favourite actor, Lawrence Fletcher, the leader of the Scottish actors whom James had defended against the kirk in his native land. Fletcher may not have been as Scottish as his patron. George Nicolson, agent of the English in Edinburgh, had described him in 1599 as one of the 'English players'. It was Nicolson's mission to report to Robert Cecil on the fitness of James VI as a future king of England, and it must have counted in James's favour that he stood firmly with Fletcher and the actors, despite the fact that 'the bellows blowers say that they are sent by England to sow dissension between the King and the Kirk'.[15] There is, in fact, little likelihood that Fletcher ever performed with the King's Men, his 'membership' being merely a sign of the king's grace and favour. He is not mentioned in the cast-list of Jonson's *Sejanus*, which belongs to this time, nor in the 1623 Folio list of actors in Shakespeare's plays. There may be a hidden story of company resentment at the attempt to impose an unwanted actor, but nothing has come to the surface. A much more significant addition to the King's Men was John Lowin, a substantial actor who joined in 1603 and remained a member for forty years.

Somewhere (not, presumably, in London) in late 1603 or early 1604, Jonson's *Sejanus* was given its first performance by the King's Men. Jonson was by now secure in the patronage of the king's cousin, Esme Stuart, Seigneur D'Aubigny, separated from his wife in London, and safe from the plague that killed their son, Benjamin, to whom he offered the moving tribute of an epitaph:

> Rest in soft peace, and, ask'd, say here doth lye
> BEN. IONSON his best piece of *poetrie*.
> For whose sake, hence-forth, all his vowes be such,
> As what he loues may neuer like too much.

Jonson did not, however, rush to comfort his wife. He was busy composing his first tragedy, and for the company that had so recently mocked him in *Satiromastix*. Although tempers were short in the Elizabethan theatre, it was not evidently mandatory to nurse grievances. But *Sejanus* failed in performance, and Jonson was mortified. In the Epistle to the readers of the 1605 Quarto edition, he confesses (or boasts?):

> I would inform you that this book, in all numbers, is not the same
> with that which was acted on the public stage, wherein a second pen
> had good share: in place of which I have rather chosen to put weaker
> (and no doubt less pleasing) of mine own, than to defraud so happy
> a genius of his right, by my loathed usurpation.

Although George Chapman is the scholars' favourite, there is no denying the possibility that the second pen was Shakespeare's. The phrase 'so happy a genius' sits uncomfortably on Chapman, but accords well with Jonson's sometimes sceptical view of Shakespeare; and we know that Shakespeare was in the original cast, called out of semi-retirement if my own speculations are well-founded, and probably bound, by verbal contract at least, to tinker with plays on behalf of the company. Typically, we have no indication of what Shakespeare thought of Jonson. Equally typically, we have several accounts of what Jonson thought of Shakespeare. 'Shakespeare wanted art', he told Drummond; and, more judiciously, he wrote in *Timber*:

> I remember, the Players have often mentioned it as an honour to
> Shakespeare, that in his writing, (whatosever he penn'd) he never
> blotted out line. My answer hath been, would he had blotted a
> thousand. Which they thought a malevolent speech.

The fulsome tribute Jonson pays to Shakespeare in the poem, 'To the Memory of My Beloved, the Author Mr. William Shakespeare', is, by contrast, uncritical, but it should not be ignored. Jonson's admiration for Shakespeare may have been tempered, may have remained 'on this side Idolatry', but it was genuine. Since his own experience was so different, he may well have envied the ease with which Shakespeare negotiated the tricky currents of theatrical politics. Jonson drank too much – it made him irascible; he ate too much – it gave him indigestion; he was constantly short of money – it made him bitter. Worst of all, he found it difficult to like theatre people. It is much more remarkable that he liked Shakespeare at all than that he did not like him utterly. He is not the only playwright who has felt like killing an actor, but he is one of the few who actually did it. That was in September 1598, when the hot-blooded Gabriel Spencer came off worse in a duel. It led to Jonson's second scrape with the law (the first was over *The Isle of Dogs* in 1597). *Sejanus* brought him a third, when he was summoned before the Privy Council to answer charges of 'popery and treason'. Jonson believed that he was a victim of the private malice of the powerful Henry Howard, Earl of Northampton, but Jonson, unlike the Earl of Northampton, made no secret of his Catholicism. He had been converted in 1598, during his spell of imprisonment after Spencer's death, and his religious adherence made him particularly vulnerable in the first year of the new king's reign, so soon after the discovery of two Catholic plots against James I (the Main and Bye Plots). Jonson would be imprisoned again in 1604 for his part in the anti-Scottish tags of *Eastward Ho!* and, as a known associate of the conspirator Robert Catesby, was again summoned before the Privy Council after the discovery of the Gunpowder Plot in 1605.[16] The contrast with Shakespeare operates here at the biographical as well as at the dramatic level,[17] and yet the two men remained persistently in contact. It may very well have been Shakespeare's gift for reconciliation that brought Jonson back to the King's Men after his humiliation in the popular response to *Satiromastix*. The pity is that the bold decision to stage *Sejanus* was not met with the applause it deserved.

1604

The King's Men were commanded to perform for their patron seven times during the Christmas and Shrovetide celebrations of 1603–4. Shakespeare had written, or was writing, *Measure for Measure*. It is a play which a politically concerned playwright might well have addressed to a politically concerned monarch, the author of *Basilikon Doron*. No king of England has ever thought more deeply about the relationship of monarch and people than James I, and few have handled it more ineptly. *Measure for Measure* advertises Shakespeare's consciousness that good government demands more than mere well-meaning, but it is too equivocal to stand as tactful thanks for generous patronage. On the available evidence, James did more for Shakespeare than Shakespeare did for James. Four of Shakespeare's plays were staged at court in 1604 – *Othello* (1 November), *The Merry Wives of Windsor* (4 November), *Measure for Measure* (26 December) and *The Comedy of Errors* (28 December). Add to these the productions, in early 1605, of *Henry V* (7 January), *Love's Labour's Lost* (some time between 9 and 14 January) and *The Merchant of Venice* (10 and 12 February), and we have remarkable evidence of Shakespeare's reputation. The only other pieces the King's Men are known to have performed at court between November 1604 and February 1605 are Jonson's two *Every Man* plays. All these plays, new and old, would also have been staged at the Globe, which means that the company could have presented, towards the end of 1604, a quite extraordinary weekly repertoire:

Monday	– *Measure for Measure* (1604)
Tuesday	– *Love's Labour's Lost* (c. 1595)
Wednesday	– *Othello* (1604)
Thursday	– *Every Man out of His Humour* (1599)
Friday	– *The Comedy of Errors* (c. 1592)
Saturday	– *Henry V* (1598–9)

And still some of the audience would have complained that there were too few new plays in the programme!

The Angelo of *Measure for Measure* would have been easily placed as an extremist Puritan by contemporary audiences. Puritanism was in the forefront of domestic politics in 1604. James I had made the gesture of welcoming leading spokesmen of the Millennary Petition to Hampton Court to discuss their grievances. Only too characteristically, having made the gesture, he spoiled it by behaving erratically. The calling of the Hampton Court Conference in January 1604 had encouraged the Puritan faction; its outcome failed to deceive them. A few changes in the wording of the Prayer Book and a few modifications in the organisation of church courts, virtually nothing pressed into effective operation, these were all the 'gains' they made. Parliament, when it met in March, was watchfully protective of its privileges and the new king equally protective of his. Whatever he may have promised in his opening speech, it was soon clear to the House of Commons that their chief privilege was that of agreeing with James I. The confrontation of king and parliament began almost at once with a dispute over the Buckinghamshire election. In May, James summoned the lower house to Whitehall and lambasted them for wasting parliamentary time on issues of privilege, and the Commons responded by appointing a committee to prepare an *Apology*, which was, in fact, not a defence but a powerfully argued justification of their actions.[18] It is in this historical context that the Duke of *Measure for Measure* is forced to reflect on the political condition of a country in which 'the prerogatives of princes may easily and do daily grow; the privileges of the subject are for the most part at an everlasting stand'.[19]

The King's Men were formally involved in the other major political event of 1604, the signing of the peace treaty with Spain. They were called to attend the Spanish ambassador, Juan Fernandez de Velasco, at Somerset House. Like the company's two previous patrons, the Lords Hunsdon, James I was well aware that actors are specialists in conspicuous display, and he was quick to use them in order to impress his foreign visitors.

Of the surviving plays from the 1604 repertoire, *Othello* is unquestionably the finest. It requires, as would *Volpone* a year or two later, two strong and contrasting central performers. We may suppose that Burbage played the title role in each of these plays, but we do not know who created Iago and Mosca: William Sly, perhaps, or the new man, Lowin.

The two anonymous plays, *The Fair Maid of Bristow* and *The London Prodigal*, are journeymen works, sharing elements of the popular prodigal son theme. Such duplication would be met with disfavour in the modern theatre, but was not uncommon in Shakespeare's day. We have only the evidence of their publication to suggest that these two plays were successful. One 'failure' of the 1604 season has disappeared without trace. Its brief history provides a fine illustration of the difficulties the players had in selecting the 'right' material. The intention, clearly, was to flatter the king by recalling an incident that had predated his ascending of the English throne. In August 1600, James had survived a plot against his life, led by Alexander Ruthven, younger brother of the Earl of Gowry. There were different versions of the story. According to one, the Scottish king had behaved with gallantry; according to another, he had been guilty of cowardice. Shakespeare's company would not have risked buying a play that showed up their patron in a bad light. Even so, as a letter from the court gossip John Chamberlain, dated 18 December 1604, records, the outcome was inauspicious:

> The tragedy of *Gowry*, with all the Action and Actors, hath been twice represented by the King's players, with exceeding Concourse of all sorts of People. But whether the matter or manner be not well handled, or that it be thought unfit that Princes should be played on the Stage in their Life-time, I hear that some great Counsellors are much displeased with it, and so 'tis thought shall be forbidden.

It was, perhaps, Sir George Buc, the efficient new Master of the Revels, who dealt with the matter by suppressing the play and silencing protest. Certainly, the King's Men ended the year in favour at court and in good pocket at the Globe.

1605

As we have seen, the Christmas festivities at the Palace of Whitehall in 1604–5 involved the King's Men in the performance of five different plays in the fortnight between 26 December and 8 January. The favour brought them at least £30 and a chance to work in the Great Hall, a room some 100 feet long and 40 feet wide. If the stage was at one end, set against the screen and below the musicians' gallery, as it probably was for the performance of *Twelfth Night* in the Middle Temple,[20] the actors would not have found conditions very different from those at the Globe. For the November performances, however, they would have had to scale up to the sublime and down to the meticulous. *Othello* was presented in the Banquet House, which was 50 feet wide and over 110 feet long, whereas *The Merry Wives of Windsor* was housed in the Great Chamber on a stage probably no more than 14 feet square.[21] It was much more important for the company to adapt than to elaborate their requirements. We know that they performed in the Great Hall on 7 and 8 January 1605, but we do not know whether any of them was present in the Banquet House on 6 January, when *The Masque of Blackness* was presented. The occasion marked the creation of the boy Prince Charles as Duke of York. The author of the masque was Ben Jonson, its designer (creator of what Jonson called 'the bodily part') was the brilliant young court architect, Inigo Jones. This was almost certainly the first occasion in England when audiences witnessed perspective scenery behind a proscenium arch, and its significance may not have been immediately apparent. The Jacobean masque was the one great theatrical innovation of the early Stuart period, serving to gratify Queen Anne's love of dancing, James I's delight in lavishness and a taste for spectacle that curiously combined classicism and mannerism. It was not until they came to occupy the indoor playhouse at the Blackfriars that the King's Men would consistently reflect in the staging of their plays the influence of the Jacobean masque; but, even at the Globe, they would have had to take account of the new court's preference for the conspicuously costly. The steady accumulation of debt was not the least damaging of James I's habits.

The ravages of the plague continued to affect the London theatres each year from 1603 to 1611, though the virulence varied with the weather. The King's Men had to maintain contingency planning at all times, and their forays into the provinces demanded effective communication with contacts as far afield as Barnstaple, one of the ports-of-call during the autumn tour of 1605. The company was out of town on 4 November, when Guy Fawkes was arrested. Having been bitten by the *Gowry* debacle, they were shy of featuring the Gunpowder Plot, but the wave of anti-Catholic feeling that swept through the capital swept through its playhouses, too. James I had never been so popular (he never would be again), and only a foolish theatre company would have neglected the opportunity for public celebration of the king's great escape. The delayed parliamentary session began in positive good humour, with James speculating on what would have happened if he had been blown to pieces:

> It should never have been spoken or written in ages succeeding that I had died ingloriously in an Ale-house, a Stews, or such vile place, but that mine end should have been with the most honourable and best company, and in that most honourable and fittest place for a king to be in, for doing the terms most proper to his office.

An ale-house was a likelier death-bed for James I than a brothel, given his inordinate fondness for alcohol and his comparative distaste for women, except as objects of contemplation, but in the heady atmosphere leading up to Christmas 1605, no one cared to point that out. The King's Men were called to perform at court ten times during the 1605–6 festivities.

We do not know which plays they performed. The London season had been seriously interrupted, and we are unsure of what Shakespeare presented to the company in 1605. *King Lear*, if not performed then, was surely in the making. Its portrait of a monarch too inflexible to benefit from wise advice is almost dangerously apposite to James I, as is its recognition of an historical transition from the old feudal kingship towards a new recognition of the rights of the king's subjects ('Oh! I have ta'en too little care of this'). It may be legitimate to doubt that Shakespeare intended anything so pointed as is here implied, but it seems unlikely that the sophisticated London audience refused to read contemporary messages in old stories. That, after all, is precisely how 'history' was then interpreted. A direct moral message was certainly intended in the two thematically linked plays that have also survived from the 1605–6 season. Both are based on the life and death of a Yorkshire landowner. In April 1605, Walter Calverley murdered or attempted to murder his wife and children. In August he was executed. *A Yorkshire Tragedy* seems to have been hastily written in the weeks that intervened between the trial and the punishment. It is an extraordinary piece, at 794 lines scarcely more than quarter-length and brutally bleak throughout. In its cut-down form, it may contain a hint about the touring practices of Shakespeare's company. In some of the provincial venues, a short play may have suited local purposes. The second quarto of *A Yorkshire Tragedy* explains to its readers that this was one of the *Four Plays in One*. Was this a typical touring package of a hard-pressed company of players? *The Miseries of Enforced Marriage* is the same story, expanded (probably by George Wilkins) to fill five acts. The possibility that the King's Men paid Wilkins to turn provincial fodder into London fare has the authentic ring of pragmatism.

1606

The fortunes of the king began their steady decline in 1606. The status of his players continued to rise. Indeed, if, as is possible, that year saw the first performance of *King Lear*, *Volpone*, *The Revenger's Tragedy* and *Macbeth*, it has fair claims to be the *annus mirabilis* of the Globe decade.

Volpone is the most extraordinary set-piece of the Jacobean dramatic imagination. Philip Brockbank has brilliantly observed its complex relationship with *commedia dell' arte* and other Italian modes:[22]

> The play is not an improvisation but it often wins the best effects associated with improvisation; it is not a masked comedy (to name another Italian type) but it often works in the same way; it has no pantomime, but acted in silence its spectacle might still be made entertaining and significant.

I know of no better summary of the fusion, in the best plays of the period, of the playwright's word and the actor's enactment of that word. An acting company that could properly exploit *Volpone* could do almost anything. We do not, of course, know that the King's Men did make the most of it, but there is cause for surprise that they staged it at all. The history of their relationship with Jonson was uneasy, and they could have been forgiven, in 1606 of all years, for steering well clear of him. Not only had he recently spent another spell in prison for his part (which he denied) in the writing of the anti-Scottish gibes in *Eastward Ho!*, but, much more seriously, he was a victim of the anti-Catholic fury that followed the Gunpowder Plot. Under pressure from the Privy Council, the Catholic Jonson had undertaken to bring before the Councillors 'a certain priest', offering him safe conduct in return for information. But Jonson's priest, not surprisingly, had gone into hiding, and Jonson was forced to return empty-handed. Almost certainly, he was still under surveillance when the King's Men agreed to present *Volpone* at the Globe. It must have taken courage to support a discredited playwright.

Macbeth, which represents Shakespeare's most strenuous attempt to flatter James I, is also indirectly linked to the aftermath of the Gunpowder Plot, one of whose saddest features was the trial and execution of the Jesuit priest, Henry Garnet, in March 1606. Garnet's prosecutors made much of the Jesuit licence to equivocate; not, that is, to tell an outright lie but to formulate ambiguous responses which concealed one truth by seeming to provide another. The king's interest in the trial was as well known as his interest in witches, and *Macbeth*, with its equivocating witches, alludes to both. Despite the darkness of the deeds it depicts, *Macbeth* is a much more hopeful play than *The Revenger's Tragedy*, in which covert guilt and public cermeony indicate an extreme of courtly decadence. We do not know how or why the King's Men bought *The Revenger's Tragedy*, nor even who from. (The old ascription to Cyril Tourneur is being increasingly challenged by advocates of Thomas Middleton.) Its tabloid excesses and its quasi-religious adherence to ceremonial signal the end of Jacobean innocence. The king's favourites, feared and hated, and James's own conduct in court and away from it would continue to offer material for more and more plays about courtly corruption. In the summer of 1606, for example, the visit of King Christian IV of Denmark became an excuse for royal misconduct, culminating in an orgy at the home of the long-suffering Robert Cecil, now Earl of Salisbury. What began as a stately performance of the masque of *Solomon and the Queen of Sheba* subsided into unseemly chaos, when performers and spectators became inebriated. The player-Queen of Sheba lost her balance and spilled food onto Christian IV's lap:

His Majesty then got up and would dance with the Queen of Sheba; but he fell down and humbled himself before her, and was carried to an inner chamber and laid on a bed of state; which was not a little defiled with the presents of the Queen which had been bestowed on his garments; such as wine, cream, jelly, beverage, cakes, spices and other good matters. The entertainment and show went forward, and most of the presenters went backward, or fell down; wine did so occupy their inner chambers.[23]

The King's Men were not present on that occasion, but they had already performed twice before the bibulous royal brothers-in-law at Greenwich, and were no strangers to James's irregularities.

1607

The year began with the by-now customary round of performances at court. The King's Men presented nine plays, including *King Lear* and *The Devil's Charter*, between 26 December 1606 and 17 February 1607. The latter play's fanciful account of a pope's league with the devil is an overt bid for Protestant applause. The author, Barnaby Barnes, was the son of a former bishop of Durham, and *The Devil's Charter* is his only known play. It may be that the King's Men bought it to please a noble patron of the author's for Barnes was certainly well-connected. From the scant surviving information about his life, he seems to have been something of a skeleton in the family cupboard, and his unhistorical slur on Pope Alexander VI may have been a prodigal's bid for a share of the fatted calf. Since it was in Durham that he was buried two years later, the bid may indeed have been successful, however brief its reward. Barnes is one among many writers for whom the Globe must have seemed like a promised land in the first decade of the seventeenth century. It is not only to *Doctor Faustus* that *The Devil's Charter* is indebted. A regular theatregoer, shrewdly calculating the ingredients of a hit, writes like this. The second-rate plays from the repertoire of the King's Men have mostly disappeared, along with the third-, fourth-, fifth- and sixth-rate. We ought not to forget that some of them might, like *Mucedorus*, have been as successful as many of Shakespeare's.

From 1604 to 1608, Shakespeare was writing tragedies. The staple diet of the audience was then, as it has always been in England, comedies. It is not likely that the company would have allowed their 'ordinary poet' to confine himself to tragedy if there were too few other writers to provide and work on comic plots. Company meetings to plan the repertoire must have been regular features of the working week. Even if, as seems possible, Shakespeare had abandoned acting for some years, he is unlikely to have absented himself from the business meetings of a company in which he was a shareholder. We do not know how he set about finding his plots, nor how much he consulted his colleagues on the choice of suitable stories.

In 1607, he returned to Plutarch – in North's magnificent translation – in order to write, with a mixture of inspiration and plagiarism, *Antony and Cleopatra*. It may be that the reference to Timon in Plutarch's life of Antony gave him the idea for his next play while he was still writing the current one. *Antony and Cleopatra* reveals an enormous confidence in the stagecraft of the King's Men, as well as an unrivalled exploitation of the freedom of the open stage of the Globe. There was, at this time, a highly talented boy in the company, a rare actor who could be trusted with Lady Macbeth and Cleopatra, prepared to hold his own with Richard Burbage. At some time in 1607, his voice broke or he left the company. A practical response was to reduce the demands on the remaining boys, as Shakespeare does in *Timon of Athens* and in *Coriolanus*.

1608

Between 26 December 1607 and 7 February 1608 the King's Men performed thirteen times at court. London was comparatively free of the plague until late in July, and the company prospered. *Coriolanus* and the much more popular *Pericles* were probably both in the repertoire before the summer closing of the theatres. *Pericles* was an effective example of collaborative writing. We do not know who provided the original 'plot', nor who were Shakespeare's collaborators. George Wilkins produced a prose version of the story in 1608, but that may have been no more than opportunism. The writer of today, who makes a novel out of a popular television show, may have had nothing to do with the original text. Like them, Wilkins was a writer in search of a living.

The winter of 1608 was mild, and plague deaths remained high until December, forcing the King's Men on to the road in late autumn. It was not they who caused the major crisis of 1608. Chapman had provided the Children of the Queen's Revels, performing at the Blackfriars, with a two-part play under the composite title of *The Conspiracy and Tragedy of Charles Duke of Byron*. Biron, Marshal of France, had visited England in 1601, and had been royally entertained. The queen was not alone in comparing him with the Earl of Essex (there was even a silly rumour that she showed Biron the skull of the earl, which she kept in her closet!). The following year Biron was arrested, charged with conspiracy against the French king, Henri IV, and executed in the Bastille. That is to say that the history was very recent, and not at all comfortable for France. It is no surprise that the French ambassador was offended. As he wrote to the Marquis de Sillery on 8 April:

> Certain actors whom I had had banned from performing the history
> of the mareschal de Biron, seeing that all the Court had left town,
> continued to play it, and not only that, but they brought into it the

Queen and Madame de Verneuil,[24] the former abusing the latter, and giving her a cuff. Having been informed of this a few days ago, I went at once to the Duke of Salisbury and complained to him, not only that these men were ignoring the ban, but also that they were adding things that were not only more important but also had nothing to do with the mareschal de Biron, and were moreover quite untrue. He was, I am bound to say, incensed by this information, and immediately ordered their arrest. However, only three were found, and they were put straight into prison, where they still are; but the principal offender, the author [*compositeur*] escaped.

The *Byron* scandal has much to tell us about contemporary theatrical conditions. The Boys' Companies had been skating on thin ice for several years. Now that their vogue was passing, the ice broke. The edict against 'representing of any modern Christian kings' may have resulted directly from the furore, but it was not the gravest consequence. James I's immediate, huffing response was to issue an order that 'no play shall be henceforth acted in London'. The threat was serious, and it seems that the King's Men were among the companies that had to gather a large sum together in order to buy off the king's displeasure. For the Children of the Revels, it was a disaster. They had to abandon their theatre in the cosy Blackfriars precinct, and take refuge in the notoriously lawless Whitefriars.

As for Chapman, in trouble again so soon after *Eastward Ho!*, he had good cause to ponder on the problems of a playwright. To his credit, he did not simply knuckle under. When the Office of the Revels denied him any chance to vindicate himself by banning publication of the *Byron* plays, Chapman wrote in eloquent anger, presumably to Sir George Buc himself, of 'illiterate Authority' that 'sets up his Bristles against Poverty'. What is more significant for our understanding of the passage of plays from desk to stage is his claim that 'I see not mine own plays; nor carry the Actors' Tongues in my mouth'. Though not in so many words, Chapman is charging the boy actors, or their adult managers, with adding words that he had not written. He is not exceptional. Unless he was, sometimes even if he was, a member of the acting company, a playwright's control over his spoken text was limited. In all probability Chapman had not seen the *Byron* plays in rehearsal – and he may not have seen them in performance either. They were, after all, commodities – and he had sold them. It is the purchaser who has the rights, not the vendor.

For the King's Men, the vacating of the Blackfriars theatre by the Children of the Revels was by far the most significant event of 1608. Richard Burbage still held the lease, and at some time during the year the momentous decision was made to add the indoor Blackfriars to the out-door Globe, thus giving the King's Men a permanent theatre with a marked resemblance to the Great Hall at Whitehall, and many of the other rooms in which they had been used to performing. For two reasons at least – leaving sentiment aside – the Globe was not abandoned. Firstly, it was profitable, and the Blackfriars capacity was much lower, even though admission charges could be higher. Secondly, the security of performance on the North Bank of the Thames was still uncertain. On 20 September 1608, Blackfriars, as well as Whitefriars, passed formally into the jurisdiction of the City of London. The dangers of renewed confrontation with the Lord Mayor and his aldermen were obvious, and it cannot have been as clear to the King's Men as it is to later historians, that James I had already effectively robbed the city of any control over its theatres.

It is characteristic of the speculative optimism of the Globe sharers that they should, at such a time, commit themselves to the new enterprise. In August 1608, a new lease on the second Blackfriars was made out to Evans (retaining an interest despite the removal of his boys, and thereby establishing a link between the Boys and the King's Men)[25] and to Cuthbert Burbage, Richard Burbage, Heminges, Condell, Shakespeare and William Sly. A week later, Sly was dead, perhaps a victim of the plague. His share was surrendered by his executrix to Richard Burbage, who seems to have divided it among the six remaining sharers. Although the Globe remained prominent in the years that followed, the end of its supremacy was in sight after 1608.

Shakespeare's career was approaching its end, too. Our uncertainty about the precise details of that career persists, despite the extraordinary and continuing labour and research of scholars. Before turning to look at three of his plays 'in performance', we can usefully summarise the probabilities of his professional life.

Shakespeare's earliest claims to attention in the London theatres were those of an actor. It was as a player in the service of the Lord Chamberlain that he achieved a rank in society. It was not unusual for actors to take a share in the literary hackwork of repertoire-building, and this was Shakespeare's likeliest route to dramatic authorship. The chances are that his earliest work is lost, or tangled in that of other writers, and that the three parts of *Henry VI* represent a progressive involvement in the preparation of texts for performance. It is a mistake, however tempting, to think of Shakespeare as a literary giant removed from the chores of script-hacking. The practical Chamberlain's Men would not have admitted as a sharer a thirty-year-old who wet his fingers with his own ink only. They would have admired his facility as a playmaker long before they began to recognise his rare skill as a playwright, so that the unstated but unmistakable shift in his status from actor to 'ordinary' dramatist cannot be historically identified. The earliest surviving playwright's contract is Richard Brome's of 20 July 1635. G. E. Bentley has examined it in detail, concluding that it is reasonable to see it as a model outcome of established practices.[26] His summary of Brome's position provides the basis for the following eight points:

1 That Brome shall write for no other company. (Shakespeare wrote for none but the Chamberlain's/King's Men.)
2 That Brome shall write three plays per year. (Shakespeare seems to have written about two plays per year.)
3 That Brome shall receive 15 shillings per week, plus the profits on the benefit performances of each of his new plays. (As sharer and house-keeper, Shakespeare would not have been paid in this way. He might even have forgone benefits, though the probability is that he took the money and smiled.)
4 That Brome shall write prologues and epilogues as required. (Shakespeare must have done this sort of thing. An objection on principle would be difficult to justify, and any other objection is irrelevant.)
5 That Brome shall add new scenes to revived plays. (The whole process of revamping old plays, adapting them for special circumstances, adding and replacing scenes, inserting and excising characters, would have needed all available hands. If Shakespeare was not available, it would be strange.)
6 That Brome shall add songs as required. (Shakespeare did this in revisions of his own plays. He could easily have done it in others. Armin and Phillips were competent poet-musicians, too.)
7 That Brome shall write introductions and inductions as required. (Webster wrote the induction for the Globe performance of *The Malcontent*. Perhaps Shakespeare had no aptitude for playhouse 'impromptus'.)
8 That Brome shall publish none of the plays written for the company. (This is a prohibition which Shakespeare accepted. Those of his plays published before the 1623 Folio found their passage into print by indirect crooked ways, or in the attempt to correct the inaccuracies of pirated editions.)

Collaboration, it may be noted, was not demanded of Brome, though it would not have been resisted. That Shakespeare wrote comparatively few plays collaboratively may owe more to the mundane detail of his habits as a writer than to his determined singularity. Of the surviving Globe plays, he might well have contributed, if only at the level of plotting, to *Thomas Lord Cromwell*, *The Fair Maid of Bristow*, *The Miseries of Enforced Marriage*, *A Yorkshire Tragedy*, and *The Revenger's Tragedy*. His failure to contribute something to these or to many of the lost Globe plays would be genuinely surprising. If the king's at home, why ask the chambermaid?

Shakespeare wrote none of his English history plays for the Globe, perhaps because he had used all the best acceptable material, or perhaps because he had lost interest. The majority of the pieces newly written between 1599 and 1608 were tragedies. That has led to some fanciful biographical speculation, but it might find a simpler explanation if it could be shown that the company was, over the same period, calling on one or two regular suppliers of comedy. It has been often enough said, but not often enough understood, that Shakespeare was a member of a theatre company. Nothing demands compromises and the cutting of corners more persistently than the staging of a play; and the number of compromises increases in proportion to the number of plays being presented within a given period.

Part II
THE PLAYS

5

TWELFTH NIGHT AND PLAYHOUSE PRACTICE

We would be less interested (or, to be accurate, less people would be interested) in theatrical conditions at the Globe if Shakespeare's plays were not so fine. It is the purpose of the three chapters that follow to approach the text of three of Shakespeare's plays with some of the considerations that have been our concern in the first part of the book in mind. The recent shift towards 'stage-centred' criticism of Shakespeare is a welcome one, and we should recognise that such criticism can provide more than a mere gloss to 'literary' appreciation. To be sure, Shakespeare would command less of our attention if he were not a great dramatic *poet*; but, as subsequent history has proved, the English theatre resists the colonial ambitions of poets. It is worth bearing in mind Cocteau's distinction between poetry *in* the theatre and poetry *of* the theatre.[1] The emphasis needs to be carefully judged. Shakespeare was a great *dramatic* poet. His was not a poetry thrust into the theatre, but a poetry that was responsive to the concrete realities of the theatre. King Lear would not have encountered a storm if the Globe could not 'create' one, nor Gloucester have lost his eyes *on stage* if the conventions of the Greek or neo-classical French theatre had held sway in England. That is not to say that the imagination of a playwright as great as Shakespeare will be constrained by the limitations of his stage. On the contrary, it will be fuelled by them.

In writing about *Twelfth Night* in the present chapter, I am concerned, firstly, with the play's music, both practically (who played, and what instruments did they play?) and thematically. Secondly, I am interested in the importance and on-stage use of hand-properties. The progression from properties to costume, from costume to casting, from casting to 'scenery', and from scenery to the place of dancing in the Elizabethan theatre, is detailed in the chapter. My final exploration, of time and place in *Twelfth Night*, though specific to that play, has a wider reference. The Elizabethan playwrights were not aiming to cajole the audience into mistaking the play for 'real life'. They thought of drama, as they thought of other arts, as 'a communication of an imagining by the artist which stimulates other people into an equivalent imagining.'[2] The claim made by Sir Philip Sidney in *An*

Apology for Poetry should not be ignored by any student of the period's literature: 'The Poet never maketh any circles about your imagination, to conjure you to believe for true what he writes.' And of drama in particular: 'What child is there that, coming to a play, and seeing *Thebes* written in great letters upon an old door,[3] doth believe that it is Thebes?'

Twelfth Night begins and ends with music. The first affective sounds of the play are not verbal but instrumental. After the theatre trumpets and perhaps the knocking of the stage have warned the audience of the players' readiness, the musicians strike up behind or above the empty platform. They play 'that lascivious, amorous, effeminate, voluptuous music' which William Prynne associated only with the theatre.[4] After a few chords, a stage door opens, and the entrance of a group of actors in livery announces that we are in a great man's house. The great man himself has the first words:

If music be the food of love, play on . . .

The conditional mood takes account of a renaissance debate about the nature of music. The Globe audience would have been familiar with the philosophical links between the macrocosmic music of the spheres and the microcosmic *musica humana* of a well-ordered commonwealth. But Orsino's interest is not so high-minded. He is speculating on the capacity of *musica instrumentalis* to stir the human spirit. 'Just as certain foods delight the palate, so in music diverse consorts stir up in the heart diverse sorts of joy, sadness, or pain,' wrote Thomas Wright in his treatise on *The Passions of the Mind* (1604). As Mary Chan has noted, the opening music of *Twelfth Night* is 'a form of self-indulgence, it is to affect Orsino rather than the audience (who may remain critical of him) and is thus contained within the play.'[5] Nevertheless, this 'overture' prepared its first audience for a play whose tone would encompass romantic extremes of joy and pain. As he listens to the music, Orsino experiences the longing for release from love (but not quite yet, please), and a premonition of the sense of futility that follows release. His progress through the play is thus foreshadowed. The highly wrought language of his first speech is designed to be a verbal accompaniment to the melody, and the melodic pull on the words continues even when the music has been silenced. *Twelfth Night* is by no means the first play in which Shakespeare uses music illustratively, but not until the late 'romances', *The Tempest* in particular, does he entrust so much to it. In the main plot, an aspiration towards harmony challenges, and eventually triumphs over, the logic of cause and effect. Against this lyrical urge, the sub-plot provides a counterpoint of bawdy ballads, catches, and discords; whilst Feste, licensed by his singing ability to establish a mood in extension, or even in contradiction, of plot, provides a sung commentary on mutability and evanescence. It seems entirely reasonable to suppose that the audience felt free to join him in the sung epilogue, 'When that I was and a little tiny boy.'

A confident theatrical practicality must underlie the new reliance on music and song. We do not know exactly who the instrumentalists were. One possibility is that, for court performances, the royal musicians played, and, at the Globe, the city waits. There are surviving records of official rebukes to the city waits for absenteeism – earning extra money at the playhouses when they should have been on civic duty. Shakespeare probably had in mind a 'broken consort', made up of 'lute; pandora and cithern (both flat-backed instruments of the guitar family, wire-strung in pairs); treble and bass viols; and flute (either the transverse flute, or the recorder)'.[6] It was for such a group that Thomas Morley prepared his *Consort Lessons* (1599). The solo voice could hold its own with such accompaniment, without any strain if the music was played inside the tiring house or, as seems peculiarly appropriate in Orsino's Hall, from the gallery above the stage doors. This, surely, was the context for Feste's singing of 'Come away, come away, death' in II.iv. The grouping on the platform stage determines itself – musicians in the gallery, courtiers formally arranged, Orsino with Viola/Cesario centrally placed, and the solo singer downstage, giving the song to the audience. 'No pains, sir; I take pleasure in singing, sir.' (II.iv.68–9)

This is the longest of the three short scenes set in Orsino's court, and the second to invite the musicians to provide a background to a discourse on love. Orsino calls for 'That old and antique song we heard last night' (II.iv.3), discovers that it was Olivia's father's jester who sang it, and despatches Curio to find him:

> Seek him out, and play the tune the while.
> (II.iv.14)

The musicians oblige instantly, and Orsino's reflex reaction is to take Cesario aside and weep words:

> Come hither, boy: if ever thou shalt love,
> In the sweet pangs of it remember me.
> (II.iv.15–16)

For nearly thirty lines up to Feste's arrival, the music continues, to be followed by the song itself. The playing of the broken consort is one of the things that distinguishes Orsino's court from the other 'places' of the play. It is quite likely, despite the absence of a confirming stage direction, that there was music behind the remaining scene set there (I.iv.). There is certainly a dramatic contrast in Feste's cheeky entrance, at the opening of Act Three, 'playing his pipe and tabor'. It is the jester's ironically humble response to the courtly music of Orsino's lovesick leisure. 'Save thee, friend, and thy music. Dost thou live by thy tabor?' (III.i.1–2) asks Viola.

Feste's instruments belong to the workaday world. His songs prescribe a limit to luxury. If Robert Armin provided his own accompaniment, it was more likely on the plebeian citherns than on the aristocratic lute.

It is no more than an assumption that the role of Feste was created by Armin, but it would be extraordinary if it was not. When Kempe left the Chamberlain's Men in 1599, it was Armin, said to be the great Tarlton's own choice as his successor, who replaced him. The resultant change in Shakespeare's characterisation – from Dogberry to Feste, from Clown to Fool – has been often noted. The likelihood that Armin played Touchstone is increased by the aptness of the name to Armin's former trade as a goldsmith; but Touchstone retains much of the Clown's demand for stage space. His disquisition on the 'seventh cause' is a stand-up comic's solo. It could be that Touchstone was begun for Kempe, and only partially adapted for Armin. In Feste, though, the move away from Kempe's style is completed. Feste is responsive rather than assertive:

> He must observe their mood on whom he jests,
> The quality of persons, and the time,
> And, like the haggard, check at every feather
> That comes before his eye.

> (III.i.70–3)

Twelfth Night is written for ensemble playing, a style unsuited to Kempe. It contains only two substantial soliloquies, Viola's in II.ii.18–42, and Sebastian's in IV.iii.1–21. Olivia has two brief, reflective monologues at the end of I.v., Antonio has one to conclude II.i., and Viola nine lines on folly in III.i.68–76. Until Feste's final song, the platform is left to a single actor for only seventy-six lines in total. It seems likely that Armin surrendered any claim to a post-play jig, accepting the wistful, sung epilogue as a more appropriate alternative. Muriel Bradbrook concludes, after a subtle analysis of his literary remains and his acting career, that there was 'some fragile timidity, or some deep-seated melancholy in Armin',[7] and that Shakespeare recognised and exploited a temperament that was very different from Kempe's. Such an adjustment would be typical of a house-writer's practical flexibility. There is interesting evidence of revision in the failure to follow up Viola's initial promise:

> I'll serve this duke:
> Thou shalt present me as a eunuch to him:
> It may be worth thy pains; for I can sing
> And speak to him in many sorts of music
> That will allow me very worth his service.

> (I.ii.53–7)

It is as unnecessary to explain this reference away as to speculate, without any hope of corroboration, on an inconvenient breaking of a boy-singer's

voice during rehearsal, or a change of intention between the first performances and a later revival. It is quite sufficient to accept that alterations to
the text might always be made during the writing or the rehearsal of a
play. Armin, the singing Fool, had earned the right to be considered a
prime asset, and Shakespeare gave him three beautiful set-piece songs, each
concerned to place the passions of the moment within a context of mor-
tality. It is the function of the philosophic fool to observe and expose the
folly of the wise. We know that Armin considered himself a 'foolosopher',
because he tells us so. His rhyming jest-book, *Quips upon Questions*
(1600) opens with the question, 'Who first began to live i' the world?' Its
fashionable interest in paradox is not enough to make the book memorable,
but the attempts of a simple man to unravel mysteries, however they may
be masked by forced wit, reach everyone's experience. Shakespeare's Feste
– and Armin's – occupies the well-trodden space between hope and hope-
lessness. Like Antonio, he is alone, but unlike Antonio, he is unruffled.
He engages in the play's activities, but is not personally engaged by them.
In that respect he is like the audience, and there is certainly a close tie in
performance between the Fool and us. It has sometimes been suggested
that the substitution of Fabian for Feste in the letter scene (II.v.) reflects
Shakespeare's nervousness that the audience might be *too* interested by
Feste, and that the scene's focus might therefore be blurred. I find that
unconvincing. Shakespeare never lacked confidence in his actors; and
Armin was certainly no Will Kempe, mercilessly improvising for the sake
of a laugh. To be sure, Olivia finds Feste's reading of Malvolio's letter,
later in the play, obstructively histrionic, and she enacts a critic's role
when she hands it to Fabian for saner delivery (V.i.312); but Feste shares
the stage with the same actors in II.iii., and does not dominate them there.
It would be a poor Sir Toby and a worse Malvolio who permitted any
Feste to upstage them in II.v. We have to accept the sudden introduction
of Fabian as a playhouse mystery, a rehearsal decision preserved in the
text. There must have been doubling of roles for the actor of Fabian,
perhaps with the Captain of I.ii., in whom Viola invites us to take a
disproportionate interest. Shakespeare had clearly thought of pairing the
Captain with Antonio, but 'lost' him somewhere. That the Captain might
have served Viola as Antonio serves Sebastian is made clearer by his brief
afterlife in Viola's cursory reference towards the play's conclusion:

> The captain that did bring me first on shore
> Hath my maid's garments: he upon some action
> Is now in durance at Malvolio's suit.

> (V.i.284–6)

An episode in the sub-plot is missing. Like the Captain, and as inexplic-
ably, Feste is absent from II.v. 'upon some action'. There is nothing in
the distinguishing characteristics of Armin's fooling, sharply noted by

Muriel Bradbrook, that would disqualify him from attendance at Malvolio's gulling:[8]

1 He attends upon ladies, rather than on lords (Armin was devoted to Lady Mary Chandois and Lady Haddington). Touchstone, Feste, Lavache share this trait.
2 He is often contrasted with a knave and he likes to prove that others are either fools, knaves or both, by means of catechism and other marks of the wise Fool.
3 He underlines or calls attention to social gradations; although living outside the social order, he enforces it. (This is a characteristic of *Quips upon Questions*.)
4 His wit is bitter and deflationary.
5 He is given to music and song.

The opposition of Kempe and Armin is figured for us in Hamlet's expostulation to the First Player:

> ... let those that play your clowns speak no more than is set down for them; for there be of them that will themselves laugh, to set on some quantity of barren spectators to laugh too, though in the mean time some necessary question of the play be then to be considered.
>
> (III.ii.43–9)

It is against the self-indulgence of the Kempe/Clown that the Armin/Fool writes in *Quips upon Questions*:

> True it is, he plays the fool indeed,
> But in the play he plays it as he must.

The musical influence is present in more than the songs and consorts of *Twelfth Night*. Emrys Jones has brilliantly analysed the movement of the letter scene (II.v.), for example, observing its timing 'musical in its strictness', and 'the abrupt scuffling interjections of the concealed spectators, who supply a kind of comic bassoon accompaniment to Malvolio's unctuous 'cello'.[9] The play has contrasting vocal parts, whose observance in performance is almost compulsory – Sir Toby and Malvolio in the bass/baritone range, Sir Andrew a nasal tenor against the purer tenor of Orsino and the lighter voice of Sebastian: Olivia, aspiring to contralto, is startled by love into her true soprano: Viola's is a mezzo-soprano part throughout, however, as Cesario, she may cling to the lower register: Maria's voice is comically linked to her physical size, either squeaky or improbably gruff in a boy so small. At its lyrical heights, the language of love moves through recitative to aria, as when Viola expresses her own concealed desire on Orsino's behalf:

> If I did love you in my master's flame,
> With such a suffering, such a deadly life,
> In your denial I would find no sense;
> I would not understand it.

OLIVIA: Why, what would you?

VIOLA: Make me a willow cabin at your gate,
> And call upon my soul within the house;
> Write loyal cantons of contemned love
> And sing them loud even in the dead of night;
> Halloo your name to the reverberate hills
> And make the babbling gossip of the air
> Cry out, 'Olivia!'

> (I.v.285–95)

It is not adequate to say of this that Viola is 'speaking blank verse'. Musical notation is almost as helpful as scansion in understanding its effect.

We have already noted that *Twelfth Night* begins in the conditional mood. We can go further. The conditional, either directly or ironically, is the fundamental mood of the play. I.ii. poses and only half rejects the question, 'If Sebastian is alive . . .?' 'Your niece will not be seen,' complains Sir Andrew in I.iii.114–15, 'or if she be, it's four to one she'll none of me.' The odds are longer than that, but 'if Sir Toby can influence his niece . . .' Sir Andrew's behaviour – and his expenditure – is motivated throughout by a flimsy conditional. In I.iv.19–20, Viola/Cesario warns Orsino:

> If she be so abandoned to her sorrow
> As it is spoke, she never will admit me.

In the next scene (s)he is admitted. Olivia is *not* so abandoned to her sorrow as she thought she was. But, far from being destroyed, the conditional mood is intensified. 'If you were the devil, you are fair,' Viola admits (I.v.272), and she begins her exquisite wooing with 'If I did love you in my master's flame . . .' (I.v.285). But Olivia's mind is firm, unless . . . 'Unless the master were the man. . . .' (I.v.315). In II.i., Viola's speculation is answered, for the audience at least – Sebastian *is* alive, though wishing he were not. It is Antonio who provides the disturbing conditional here: 'If you will not murder me for my love, let me be your servant' (II.i.36–7). The conditional clause may sound like a throw-away, but III.iv. will bring it perilously close to fulfilment. Olivia's ring contributes a physical aspect to the conditional mood in II.ii. Malvolio introduces it by dropping the love-token: 'If it be worth stooping for, there it lies in your eyes; if not, be it his that finds it' (ll.16–17). As a ring, it is presumably valuable; but Viola knows, as we know, that it is worthless as a love-

97

token. II.iii. ends with a flurry of conditional clauses, identifying the carelessness with which Sir Toby gulls Sir Andrew:

SIR ANDREW: If I cannot recover your niece, I am a foul way out.
SIR TOBY: Send for money, knight: if thou hast her not i' the end, call me cut.
SIR ANDREW: If I do not, never trust me, take it how you will.

(II.iii.203–8)

Irony dominates the conditionals of II.iv., from Orsino's 'if ever thou shalt love . . .' (l.15) to Viola's:

My father had a daughter loved a man,
As it might be, perhaps, were I a woman,
I should your lordship.

(ll.109–11)

It is this irony that affects the tone of the second half of the play, supplying the drama in Olivia's elliptical conditional:

But, would you undertake another suit,
I had rather hear you to solicit that
Than music from the spheres.

(III.i.120–2)

and the whole ensuing dialogue, as well as in Sebastian's euphoric:

What relish is in this? how runs the stream?
Or I am mad, or else this is a dream:
Let fancy still my sense in Lethe steep:
If it be thus to dream, still let me sleep!

(IV.i.64–7)

Only in the plays of Chekhov, perhaps only in *The Three Sisters*, is the conditional mood as predominant as it is in *Twelfth Night*; and it is no accident that Chekhov's work has been so often discussed in musical terms. The conditional mood, because words are necessarily inadequate to encompass it, reaches out towards music.

It is my contention that Shakespeare, having tackled the theatrical problems of providing *Twelfth Night* with effective musical interludes, found his attitude to his material changed. An episodic story became in his mind a thing of dreams and themes, its title borrowed from the Feast of the Epiphany, the celebration of a mysterious revelation generously made and joyfully received.[10] It was not a matter of conscious decision so much as an exercise of the free imagination. It would be anachronistic to ascribe to Shakespeare a musical sophistication beyond his scope – Monteverde's harmonic innovation was too recent to have affected any but the most progressive musicians in Tudor England. We will not find symphonic form in *Twelfth Night*, as some have sought it in Chekhov. Even so, the control of the story is consistent with its musical framing. Two themes, crudely divisible into an 'Olivia' theme and a 'Viola' theme, are repeated with variations through the play, but the first is dominant from the moment it is encountered in I.i. almost until the end. Olivia is, after all, the obvious romantic centre, 'loved' by three men, loving a fourth, and the eventual love-prize of a fifth. I.ii. introduces the Viola theme in a minor key, and circumstances conspire to keep it there. But Viola is the true centre of the play. We *know* this by II.iv., when her delicately poised responses to Orsino declare her certainty, but we may not remember finding it out. Shakespeare has worked openly, but with discretion. The ordering of the scenes in Act One has silently advised us:

Scene 1 – We meet Orsino. He talks of Olivia.
Scene 2 – We meet Viola. She talks of Sebastian.
Scene 3 – We meet Olivia's household, but not Olivia.
Scene 4 – Viola talks with Orsino about Olivia.
Scene 5 – Viola talks with Olivia about Orsino.

An act which *seems* to be dominated by the star-crossed love of Orsino for Olivia is, in fact, dominated by Viola. It is never as sure a dominance as Rosalind's in the Forest of Arden, partly because Viola spends so much of the play on the verges of misery – but she grows with the unfolding action. The Olivia theme recedes to a minor key for its last appearance in Act Five, outmanoeuvred even by the 'recognition-music' of Viola and Sebastian. The Viola theme rises to an ecstatic majority as she 'becomes' the woman she first and last was in I.ii. It is her reversion to womanhood that completes the story, releasing all its tensions. In the relaxation that follows release, it is possible to deal kindly with Malvolio.

I have dealt at some length with the music of *Twelfth Night* because it strikingly illustrates the ease of contact in Shakespeare's work between play-house practice and dramaturgy. Discussion of the play's hand-properties can be briefer. A props-list for *Twelfth Night* would include:

Large cups or 'stoups' (II.iii.14) for wine	I.iii. and II.iii.
Pipe and tabor for Feste	(I.v.) and III.i.
Ring (presumably not the Lucrece seal-ring)	I.v. and II.ii.
Veil for Olivia	I.v.
(? Cithern) for Feste	II.iii. and V.i.
Chain of office for Malvolio as steward	II.iii. and passim.
Purses (for Orsino, Viola, and Antonio)	II.iv., III.i., III.iii. and V.i.
Jewel for Orsino to give to Viola to give to Olivia	II.iv.
Sealed letter thrown in Malvolio's path	II.v.
Written challenge (brought on by Sir Andrew)	III.iv.

Jewel containing Olivia's portrait	III.iv.
Dagger for Sebastian	IV.i.
Gown and beard to disguise Feste	IV.ii.
Letter (written by Malvolio)	V.i.
Swords	

(Yellow stockings and cross-garters would be the responsibility of the tireman.)

Hand properties are important in any theatre, and where the audience is as close to the action as it was in the Globe, there is no room for slipshod half-measures. We can assume that a list was posted in the tiring house detailing the actors responsible for carrying each property on to the platform. The most important items on this list merit separate treatment. Olivia's ring is vital to the effective playing of II.ii. When Malvolio drops it, we need to hear it fall. The implication is that, mourning or not, Olivia retains the vanity of a flashy dresser. Malvolio's chain of office may pass unnoticed on his first appearance in I.v. It cannot do so in II.iii. when it incongruously adorns his night-dress, nor at the moment in II.v. when he fingers it forgetfully while talking to himself:

> Seven of my people, with an obedient start, make out
> for him. I frown the while; and perchance wind up my watch,
> or play with my – some rich jewel.

$$(ll.65–8)$$

At Stratford in 1974, Nicol Williamson filled the hiatus between 'my –' and 'some rich jewel' with a gesture sharper than an editor's footnote. Of the purses, only Antonio's has real significance. It comes to represent friendship and loyalty in III.iv., when Antonio finds himself shatteringly rejected by the man he believes to be Sebastian. That means that his passing the purse to Sebastian in III.ii. must be memorable. It is the job of the actors to make it so. The Lucrece seal on Maria's gulling letter is worth a groundling's giggle. What is the chaste Olivia doing with a seal whose pictured lady is better known for being raped than for being chaste? As a prominently displayed property, the letter needs to be physically distinct from Sir Andrew's inept written challenge, and from Malvolio's complaint. The jewel intended for Olivia invites some undefined stage business. Orsino intends it as evidence that 'My love can give no place, bide no denay' (II.iv.126), but the evidence is not produced when Viola meets Olivia in III.i. Olivia silences Viola's attempts to plead Orsino's case before there is any opportunity to present the jewel. But Viola has it, and we should remember it in a later scene, when Olivia asks her to 'wear this jewel for me, 'tis my picture' (III.iv.231). The two jewels are physical reminders of the way in which Viola is asked to carry the loves of both Orsino and Olivia, almost like a commodity. Both these jewels are tainted in comparison with the pearl Sebastian holds up in IV.iii.2: 'This pearl she gave me, I do feel't and see't.'

Shakespeare's recognition of the importance of costume in his theatre is a feature of many of his plays. We know how much Henslowe's company was prepared to spend on cloaks and gowns, taking account of the audience's particular interest in dress. The wardrobe-master (tireman) was a powerful and important member of the Chamberlain's Men. Whoever he was, he was a craftsman as well as an administrator. We must assume that he checked the appropriateness of the costumes selected by the leading actors, as well as supplying the extras, the boys, and perhaps the hired men out of stock. We must also assume that it was he who took note of any requirements written in by the author. Consider the case of Olivia. When we first meet her, in I.v., she is dressed in mourning black, and modestly enough not to be immediately distinguishable from Maria. 'The honourable lady of the house, which is she?' asks Viola (I.v.178). But a change, or at least an adjustment, of costume is indicated for her next appearance, in III.i. She is dressed to kill. Her metaphorical confession of her transparency – 'a cypress, not a bosom,/Hides my heart' (III.i.134–5) – would be provocatively reinforced by the wearing of a thin gauze at the throat. There is a further change of costume for Olivia in IV.iii. She would not marry in mourning. And a rich dress in V.i. would amply justify Orsino's salute: 'Here comes the countess: now heaven walks on earth!' (V.i.101). By such attention to costume, the progress of the story is enhanced. Malvolio would have been the tireman's delight. Sober-suited in I.v., grotesquely wrapped for the night in II.iii, then yellow-stockinged and cross-gartered for his imagined triumph in III.iv. Maria's trick would not work so well, nor be so appropriate, if Malvolio were not excessively clothes-conscious. In his fantasy marriage to Olivia, before he has found the fatal letter, he pictures himself 'in my branched velvet gown' (II.v.54), not forgetting that 'the lady of the Strachy married the yeoman of the wardrobe' (II.v.44). And he is as conscious as a panto-mime dame of the damage clothes can do to a body – 'this does make some obstruction in the blood, this cross-gartering' (III.iv.22–4). The dishevelled final entrance and departure of Malvolio is a demeaning experience for a man who likes to define himself by what he wears. The dressing of the look-alike Sebastian/Cesario was largely a technical matter for Shakespeare's tireman, but not the less important for that. The Globe audience might have been more easily satisfied by a tentative resemblance than a modern one, but the impact of the play is heightened if there is even a split-second of uncertainty on Sebastian's carefully timed entrances. The stage doors of the Globe, distantly framing the costumed actor, would be an asset. We see Viola in woman's dress only for one brief scene. There is no repeat of the magic moment in *As You Like It* when Rosalind, having shed Ganymede, is led in by Hymen. Instead, we are abruptly informed that the Captain who brought Viola to Illyria 'hath my maid's garments' (V.i.285). We need, at that point in the play, to remember how she looked in I.ii. That scene is short, but the tireman would have had to give thought to Viola's dress.

Costume is important in *Twelfth Night*, but not unusually so. What is more particular to the play is its insistence on the physical appearance of certain of its characters. Feste is guiding the audience as well as Olivia when he warns that '*cucullus non facit monachum*' (I.v.61). As Sir Thopas, he will later give the Latin tag (Armin liked to display his Latin) graphic illustration. It is not just a question of costume. That people are not always what they seem is a thematic centre of the play. Because it is a comedy, the happy truth is that the reality is better than the appearance; but there are threatening moments, as Olivia realises after her first encounter with Cesario:

> I do I know not what, and fear to find
> Mine eye too great a flatterer for my mind.
> (I.v.329–30)

The visual aspects of the play are emphasised in the text. It is not only Olivia whose mind is led by her eye. The audience, too, is given strong visual leads. Shakespeare wrote the play with the physique as well as the voices of the members of the Chamberlain's Men in view. Sir Andrew and Sir Toby are prototypes of Laurel and Hardy, the thin nitwit and the fat, bungling blusterer. You cannot reverse such roles. If Sir Andrew is a 'thin-faced knave' (V.i.215) whose hair 'hangs like flax on a distaff' (I.iii.110) and whose legs are irresistibly comic 'in a flame-coloured stock' (I.iii.146), Sir Toby must be stout-cheeked, dark, and thick-legged. And whilst it might be defensible, in modern performance, to play down the references to Maria's size, Shakespeare had clearly in mind a boy whose smallness and accompanying vivacity endeared him to audiences. Something is lost if Maria is not vividly the smallest member of the cast. There ought, for example, to be some incongruity in the idea of Sir Toby's marrying her. But it is no longer possible to revive the impact on the play's first audience of the original boy's chirpy precocity. There is something about *little* little boys that plucks at adults. Marston relies on it in his treatment of the 'treble minikin' who created Catzo for the Boys of St Paul's in *Antonio and Mellida* (1599/1600). Shakespeare wrote *Twelfth Night* in the confidence that his company had three strong boys, one of them decidedly smaller than the others. A good Rosalind ('I am more than common tall', *As You Like It*, I.iii.118) would be well equipped to play Viola, and the actors of Celia and Phebe would enjoy the new demands of Olivia and Maria. The play seems to require that its characters should signal their temperaments by their shape, gesture, and demeanour, and that means that Shakespeare must have written with particular actors in mind. We do not know the original cast, though T. W. Baldwin has boldly suggested the following:[11]

Sir Toby Belch (401)	Thomas Pope
Feste (347)	Robert Armin
Malvolio (311)	Augustine Phillips
Orsino (219)	Richard Burbage
Sir Andrew Aguecheek (179)	Richard Cowley
Sebastian (131)	William Sly
Fabian (130)	John Heminges
Antonio (107)	Henry Condell
Captain (32)	William Shakespeare
Viola (354)	Ned (Shakespeare?)
Olivia (323)	Samuel Gilburne
Maria (171)	Samuel Crosse

The list is no worse than any fond speculation might be, for all its dependence on highly questionable lines of argument. What is perhaps more interesting is the implication of Baldwin's line-count (the bracketed figures in the cast-list). There is no single 'big' part. Eight actors have 150 lines or more. The spread and distribution of lines are unique, even in those plays written for performance in the years around 1601.[12] *Twelfth Night* is an uncommonly ensemble piece. We can be sure that Shakespeare's belief in his fellow-actors was rising high in 1600/1601.

Twelfth Night was intended for easy staging in any of the spaces in which the Chamberlain's Men might be asked to present it. We know that it was performed in the Middle Temple in February 1602. Almost certainly it was seen at court, though probably not on 6 January 1601, as Leslie Hotson argues in *The First Night of Twelfth Night* (1954). Later court performances are recorded in 1618 and 1623. As a popular play, it would have been a stand-by at the Globe and the indoor Blackfriars, and it would be surprising if it was never part of the touring repertoire. For the scenes set in Orsino's court, and for those in which Olivia plays formal/ informal hostess, the platform stage, backed by the screen of the tiring-house facade, the gallery, and the two stage doors, is an almost naturalistic setting. The outdoor scenes are created by words and by convention. Only two 'design' questions of any significance arise. Was there a box-tree to conceal the sniggering spies in II.v.? And was the imprisoned Malvolio visible in IV.ii.? There was certainly nothing to stop the Chamberlain's Men bringing on a 'tree', nothing offensive in the notion of Sir Toby, Sir Andrew, and Fabian carrying on one each, to form a decoratively spread broken hedge. The intention would not be to conceal the actors, but to amuse the audience. The Chamberlain's Men were happy to work on an empty platform, but they did not idolise emptiness. They would have known how to represent Malvolio's imprisonment by thrusting on a curtained enclosure, a 'discovery-space' used in this instance mostly for concealment. The strongest evidence against such a suggestion is the folio stage direction, 'Malvolio within', but the provenance of Shakespearean stage directions is never certain, and what was done once may never have been done again. Feste and Malvolio both call the prison a *house* (IV.ii.39 and 46). Beyond that, we know only that it is dark. The fact that Feste goes to the length of dressing up in order to play Sir Thopas would indicate, to a modern audience, that the prisoner could see out on to the stage; but the Elizabethans would have been less scrupulous. The Globe audience did not watch Feste disguising himself to deceive Malvolio, so much as Robert Armin getting ready for his big scene.

There is no formal dance to bring the accidents of *Twelfth Night* to an ordered end, though a simple decision on Shakespeare's part to make Viola's 'maid's garments' more immediately recoverable would have made one possible. The squeezing in of the perfunctory reference to the neglected Captain (V.i.284–6) – imprisoned with a dress – seems to indicate a positive determination of Shakespeare's that this comedy, unlike *A Midsummer Night's Dream*, *Much Ado About Nothing*, and *As You Like It*, will not end with a dance. It may be no more than a playwright's unwillingness to repeat himself, or it may be evidence of a sadder, wiser mood. The substitution of Feste's song for the patterned image of harmony that dancing would have represented to the Elizabethan audience is 'wholly in the spirit of a play which evokes, and makes us free citizens of, a world of mirth, and yet at the same time keeps us aware of a world where malice is seldom "sportful", nor time golden'.[13] The dance of the sun, moon, planets, and stars to the music of the spheres reassured the Elizabethans that the world was ordered. In human imitation, people were urged to dance, as Antinous urges Penelope in Sir John Davies's *Orchestra* (1594):

> Dauncing (bright Lady) then began to be,
> When the first seedes whereof the world did spring,
> The Fire, Ayre, Earth and Water did agree,
> By Loves perswasion, Natures mighty King,
> To leave their first disordered combating;
> And in a daunce such measure to observe,
> As all the world their motion should preserve.

Queen Elizabeth was fond of dancing galliards well into her middle age, but it was presumably in the slow and stately pavan that she opened a ball at Richmond in 1602 with the French Duke of Nevers. The showy incorporation of dance into court masques was a feature of James I's reign – an indulgence to the wife he neglected – and Shakespeare's later plays match the mood with their increasing use of dancing. It is unlikely that the Chamberlain's/King's Men needed a choreographer. The ability to dance was one of an actor's skills, and John Lowin, who joined the company in 1603, was the author of a pamphlet called *Conclusions upon Dances, both of this age and the olde* (1607). The platform stage was well able to accommodate dances, from the processional pavan to the rapid travel of the galliard (or cinquepace), the lavolta, and the coranto, as well as the country dances which probably served as a base for the post-performance jigs. It was against such a background of experience that the Globe audience saw Sir Andrew's risible contortions in I.iii. The 'caper' that Sir Andrew claims to cut in a galliard (l.131) would involve him in a high leap with rapid foot movement in mid-air, a grotesque exposure of comic legs. The 'back-trick' (l.133), however Sir Toby's innuendo may enforce its sexual connotations, was, for the ingenuous Sir Andrew, no more than a variation on the caper. In this conversation with Sir Toby, Sir Andrew is laying claim to gentlemanly skills in the dance, and at the same time falling ludicrously short in their demonstration. There is an implicit promise, or delusion, that once Olivia starts dancing again, she will be Sir Andrew's for the taking! But it is not only Olivia's grief that obstructs dancing in her house; there is also Malvolio's disapproval, the frowning on pleasures of the body of a man who is 'sometimes . . . a kind of puritan' (II.iii.153). To illustrate the implied attitude of Malvolio to dancing, Alan Brissenden quotes a splendid passage from Stubbes's *Anatomie of Abuses* (1583):[14]

> Dauncing, as it is vsed (or rather abused) in these daies, is an introduction to whordom, a preparatiue to wantonnes, a prouocative to vncleanes, & an introite to al kind of lewdenes, rather than a pleasant exercyse to the mind, or a holsome practise for the body . . . For what clipping, what culling, what kissing and bussing, what smouching & slabbering one of another, what filthie groping and vncleane handling is not practised euery wher in these dauncings? . . . But, say they, it induceth looue: so I say also; but what looue? Truely, a lustful looue, a venereous looue, such as proceedeth from the stinking pump and lothsome sink of carnall affection and fleshly appetite, and not such as distilleth from the bowels of the hart ingenerat by the spirit of God.

Malvolio's vocabulary of abuse is only a little less colourful than Stubbes's. He attacks the willingness of his 'masters' to 'gabble like tinkers,' and to 'squeak out your coziers' catches' (II.iii.97 and 99), and his rhapsodies in II.v. include an imagined reproof to 'Cousin Toby' – 'you waste the treasure of your time with a foolish knight' (ll.85–6). But, trapped into compliance, he will later perform his own peculiar dance, smiling in yellow stockings and cross-gartered.

We turn, finally, to a consideration of playhouse practice on matters of time and place. There is, of course, a vast and curious body of writing on Shakespeare's dramatic treatment of time. Emrys Jones has usefully concluded that:[15]

we must think of time in terms of a more illusionist and mimetic system in which the primary concern is not duration but continuity, and above all continuity of scenes.

The point is well illustrated by Shakespeare's deployment of Sebastian in *Twelfth Night*. We hear about him first when the Captain tells Viola:

> I saw your brother
> Most provident in peril, bind himself
> (Courage and hope both teaching him the practice)
> To a strong mast that liv'd upon the sea;
> Where, like Arion on the dolphin's back,
> I saw him hold acquaintance with the waves
> So long as I could see.
>
> (I.ii.10–16)

The association with Arion, whose music charmed the dolphin that saved his life, follows appropriately on the consort of the previous scene. It offers Sebastian a part in the music of the play. But it is very much a solo part. Until Act Four he is held in isolation from all but Antonio, himself an isolate, and he lives in a time-scheme that has no extra-dramatic reality. II.i., Sebastian's first scene, is structurally linked to I.ii., Viola's first scene. In the silent cinema they might have been connected by an admonitory, 'Meanwhile, on another stretch of Illyria's sea-coast . . .' But within the duration of the play Viola has already had time to establish herself as Orsino's favourite, and to flutter the sad heart of Olivia. If there is any explanation for Sebastian's delayed arrival in Illyria, Shakespeare has not bothered to give it. Clearly he felt no need to. The play is not ready for Sebastian until it has established Viola. His introduction is timed by the story, not by the clock. The Globe audience could accommodate the disparity between Viola's time and Sebastian's. It is asked to do so throughout the play. They have to be held apart until the story allows their bringing together. At the end of II.i., Sebastian tells Antonio, 'I am bound to the Count Orsino's court' (II.i.45). If he were to go straight there the play could end in II.ii., or certainly in II.iv. Instead, he disappears until III.iii. Naturalism would demand some explanation of his failure to reach Orsino's court. Shakespeare ignores it, turning Sebastian from a purposeful visitor to an idle tourist:

> What's to do?
> Shall we go see the reliques of this town?
> (II.iii.18–19)

The scene serves only two ends. It keeps the audience aware of Sebastian's proximity to the leading characters, and it permits the exchange of a hand-property that will be important later, Antonio's purse. The first is the more important. In the timing of the story, Sebastian must be gathered in for the dénouement. He has so far inhabited only his own places in only his own time. The second is more concerned with the uneasy possessiveness of Antonio, whose need for Sebastian's love is never resolved in Illyria. The setting for III.iii. is singular, a somewhere-street occupied by the play's two strangers. It is not until IV.i. that Sebastian strays into the time and places of the other characters. Antonio beats him to it by about eighty lines, and perhaps (at the Blackfriars, if not at the Globe) an interval. What has become, for the audience, the 'real' world is a bewilderment to the two time-travellers. Antonio thinks himself rejected by his friend. Sebastian is quizzed by a jester who claims to know him, struck by a gangling idiot he has neither seen nor spoken to before, and invited indoors by a beautiful woman who shows every outward sign of loving him. 'Are all the people mad?' (IV.i.29) Sebastian's resolution to accept 'this accident and flood of fortune' (IV.iii.11) provides the solution Viola had hoped for in the soliloquy that concludes II.ii. The words of the scene's final couplet are significant:

> O time, thou must untangle this, not I,
> It is too hard a knot for me t'untie.

It is Sebastian who does time's job. Mysteriously out of sequence with the play's events until his final entrance, he has the power to harmonise. He is crucial to the play's dramatic syntax, and astonishingly at ease – the only character other than Feste who is.

Before turning to Sebastian's final entrance – the moment at which time will stand still – we have two small irregularities to consider. They take us back to the parting of Sebastian and Antonio in III.iii., and to their surprisingly detailed plans – surprising, that is, in a play not much concerned with details of time and place. This is how the scene ends:

ANTONIO: Hold, sir, here's my purse.
　　　　　In the south suburbs, at the Elephant,
　　　　　Is best to lodge. I will bespeak our diet
　　　　　Whiles you beguile the time, and feed your knowledge.
　　　　　With viewing of the town. There you shall have me.
SEBASTIAN: Why I your purse?
ANTONIO:　Haply your eye shall light upon some toy
　　　　　You have desire to purchase; and your store,
　　　　　I think, is not for idle markets, sir.
SEBASTIAN: I'll be your purse-bearer, and leave you for
　　　　　An hour.
ANTONIO:　　　　To the Elephant.
SEBASTIAN:　　　　　　　　I do remember.

(ll.38–50)

At the Elephant in one hour. Nothing could be more specific. But Antonio does not stay at the Elephant. Half an hour later by his own timing (V.i.96), he has found his way to Olivia's house, rushed to protect 'Sebastian' from Sir Andrew, only to be denied by 'That most ingrateful boy' (V.i.81), and immediately arrested. The audience has watched him walk in on a farce like someone from another genre. *Meanwhile*, the real Sebastian is looking for him:

> Where's Antonio, then?
> I could not find him at the Elephant,
> Yet there he was, and there I found this credit,
> That he did range the town to seek me out.
>
> (IV.iii.4–7)

It is the only occasion in the Sebastian/Antonio sub-plot on which Shakespeare has pandered to plausibility. Is it worth it? It all seems oddly cumbersome. The second irregularity comes with the entrance of Sir Andrew and Sir Toby in V.i.175. When are we to suppose that Sebastian gave Sir Toby 'a bloody coxcomb too'? Not in IV.i., when Sir Andrew is soundly beaten, unless Sir Toby is uncomplainingly bleeding through IV.ii. An off-stage battery so soon after the splendid on-stage confrontation of IV.i. is a surprisingly tired device. All that can be said is that it allows Sebastian to make his magnificently timed final entrance with an easy excuse for not noticing anyone except Olivia: 'I am sorry, madam, I have hurt your kinsman' (V.i.219). But a better pretext for this important failure would not have been hard to find. It seems likely that Shakespeare was careless of all but the entrance itself.

This is one of the magical stage moments in the history of English comedy. Wycherley's *The Country Wife* has one which operates in reverse. Its concern is to avert the threat of sudden clarification. The focus is Margery Pinchwife, innocent among sophisticates, fresh from the discovery of sex that her husband could not provide, dancing to the tune of Horner's whore-pipe – and here they all are, saying that Horner is impotent. Why are they all telling lies? How can Dorilant, who ought to know better, call Horner 'an arrant French capon'? She can stand it no longer: ' 'Tis false, sir, you shall not disparage poor Mr. Horner, for to my certain knowledge –' 'Oh, hold!' shouts Lucy. 'Stop her mouth!' whispers Mrs Squeamish. And she is forced to participate in the face-saving lie. It is a tableau of deceit, with every eye turned on Margery Pinchwife. Had she finished the sentence, she would have 'created' two cuckolds, two fornicators, two adulteresses, and a proven lecher. The society of the play could not bear so much truth. Quite differently in *Twelfth Night*, everyone looks at Sebastian. His entrance removes the scales from the eyes of all the on-stage characters. So much of the play has circled round the anguish of rejection: Olivia rejects Orsino, Sir Andrew, and Malvolio: Viola rejects

Olivia and Antonio; Feste as Sir Thopas rejects Malvolio; we have just witnessed the rejection of 'Cesario' by Orsino and of Sir Andrew by Sir Toby: now the rejections are over. The characteristic movement of one human being in hope towards another only to be met by a rebuff is suddenly changed when the stage door opens, and Sebastian walks on to the platform. His own obliviousness is a masterly embellishment, but the entrance itself is the true mark of the actor-dramatist. It is based on an apprehension of the difference between the actor within the tiring house waiting for his cue, and the actor opening the door to show himself to an audience. The effect need not be lost on modern stages, but the arrangement of the Globe platform, and the time it took for an actor to travel from the stage door, must have enhanced it. When Sebastian is suddenly slotted into the whole scheme of the play, time has, as Viola said it must, 'untangled' the knots.

In the performance of any play, actors walk into and out of acting space. Once it became conventional to establish scenically a particular place, dramatists had to invent plausible reasons for each actor to make his entrance. Were it not for the glass slipper, what could bring Prince Charming to Cinderella's kitchen? Shakespeare had no significant scenic constraints. It is not often that an Elizabethan actor is asked to explain what he is doing here, or how he got in. The mock-duel between Viola and Sir Andrew, for example, is taking place somewhere on Olivia's estate, and yet Antonio stumbles into it, and two civic officers appear to take him away from it. Place on Shakespeare's stage is a fluid concept. His concern is to provide occasions for characters to meet, and to construct scenes out of those meetings. The characteristic entry of an Elizabethan actor is not to a place but to or with people. If place is significant, it will be quickly established. 'What country, friends, is this?' asks Viola to open the second scene of *Twelfth Night*, 'This is Illyria, lady.' The extras are costumed as sailors, the Captain presumably a sea-captain, identifiable as such by his costume, and the talk is of shipwrecks. It feels like the sea-coast. The various locations in *Twelfth Night* are defined by the people who dominate them. That is not to say that mobile scenic properties were never used, merely that they were not necessarily used. J. L. Styan has interestingly seen Shakespeare's treatment of location as evidence of the distinction between what he calls representational and presentational drama:[16]

> Representational drama must account for the place where the actors find themselves. Presentational drama asks only that the actors adjust their relationships with each other; the stage they stand on remains the same.

There is a distinction also in the way the actors would address their surroundings. A scenic piece would affect the grouping of the characters, but not their presentation of the story.

Orsino's court might have had its chair of state as well as its musicians, though the scenes are short and the fact that Orsino himself is never absent from the stage during them would make the lowering and raising of the throne fussy and unnecessary. Most of the play takes place in and around Olivia's house. Even so, Shakespeare's fondness for alternating his locations (indoor followed by outdoor scenes, particularised places by generalised) is evident. Only once do successive scenes seem to share the same place, albeit a generalised one – I am thinking of III.iv. and IV.i. By alternating locations, Shakespeare freed himself from the constraints of time. If IV.i. happens in the same place as III.iv., its events must necessarily follow those of III.iv. There is no scope for a 'meanwhile' scene, or for one subtly removed from the play's overt time-scheme. What is worse, there is a technical problem about clearing the place of actors only to re-fill it again with other actors (to re-fill it with the same actors is, of course, against convention). There are two plausible explanations for the place-sharing of III.iv. and IV.i. The first is that there was an interval between them, deliberately timed to delay Sebastian's arrival for his first sharing of the stage with any of the characters from the main plot – but evidence does not readily support a claim that there were intervals at the Globe. The second is that Shakespeare did not intend the scenes to be divided. There is certainly no *need* for any division, and it could be argued that a clearance of the stage (the emptying of the stage for a moment was, most likely, the conventional way of signalling to the audience a change of scene) interrupts the easy flow of the play at this point from peril to romance. The act and scene divisions of Shakespeare's printed texts can be dangerously misleading. They are not always Shakespeare's, and they are not authoritative.

Of the eighteen scenes into which the play is normally divided in modern editions, twelve are set in, or in the vicinity of, Olivia's house, three are set in Orsino's court, two on Illyria's sea-coast, and one in the streets of an unspecified Illyrian city. The presence in its southern suburbs of an Elephant Inn (there was one in Southwark that the Globe audience would certainly have known) betrays Shakespeare's inner vision of a city like London, and allows the speculation that he thought of Orsino's court in terms of one of the London palaces, and Olivia's in terms of one of London's walled houses. He could have looked across the river from the Globe to see Somerset House, Arundel House, or Essex House. Such speculation is only interesting insofar as it indicates something of the play's implicit sense of distance, proximity, and accessibility. Three of the 'Olivia' scenes have their location defined by Sir Toby, three equally clearly by Olivia, and the remaining six are probably outdoors. Of these six, one certainly indicates a garden (II.v.), four others seem better suited to an outer courtyard, and one (IV.ii.) to an inner courtyard. They can be listed as follows:

	Location	Defining character(s)	Scenic properties
I.i.	Orsino's court	Orsino	Chair of state
I.ii.	Sea-coast of Illyria	Captain and sailors	None
I.iii.	Olivia's house	Sir Toby	Table and chairs
I.iv.	Orsino's court	Orsino	Chair of state
I.v.	Olivia's house	Olivia	Elegant chair
II.i.	Sea-coast of Illyria	Antonio/Sebastian	None
II.ii.	Olivia's outer courtyard	Malvolio	None
II.iii.	Olivia's house	Sir Toby	Table and chairs
II.iv.	Orsino's court	Orsino	Chair of state
II.v.	Olivia's garden	Malvolio	Box-tree
III.i.	Olivia's outer courtyard, then her house	Olivia	Elegant chair brought on
III.ii.	Olivia's house (or courtyard)	Sir Toby	None
III.iii.	City street	Antonio/Sebastian	None
III.iv.	Olivia's outer courtyard	Olivia/Sir Toby	None
IV.i.	Olivia's outer courtyard	Sir Toby/Olivia	None
IV.ii.	Olivia's inner courtyard	Malvolio	(Curtained discovery space)
IV.iii.	Olivia's outer courtyard	Olivia	None
V.i.	Olivia's reception room	Olivia	(Drapes and strewn rushes)

We do not know whether the different locations within Olivia's house were distinguished from each other by appropriate properties. Indeed, it scarcely matters. Sir Toby is wherever the drink is. His 'room' is created when he enters it drinking, as he does in I.iii. and II.iii. It was a readily acceptable practice for stage-hands to carry on stools, chairs, tables – or box-trees – as appropriate. Even the tireman might be pressed into service, as is clear from the opening stage direction of the Induction (specially written for the Globe) to Marston's *The Malcontent*: 'Enter Will Sly, a Tireman following him with a stool.'[17] Most scenic properties were brought on and taken off in this way. It might have saved trouble, as Bernard Beckerman points out,[18] if stools were distributed about the Globe stage throughout the performance. That definition of a place could change during a scene is illustrated by the conduct of III.iv., where the atmosphere is initially established by Olivia, but shifted through Malvolio's 'madness' into the keeping of Sir Toby. It is not the place itself that changes here, but the control of the place. The remarkable flexibility of location on the Globe stage is clearer in III.i. The scene begins 'outdoors', when Viola and Feste enter, probably at opposite stage doors. (The entry of Sebastian and Feste at the opening of IV.i. will be a visual echo of this.) The place is neutral, unspecific; the 'platea' of mediaeval tradition. Since the audience knows of Viola's mission, it will assume that the scene is set close to Olivia's house, but that is not confirmed until Sir Toby's entrance and invitation: 'Will you encounter the house? my niece is desirous you should enter, if your trade be to her' (ll.83–5). The dialogue that follows contains some intriguing implicit stage directions:

VIOLA: I am bound to your niece, sir; I mean, she is the list of my voyage.

SIR TOBY: Taste your legs, sir, put them to motion.

VIOLA: My legs do better understand me, sir, than I understand what you mean by bidding me taste my legs.

SIR TOBY: I mean, to go, sir, to enter.

VIOLA: I will answer you with gait and entrance; but we are prevented.

Enter OLIVIA *and* MARIA

Most excellent accomplished lady, the heavens rain odours on you!

SIR ANDREW: That youth's a rare courtier: 'rain odours' – well.

VIOLA: My matter hath no voice, lady, but to your own most pregnant and vouchsafed ear.

SIR ANDREW: 'Odours', 'pregnant', and 'vouchsafed': I'll get 'em all three all ready.

OLIVIA: Let the garden door be shut, and leave me to my hearing. Give me your hand, sir.

VIOLA: My duty, madam, and most humble service.

(ll.86–107)

The Folio carries no stage direction for the exit of Sir Toby, Sir Andrew, and Maria, but modern editors rightly place it between Olivia's request that the garden door be shut and her turning to ask Viola for her/his hand. The place is transformed from public to private, from generalised 'platea' to specific 'locus', by the shutting of the stage door. The feeling is of an indoor scene now, with the garden shut out. Rather than moving Olivia and Viola to a private place, Shakespeare has moved a private place to them. Such is the scenic scope of the open stage.

It has been the attempt of this chapter to show ways in which the asking of theatrical questions can enhance the reading of a Shakespearean text, as well as setting new challenges for its performance through the recovery of old answers. I am not advocating historical reconstructions, but I am recommending an investigation of the spirit of the original performances. Playhouse practice at the Globe was not careless, but neither had it the well-oiled impersonality of modern stage management. Performance was risky and volatile. The actor stood before a day-lit audience, and shared space with them. There were no 'mysteries' other than the mystery of talent and the surprise of resourceful improvisation. It was a theatre in which everything was open and exposed – the musicians as well as the singers, the scene-shifters as well as the actors. You do not 'get away' with things in such a theatre, you get on with them. The platform, visualised by the playwright and tended by the stage hands, belongs to the actor. It is to him that we will pay particular attention in the next chapter.

6

HAMLET AND THE ACTOR IN SHAKESPEARE'S THEATRE

At the opening of IV.v. of Marston's *The Malcontent*, the disguised Duke
Pietro and the double-disguised Malevole enter 'at several doors', and
Pietro launches himself into two lines of rhetorical lamentation. He is cut
short by Malevole:

> O, do not rant, do not turn player. There's more of them than can
> well live by one another already.

We do not know just how overcrowded the actor's profession was at the
beginning of the seventeenth century, when *The Malcontent* and *Hamlet*
were written, but a glance at Edwin Nungezer's *Dictionary of Actors*
(1929), which is necessarily restricted to those actors known by name
from scattered references, will show that there were enough to stock the
known London companies several times over. Marston knew what he was
talking about. For the leading members of Shakespeare's company the
profession was a rewarding one, but there were sufficient unemployed and
irregularly employed actors to keep them on their toes: and there were,
in addition, all the uncertainties of London's theatrical life to cope with.
The Elizabethan actor had to be resourceful.

The resourcefulness of the players who visit Elsinore is an outstanding
characteristic. They can pull an old play out of their repertoire, accommodate an unrehearsed speech, and perform in whatever space the court-
chamberlain Polonius appoints. Hamlet's first assumption, when
Rosencrantz announces the actors' imminent arrival, is that he will be seeing
a lick-and-promise roadshow with an established line in type-casting:

> He that plays the king shall be welcome; his majesty shall have
> tribute of me; the adventurous knight shall use his foil and target;
> the lover shall not sigh gratis; the humorous man shall end his part
> in peace; the clown shall make those laugh whose lungs are tickle
> o' the sere; and the lady shall say her mind freely, or the blank verse
> shall halt for 't.

> (II.ii.341–8)

But he is wrong. This is no fifth-rate stock-company. It is 'the tragedians of the city', the very company he was 'wont to take such delight in' (ll.350–1). There is no doubt at all, and would certainly have been none in the minds of the play's first audiences, that the allusion is to the Chamberlain's Men. 'How chances it they travel? their residence, both in reputation and profit, was better both ways' (ll.352–4). Hamlet is asking a question, and making a point, that Shakespeare would like the theatre audience to take note of. Touring was inconvenient and comparatively unprofitable (so please put a penny in the old man's hat?), and it was not from choice that the Chamberlain's Men deserted their London audiences. Nevertheless, a good company travelled in good order. It was probably a group led by Robert Browne that Paumgartner saw at the Frankfurt Autumn Fair in 1592. He wrote to his wife:

> Here are some English actors whose plays I have seen. They have such splendid good music, and are perfect in their dancing and jumping, whose equal I have never seen. There are ten or twelve of them, all richly and magnificently clothed.

Shakespeare so contrives it that we do not need to see the whole company, but we can assume with the Globe audience that Elsinore played host to ten or twelve actors 'all richly and magnificently clothed'. The whole episode is a delicately framed celebration of the talents and versatility of the Chamberlain's Men. Muriel Bradbrook's suggestion that the First Player was made up to look like Richard Burbage is wonderfully poignant.[1] Burbage as Hamlet draws attention to his old friend's new beard – 'Thy face is valanced since I saw you last' (II.ii.451–2) – and it would have been no difficult job for the tireman[2] to provide the unknown actor with a pointed beard like the one Burbage wears in the Dulwich self-portrait. It is a charming inset – Burbage as Hamlet exchanging memories with the First Player as Burbage. I am less certain about Professor Bradbrook's second suggestion – that the exchange between Polonius and Hamlet quoted below made playhouse capital out of the audience's knowledge that the actor of Polonius was the company's Julius Caesar and Burbage its Brutus:

HAMLET: My lord, you played once i' the university, you say?
POLONIUS: That did I, my lord, and was accounted a good actor.
HAMLET: And what did you enact?
POLONIUS: I did enact Julius Caesar: I was kill'd i' the Capitol; Brutus killed me.
HAMLET: It was a brute part of him to kill so capital a calf there.

(III.ii.103–12)

'The point of the exchange,' proposes Professor Bradbrook, 'depends on the identity of the actors.'[3] It is a shrewd suggestion, but it underrates the alternative and stronger point of Hamlet's phoney jocularity and the execrable final puns. An actor speaks such a line in order to force a laugh out of the audience, because he knows that the discomfort that people feel when they laugh without being amused is important to the scene. Professor Bradbrook's other playhouse inference[4] is, perhaps, the most poignant of all. It comes with the graveyard reminiscences of Yorick (V.i.188–211). On the assumption that Armin played the First Gravedigger, and in the knowledge that he was popularly reputed to have been Tarlton's choice as his successor, we have here the image of Armin and Burbage, each with a hand on Tarlton's skull – the present leaders of the theatre remembering their heritage.

Shakespeare does not habitually indulge in theatrical in-jokes, though there are certainly more in the work than we can now hope to recognise. *Hamlet* is, however, among many other things, a play about acting, and the contemporary references are peculiarly appropriate. Elizabethan play-wrights were rarely averse to the cheap laugh, and actors were often asked to speak scurrilous lines about their profession. More often than not, the metaphorical references are belittling – acting is 'seeming', the actor a 'shadow', the play a deception. But in *Hamlet*, the play is the thing, not the thing's shadow, and the passion of the First Player is singularly without deception:

> Tears in his eyes, distraction in his aspect,
> A broken voice, and his whole function suiting
> With forms to his conceit.
>
> (II.ii.589–91)

I have the impression that Shakespeare, in direct reference and metaphor, is kinder to actors than most of his contemporaries are. It is the seriousness of Peter Quince's amateur company, however misplaced their emphases, that comes through in the end, almost to shame the fashionable on-stage audience in *A Midsummer Night's Dream*.[5] The players in *Hamlet*, unlike Peter Quince's, are true professionals – a credit to the theatre – and it is evidence of Shakespeare's pride and confidence that he could exhibit them so openly. There remains some uncertainty about what has brought them to Elsinore. An outbreak of plague in the city would have provided a pretext well suited to the imagery of disease that permeates the play, but Shakespeare steers clear of that disturbing reality. The Quarto edition of 1604 (the good quarto, generally known as Q2, which provides the basic copy to most modern editors) ascribes the leaving of the city to an 'inhibition' brought about 'by the means of the late innovation' (II.ii.355–6), which *may* refer to the Privy Council order of 1600, limiting London to two theatres and those theatres to two performances a week; but the supposition is not strengthened by the fact that the order was largely ineffective. Much more interesting is the dialogue included in the pirated 'bad' Quarto of 1603:

HAMLET: How comes it that they travel? Do they grow resty?
GILDERSTONE: No my Lord, their reputation holds as it was wont.
HAMLET: How then?
GILDERSTONE: I' faith my Lord, novelty carries it away,
              For the principle public audience that
              Came to them, are turned to private plays,
              And to the humour of children.

(ll.975–81)

There is very little authority in the text of this Quarto, but this bald statement of the adult actors' complaint has a lot of felt life in it. It was the same sort of craze that disgruntled John Philip Kemble two centuries later, when Master Betty, the Young Roscius, drew his audiences away – to watch a ten-year-old play Hamlet! The Folio version of the play picks up the reference to the children. It is, indeed, much fuller, with its attack on the 'little eyases' who 'berattle the common stages', and its allusion to the war of the theatres (II.ii.361–87), but it is too ornate and wordy to speak as effectively for the bitterness of actors. This is one of those cases in which we cannot be sure what was actually said on the Globe stage, when and how often it was updated, and how the original audience would have responded to the lines.

Something about Elizabethan acting *ought* to be made clearer by the popularity of the boy players, yet that something remains elusive. Shakespeare's attitude to their fashionable resurgence at the turn of the century shows common sense as well as some professional fury. Unlike all his best-known contemporaries, he never wrote for boys – though the demands he made on the ones in his own company suggest an appreciation of talent where he saw it, and where he felt it to be appropriate. We cannot recover a past taste, however we may try to account for it. The peculiar archness of young children, when asked by adults to perform, is generally repellent, though there may be something of a modern parallel in the success of Alan Parker's film *Bugsy Malone* (1976). The plays written for the boys' companies were plays about adults. The revealing disparity is that between the childlike behaviour of the actors and the adult motives and effect of the characters. To 'be' a boy but to 'present' the lust or bitterness of a man is to invite an audience to scrutinise lust and bitterness. That is to say that the play itself is thrown into relief by the performance. This does more to explain the willingness of Jonson and Chapman to contribute to the boys' repertoire than it does to account for the delight of the fashionable audience. Michael Shapiro's investigation of the inherently saturnalian atmosphere of the performances is informative.[6] He has noted the incidence of praise and abuse in the children's plays of the first decade of the seventeenth century, linking it with a 'festal impulse' in the psychology of courtly and aristocratic audiences of the period. It is certainly possible that the fascination sprang from the spectators' sense that they were themselves being 'dramatised' as they filled the gap between the boys' perceptions and the words they spoke.

There is some danger in all this of underrating the skills of the trained boy-actors. They were genuine rivals to the adults in an age that wasted little time on protecting the under-privileged. They were trained to speak well in indoor theatres that did not overtax their voices. (Even so, the vocal range of the treble voice is limited, and we cannot presuppose a sensitivity to tempo, since that must depend on the deeper perception of meaning.) They were choirboys, and their theatres were musically more ambitious than Shakespeare's. The snobbishness that now attaches itself to music more readily than to theatre had its precedent in Elizabethan England, and may have drawn in some of the audience. Better instructed in syntax than modern schoolboys, these may have avoided the false stresses and sudden breathlessness that we are likely to hear in school Shakespeare. But however skilfully, it was the mechanism of 'received' performance that they must have exhibited, spiced with naughtiness, and with a gift for sparky satirical touches that belongs to children at the cross-over point between naivety and knowingness. The mechanical imitation of adult performance was inherently mocking, and it is for this that Hamlet takes them to task in the Folio text:

> Will they not say afterwards, if they should grow themselves to common players (as it is most like if their means are not better), their writers do them wrong to make them exclaim against their own succession.

> (II.ii.372–6)

Shakespeare is offended by writers who, whilst exploiting the boys, damage the profession. He fears that the eventual effect of providing vehicles for child-actors 'consciously ranting in oversize parts'[7] will be to downgrade the theatre. Perhaps it was. It carried a certain jokiness forward into the Caroline theatre and on into the Restoration. As for the boys themselves, the career of Ezekiel Fenn provides an interesting footnote to Hamlet's admonition. Fenn was a leading member of Queen Henrietta's company in 1635, and subsequently joined Beeston's Boys. He is known to have played Sophonisba in Nabbes's *Hannibal and Scipio* and Winnifrede in *The Witch of Edmonton*. But he grew up. In about 1639, Henry Glapthorne wrote a prologue 'For Ezekiel Fen at his first Acting a Mans Part', in which Fenn's nervousness is compared to that of a merchant embarking on an untried vessel. There is no further record of Fenn, either before or after the closing of the theatres. Did his adult nerve fail? Or was he simply not a good enough actor to make the transition? We have to recognise that Shakespeare's instinct was probably sound: the vogue for boy-actors, however helpful it may have been to some notable drama-tists, was probably detrimental to the profession of both actor and play-wright. The boys were asked, for the most part, not to sustain passion, but to flash it. Marston explains the problem in a speech he gives to the boy who played the stoical Pandulpho in *Antonio's Revenge*:

> Man will break out, despite philosophy.
> Why, all this while I ha' but play'd a part,
> Like to some boy that acts a tragedy,
> Speaks burly words and raves out passion;
> But when he thinks upon his infant weakness,
> He droops his eye. I spake more than a god,
> Yet am less than a man.
>
> (IV.ii.69–75)

It is a touching speech, but it leaves Marston accused of writing plays towards the deficiencies rather than the qualities of the actors. It is some-thing that Shakespeare sets himself firmly against, in *Hamlet* and else-where. He expects as much of the boys as he does of their elders. (The disparaged 'little eyases' are, incidentally, the nearest *Hamlet* gets to intro-ducing children. They are the sole representatives of a missing generation, barred from the Danish court by the forced interruption of Hamlet's relationship with Ophelia. If there are to be royal children in Denmark, they will belong to the warlike stock of Fortinbras). From one point of view, the occupation of the Blackfriars by the King's Men in 1608 was a sign that the adult companies had won. From another, it signalled their preparedness to join what could not quite be beaten.

Antonio's Revenge, written for the Paul's Boys, and *Hamlet* written for the Chamberlain's Men, tell similar stories, but the telling takes them worlds apart. That *Hamlet* is incomparably finer owes more to the quality of Shakespeare's genius than to the quality of the actors he wrote for; but it owes something to that. He wrote something to order, and sometimes carelessly, but he never wrote *down*, as Marston did. It is only in its open references to the contemporary theatre that *Hamlet* approaches the mood of the children's stage. The Elizabethans were familiar with the idea of the world as a theatre, and familiar too with much of the metaphorical language inspired by it:[8]

> Convinced, even if they sometimes disapproved, that illusion had power over reality, Elizabethans must have understood intuitively why Hamlet, conscious all at once of his own susceptibility, begins to speculate so ominously upon the use of the stage.

Shakespeare's preoccupation with the world of the play and the play of the world was never more intense than during the writing of *Hamlet*. It

119

wells up into the action as well as into the imagery. The English language is notoriously hospitable to theatrical metaphors, and in Shakespeare's England they were not yet detached from their origin. Men played their parts on the world's stage, and did not leave them behind when they crossed the Thames to attend performances in a playhouse significantly called the Globe. 'Sit in a full Theater,' wrote Webster in his Character of 'An Excellent Actor',[9]

> and you will thinke you see so many lines drawne from the circumference of so many eares, whiles the *Actor* is the *Center* . . . All men have beene of his occupation: and indeed, what hee doth fainedly that doe others essentially: this day one plaies a Monarch, the next a private person. Heere one Acts a Tyrant, on the morrow an Exile.

Take him for all in all, the actor was a man, and had to be attended to.

For all the work of scholars, we cannot claim to know how Shakespeare's plays were originally acted. Little contemporary comment has survived, and what there is tells us of the effect rather than the means by which that effect was produced. The absence of detail has permitted widely divergent views. At one extreme are the formalists, who see Elizabethan acting as a branch of rhetoric. At the other are the naturalists, who believe that off-stage Burbage was not so different from on-stage Burbage. Both schools neglect a feature of all genuinely popular forms – their impurity. There was no *single* style in the acting tradition inherited by the Elizabethans, though attempts were made to impose one through the scholarly drama of the mid-sixteenth century. These attempts were doomed to failure. They were the pipe-dreams of an intelligentsia. The Elizabethan plays that continue to engage us embody a popular resistance to scholarly purism. It seems reasonable to suppose that the acting styles were similarly mixed. The earliest visual evidence we have is a drawing, probably by Henry Peacham, of a scene from *Titus Andronicus*. The first thing that strikes is the grouping; a formal arrangement to provide a focus on the confrontation of Titus and Tamora, but with a sensationally black Aaron as a challenge to symmetry. The second is the costume; a mixture of Roman and Elizabethan, but lavish. The third is the quantity of weaponry; spears, swords, shields, poleaxes, etc. were properties so familiar as to be inconspicuous. The fourth is the full-arm sweep of Titus's gesture (formal?) and the much more ragged right arm of Aaron (natural?); the three on-stage figures of the de Witt drawing display a parallel contrast of the stately and the exaggerated. Neither drawing is at all definitive, but neither contradicts an impression of mixed performance styles such as might be expected from the plays. If, as the 'rhetoricians' seem sometimes to argue, Shakespeare had expected his plays to be finely spoken throughout, with fully developed and reasoned variations of pitch, tone, and emphasis, he would have written them differently. We ought to allow

Burbage the intelligence to discriminate between the range of voice and gesture required by 'who would bear the whips and scorns of time,/The oppressor's wrong, the proud man's contumely' (II.i.70–1) and 'Do you see yonder cloud that's almost in shape of a camel?' (III.ii.400).

The urge to purify performance is a sophisticated one. When a theatre yields to it, it ceases to be popular, as has the Noh theatre of Japan. It may remain religious, as Greek tragedy did, but it will quickly forfeit its ingredient of folk-art. Students of Shakespeare are too often a rotten audience for his plays, and an ignorant nostalgia contributes to that rottenness. There is a belief that the plays should be performed 'straight', as they were by the Chamberlain's Men. This is sentimental clap-trap. Shakespeare's plays were first performed, to the best of their ability, by a group of actors who had to keep an eye on their audience, to adapt the staging to a variety of spaces, to double and treble parts, and to separate in their heads the lines they spoke in yesterday's play from the lines they must speak today but not repeat tomorrow. They went out on to the platform to deliver the next episode in a story. To help them get the order right, the book-keeper wrote out a 'plot', and hung it somewhere in the tiring house. One or two of these 'plots' have survived, though none from Shakespeare's company. Written on foolscap, divided into two columns, with marginal notes on properties and sound effects, they noted the names of the actors as well as the characters they were impersonating (in case they had forgotten?) against the episodes that would require them to be on stage. They were then pasted on to a thin pulp board, pierced at the top for hanging. There can have been little time, and little call, for elaborate rehearsal. The actor relied on his experience, and excelled if his sensitivity and responsiveness were keyed up. The likelihood is that special attention was given to certain scenes and exchanges, but that the rest were left unrehearsed. The lines were learned, but the positions on stage were not 'blocked' as they come to be in the modern theatre. The physical on-stage relationships of characters were decided by tradition – the Peacham drawing suggests as much – so that a socially inferior character would assume automatically his customary place on the platform. There is a distinction between the set-piece (*Hamlet* I.ii. – the Council) and those with an extempory air (Hamlet with the Gravedigger, V.i.). Some rehearsal on the first might be expected, none on the second. There is no doubt that Elizabethan actors had fine memories. Where they failed in the 'set-piece' scenes, a prompter would be needed, whereas the extempory scenes could survive paraphrase. It may be that the Chamberlain's Men were superior to the players of Lord Letoy's household in Brome's *The Antipodes* (1636) – though they, too, are splendidly resourceful – but it would be pious to suppose that none of Shakespeare's colleagues ever had recourse to the kind of 'fribbling' to which Letoy refers:

Well sir, my actors
Are all in readiness, and, I think, all perfect
But one, that never will be perfect in a thing
He studies: yet he makes such shifts extempore,
(Knowing the purpose what he is to speak to)
That he moves mirth in me 'bove all the rest.
For I am none of those poetic furies,
That threats the actor's life, in a whole play,
That adds a syllable or takes away.
If he can fribble through, and move delight
In others, I am pleas'd.

(II.i.14–24)

This fribbler, however imperfect his memory, is a good actor because *he knows 'the purpose what he is to speak to'*. It was on this knowledge that effective Elizabethan performance depended. The 'straight' for them was too narrow, and they had no time to fix all the moves – but they could check their entrances on the hanging 'plot', and knew to exit when they had fulfilled their purpose.

The eight boys who bustle out for the Induction to *Antonio and Mellida* (1590/1600) each carry a 'part' with them. 'Faith, we can say our parts,' says the boy who is going to play the important role of Piero, 'but we are ignorant in what mold we must cast our actors' (ll.3–4). It is to be hoped that the adult actors did not go through the mechanical act of memorising lines without reference to character, though boys might well have done so if good leadership was wanting. Marston is, of course, exaggerating for the sake of an in-joke. The Paul's Boys were tolerably drilled. They would not have been given their parts to learn in total isolation, and asked to come together for the first time in public perform-ance – although a legal fiction of the time called the boys' performances 'rehearsals'. The Chamberlain's Men would have been better informed. They knew the plot before most of their plays were completed, since it was stories, not literature, that they bought. But subsequent practice was the same for them as for the children. The playhouse scribe would write out the play from the author's copy. (In the case of *Hamlet*, that is a big job.) Each actor must get his lines as quickly as possible. The scribe's copy was chopped into 'parts', and the parts pasted together in sequence. Only the briefest of cues were written in, since time and labour permitted no more. Alleyn's part in Greene's *Orlando Furioso* (1591) has survived. It forms a roll about 17 feet long, marks no scene divisions, has two-word or three-word cues (sometimes only one), short stage directions in Latin (longer ones in English), and carries numerous alterations in Alleyn's own handwriting. To 'possess' a part in an unpublished play, an actor had to possess the roll that carried it. If the roll was lost, if an unscrupulous actor left with it to join another company, a new one would have to be written out. It was part of the book-keeper's responsibility to keep an eye on the 'parts'. The prompt-copy, which he also held, was the company's property, and, in the absence of copyright controls, its only security against piracy. That meant that it was much too valuable to be entrusted to any new actor wishing to learn an old part.

The format of Alleyn's 'part' in *Orlando Furioso* is a warning to those who believe too readily in Elizabethan ensemble playing. Alleyn may have been more of a soloist than Burbage, but the sense remains of leading actors seeking their own space from which to speak their 'arias'. It was said of the nineteenth-century actor Edmund Kean (or said *by* him) that he was prepared to play opposite anyone when touring his favourite Shakespearean roles, provided no one came within an arm's length of him. We cannot be sure that Burbage's method was so different, particularly in the spoken arias in which he would most have relied on his rhetorical skills. 'Give us a taste of your quality,' says Hamlet to the First Player, 'come, a passionate speech' (II.ii.460-1); and the Player turns on passion in order to meet the test. He would have looked for room on the platform as well, knowing that a passionate speech cannot be delivered cheek-by-jowl with other actors. It was a near approach to the art of the rhetorician, but a recognition of the *difference* is crucial to our understanding of Elizabethan acting. The contemporary word was 'personation'. Antony, when he *acts* the orator in *Julius Caesar*, stays cool while he inflames the crowd. Not so the Player, who:

> Could force his soul so to his own conceit
> That from her working all his visage wanned,
> Tears in his eyes, distraction in 's aspect,
> A broken voice, and his whole function suiting
> With forms to his conceit.
>
> (II.ii.587–91)

The Hecuba speech, let it be said, is closer to those Alleyn spouted than to any that Shakespeare asked of Burbage. (It is generally true that the highest rhetorical flights in Shakespeare are undertaken by comparatively minor characters.) Even so, the ability to switch on and *feel* a passionate speech at will is a characteristic we cannot ignore. The achievement of *personation* is to make personal the words and figures of speech that comprise a 'part'. The possession of a part meant the possession of its words – and Shakespeare would not have written Hamlet for an actor who was prepared to substitute his own. And yet there is an anomaly here. It is most unlikely that *Hamlet* was ever performed on the Elizabethan stage in the form in which it has been preserved in Q2 or the Folio. It is too long. The garbled version of Q1 is closer to playhouse norms. But we do not know what was cut, and find it hard to locate the cuttable. It seems unlikely that Burbage would willingly have surrendered much of his part. He had never had a better one.

We shall not get very close to an appreciation of Elizabethan acting styles if we think in terms of whole plays, as a modern director or critic will. The notion of *consistency* is a bugbear, carried into the twentieth century by the excellence of Stanislavsky's precepts. Coleridge's observation of Edmund Kean takes us closer to the spirit of Elizabethan performance:[10]

> His rapid descents from the hyper-tragic to the infra-colloquial, though sometimes productive of great effect, are often unreasonable. To see him act, is like reading Shakespeare by flashes of lightning.

But Kean was disorderly, and his disinclination to sustain a grand style owed as much to alcohol as to principle. Knowing the limitations of his stamina, he tended to coast towards and away from big scenes, striking hard while his breath and passion held. Burbage was, by contrast, disciplined. The discipline, though, was that of the scene or episode, not of the 'act' or 'play'. It was not the unity of a work of art but the variety of a story that the actor served. This is a crucial recognition. The rapid transition on the open stage from scene to scene allowed also a rapid transition from style to style. The acting required in the opening scene of *Hamlet*, in which the blank verse scurries towards prose until the Ghost has come and gone, struggles to establish itself, is knocked awry by the Ghost's re-entry, and finally overstretches for an inappropriate lyricism, is not at all the same as that required for the second scene. Marcellus, Bernardo, and Horatio are not allowed the leisure to establish a level of rhetoric: the scene in the theatre is dominated by the impertinent Ghost. But with the emptying of the stage, the lowering of the throne, and the bringing on of a council table, a new formality is immediately promised in I.ii. The conventions of courtly decorum, with which the Globe audience was familiar, may well have been a theatrical approximation to actual courtly decorum, but they represented a potent reality when the monarch was active. This is the first of the play's four formal, courtly occasions – familiar pretexts for the filling of the stage with liveried actors attractively grouped – and the only 'innocent' one. It would be a stuck-fast, type-cast company that gave away Claudius's guilty secret so early. His is the sweetness and light at this council meeting, and Hamlet's the sullenness. The actor of Claudius is invited to speak diplomat's rhetoric, sincere and nicely polished; but he has to share the audience's attention with the silent Hamlet, the kind of committee member no chairman would relish at a meeting. The notes Hamlet strikes jar against the audience's ready acceptance of courtly norms, established by theatrical convention. (Cordelia's 'Nothing, my Lord' jars similarly in the atmosphere of King Lear's court.) We should bear in mind that a scenic unit – episode is a better word –

in Shakespeare may not coincide with the accepted scene divisions. The French style of beginning a new scene with the entrance of a character is often a better guide. The council scene properly ends with the exit of Claudius, accompanied by a trumpet flourish and probably by gunfire. (The same sounds, and the same empty throne, will signal the end of the play.) It is a paradoxical moment in performance. Overjoyed that Hamlet has agreed to stay at court, Claudius calls for a celebratory carousal and a volley from the great guns of Elsinore every time he takes a drink – and walks off without Hamlet. There is some meaning in this oversight. The apostrophe with which Hamlet now begins his first soliloquy announces a change of style. The secular court is challenged, its complacent assumption that all the seams can be tucked in without reference to higher authority defied. Here, for the first time, is the rhetoric of passion, asking of the actor those detailed gestures which were believed to be the appropriate, and in this special sense the 'natural', physical counterpart of deep feeling. It was probably at such peaks that Elizabethan acting moved furthest from what we would call naturalism, but the idea that the human body might remain comparatively still while the passions race is fairly new to England. The change occurred later on the English stage than it did in the English middle-class home, perhaps between the Hamlet of Irving and the Hamlet of Forbes-Robertson. The fascinating notes made by James Hackett on Edmund Kean's playing of Richard III are evidence of an older tradition.[11] Kean's succession of gestures and moves are closely tied to the text, but they would not be seen as 'necessary' by a modern audience, now that the Victorian cult of the strong and silent man has encouraged actors to carry the stiff upper lip principle as far as a virtual paralysis of the limbs. Burbage strutted and fretted in this soliloquy.[12] The words demand it, and the audience expected it. The passionate speech was the actor's aria. (It is, quite simply, 'a passionate speech' that Hamlet invites the First Player to deliver.) The appropriate gestures were known and admired. The boy who played Ophelia would rely on conventional gestures of madness to point his performance. Webster relied on the common stock when supplying, as a stage direction in *The White Devil* (V.iv.90), 'Cornelia doth this in several forms of distraction.' The forms may have been variable, but they were well enough known to be drawn upon at will.

We should not be fooled by critics who assert the primacy of the voice in Elizabethan acting. Physical grace and accuracy were at least as important. At one extreme is rhetoric, at the other dance. The actor was expected to have some expertise in both. It was certainly not enough to be able to speak well. Jonson would not otherwise have written of Alleyn that 'others speak, but only thou dost act.'[13] He may have had in mind Alleyn's powers of *personation*, but there is some substance in Alexander Leggatt's comparison of the temperament of the Elizabethan actor with that of a competitive athlete.[14] In one of his rare sallies into unnecessary invention, Shakespeare provided Claudius and Laertes with this passage of dialogue:

> CLAUDIUS: Two months since
> Here was a gentleman of Normandy:
> I've seen myself, and serv'd against, the French,
> And they can well on horseback; but this gallant
> Had witchcraft in't, he grew unto his seat,
> And to such wondrous doing brought his horse,
> As he had been incorps'd and demi-natur'd
> With the brave beast; so far he topp'd my thought,
> That I, in forgery of shapes and tricks,
> Come short of what he did.
>
> LAERTES: A Norman was't?
> CLAUDIUS: A Norman.
> LAERTES: Upon my life, Lamord.

$$\text{(IV.vii.81–92)}$$

This is a lot of words to expend upon a character whose sole claim to relevance is that he once conveyed to Claudius the information that Laertes had become an accomplished fencer. It is an indication of the lengths to which Claudius will go to prepare the ground for his big lines; but also, knowing the value that the Elizabethan actor placed on physical prowess, it is not extravagant to see in Lamord the *beau idéal* of the performer, one who would spring to life on the English stage two centuries later in the person of the horseman Ducrow.

Hamlet's advice to the players has been the centre-piece of many an argument about Elizabethan acting, but it is, in truth, pretty commonplace stuff if taken out of its context in a play densely concerned with the human implications of acting. Brome sharpened it thirty years later, when he had the charmingly eccentric Lord Letoy of *The Antipodes* advise his players:

>   Let me not see you act now
> In your scholastic way you brought to town wi' ye
> With seesaw sack-a-down, like a sawyer;
> Nor in a comic scene play *Hercules Furens*,
> Tearing your throat to split the audient's ears.
> And you, sir, you had got a trick of late
> Of holding out your bum in a set speech,
> Your fingers fibulating on your breast
> As if your buttons or your band-strings were
> Helps to your memory. Let me see you in't
> No more, I charge you. No, not you, sir, in
> That over-action of the legs I told you of,

126

> Your singles and your doubles. Look you, thus –
> Like one o' th' dancing masters o' the Bear Garden.
> And when you have spoke, at end of every speech,
> Not minding the reply, you turn you round
> As tumblers do, when betwixt every feat
> They gather wind by firking up their breeches.
> I'll none of these absurdities in my house,
> But words and action married so together
> That shall strike harmony in the ears and eyes
> Of the severest, if judicious, critics.
>
> (II.i.16–37)

The engaging particularity of his rebuke contrasts with the generality of Hamlet's. All that we could really have learnt from Hamlet's speech is buried in the lost gesture that followed Burbage's 'do not saw the air too much with your hand thus' (III.ii.5). No one on stage or in the audience would have been likely to take exception to Hamlet's counsel of temperance. Involved in the world of the play, Hamlet is talking as much about living as about acting. The metaphor is a truism: he who acts well and modestly will live well and modestly. The play-within-a-play will test the further assumption that the ability to appreciate a good play is a sign of a good man. In commending a middle way between tempestuousness and tameness, Hamlet is, nevertheless, inviting the actors to realise as well as to restrain their passions. They cannot simply let themselves go, but neither can they bury themselves in their technique. The critical search for a descriptive adjective midway between 'rhetorical' and 'naturalistic' has produced, from Bernard Beckerman, 'ceremonial',[15] and, from J. L. Styan among others, 'presentational'.[16] The actuality of the second is attractive. The Elizabethan actor came out of the tiring house to present himself, and to present a necessary part of a story. How he behaved, what he actually did, was conditioned by the needs of the story. Given the opportunity to excel, he would have taken it, with the image of perfect performance, utter ease and appropriateness like Lamord's, as an incentive. The rogue tradition had not been stifled by respectability, and the players remained showmen and entertainers.

It is with a trumpet flourish, and probably a kettledrum accompaniment, that the players announce their arrival at Elsinore. As publicly proclaimed disguisers, they do not know that they are entering a world of surreptitious disguises. The way in which their advent and performance intensify and release the forces at work there has been much analysed, and often finely. Nigel Alexander rightly points to the central fact that 'the inner-play forces the audience on stage to reveal the parts that they have chosen for themselves in the theatre of the world, both in the past and for the future.'[17] That is to say that the performance of *The Mousetrap* relates the events that occurred in the pre-history of the play proper to events that have not yet occurred. The clarity of its retrospect – it is by far the clearest thing that has yet happened in *Hamlet* – promises a clear prospect; until the view is blocked by the king's interruption of the performance. The original audience would not have been surprised by Hamlet's belief in the play as a detective of his uncle's guilt. The efficacy was proverbial. For the Chamberlain's Men, though, it must have had a particular significance after 7 February 1601, the day on which they foolishly agreed to stage *Richard II* at the request of supporters of the rebellious Earl of Essex. When the actor of Claudius stirred, 'frighted with false fire' (III.ii.282), he might have remembered Queen Elizabeth's comment to William Lambarde, 'I am Richard II, know ye not that?' They knew a thing or two about *lèse majesté*.

The play-within-a-play provides the second occasion for the formal assembly of the Danish court, and once again Hamlet's behaviour challenges and distorts the image of symmetry and harmony. According to the time-honoured ritual of court ceremony, Claudius and Gertrude should be the focus of the performance, but Hamlet's obscene by-play with Ophelia desecrates decorum. The dumb show comes as both a relief and a puzzle, a relief because the pressure Hamlet puts on Ophelia is almost unbearable, and a puzzle because this dumb show is, as we will see, eccentric. Q2 has it introduced by trumpets, the Folio more appropriately by hautboys. (The Elizabethans readily associated the 'loud and shrill' oboe with the gruesome and the ominous. Hautboys celebrate the arrival of Titus Andronicus, 'dressed like a cook', to serve Tamora with the pie containing selected portions of her sons, and announce to Macbeth the disquieting parade of 'eight Kings and Banquo'.) The vogue for introductory dumb shows had passed by the time Shakespeare wrote *Hamlet*. We can surmise both that the first audience would have picked up the point that this was a revival of a fairly musty play, and that they would not have been surprised by young Ophelia's bewilderment. She was not old enough to have seen anything quite like it. Claudius is another matter. Why, having seen the dumb show, does he allow the play to continue? The suggestion that he is not looking, first made by Dover Wilson,[18] has no warranty in the text and is theatrically silly. There are three simpler explanations. Firstly, he is in no hurry to jump publicly to fearful conclusions: secondly, unlike the theatre audience, he does not know what Hamlet knows: and thirdly, if, like the older members of the audience, he has some experience of dumb shows, he will be aware of their tendency to be allegorical rather than as literal as this one proves to be. A dumb show prefiguring a whole play is a rarity indeed. Perhaps we are seeing the action of the first part only, the outermost of the Chinese boxes whose progressive unpacking would reveal that *The Mousetrap* ends with a duel in which all the main characters die. Of one thing we can be certain. Dumb shows required particularly careful rehearsal, since any intrusive or random movement would blur their effect. They are vivid evidence of the store set by visual features on Shakespeare's stage.

We have already witnessed a kind of dumb show in the silent apparition of the opening scene. It was asking a lot of a theatre company to write in, at the opening of a play, an entrance for a Ghost, to provide that Ghost with no words of self-explanation, and still require it to be impressive rather than comic. The suit of armour would need to be striking, a first and important call on the tireman. (The legendary king whose image recurs in the illustrations to Holinshed's *Chronicle* has the necessary weight.[19]) An armed figure frequently appeared in Elizabethan dumb shows – an obvious emblem for war – and it is to thoughts of war that the apparition turns Horatio and Marcellus. It is an image that we ought to remember when the armed figure of Fortinbras closes the play. The echo is louder and more resonant than that. Stirred to reminiscence in the opening scene, Horatio reminds Marcellus and informs the audience that:

> our last king,
> Whose image even but now appear'd to us.
> Was, as you know, by Fortinbras of Norway,
> Thereto prick'd on by a most emulate pride,
> Dar'd to the combat; in which our valiant Hamlet –
> For so this side of our known world esteem'd him –
> Did slay this Fortinbras; who, by a seal'd compact,
> Well ratified by law and heraldry,
> Did forfeit with his life all those his lands
> Which he stood seiz'd of, to the conqueror.
>
> (I.i.80–9)

At the end of the play, old Hamlet's son, killed in a duel, has ensured the election of old Fortinbras's son to the vacant throne of Denmark. The armed figure who ought still to be king at the beginning of the play is replaced at its end by the armed figure who will be king. The costume is part of the pattern.

The play's martial frame, pictorialised so vividly by armour, is partly reinforced by music. No sound effect beyond the crowing of a cock is specified in the eerily muted opening scene, but the second begins with a military flourish of trumpet and kettledrum, and invites the firing of the theatre cannon. Martin Holmes has drawn attention to the contemporary fame of the Elsinore guns.[20] The play will not finish until the sound of their firing has died away. A stage direction, 'A march afar off' (V.ii.363), anticipates Hamlet's death by ten lines, but the clash of martial music and the music of the spheres is further underlined by Horatio's juxtaposed lines:

flights of angels sing thee to thy rest.
Why does the drum come hither?
(V.ii.374–5)

Music and sound effects in *Hamlet*, from the first cock-crow through the song-snatches of Ophelia and the Gravedigger's dirge at her empty grave to the final peal of ordnance, are employed to increase the audience's discomfort.

Costume and music are aids to the self-display of the actor and to the clear delineation of the story. They attracted the Elizabethan audience off stage as well as on it. But the greater concern of *Hamlet* is with the temperament of the actor, his motive for disguise. The play's setting, let it be noted, is the intensely theatrical court of Claudius, King of Denmark. It is a play that, in performance, draws on the histrionic impulse of the actor himself as well as revealing the histrionic impulse of the character he plays. Much of the language of *Hamlet*, and most of its tension, are associated with the processes and practice of 'seeming' and of 'watching'. Let us consider *seeming* first.

Of the various synonyms for acting, 'seeming' is the least attractive. It sounds unpleasant, and it implies the wish to gain an unfair advantage by pretence, to deceive for personal profit. Marston has an instructive stage direction for the boy who plays Piero in *Antonio's Revenge*. He has just killed Andrugio, and must feign horror at the news of his death. 'Give seeming passion' is the author's direction (I.ii.241). The probability is that Elizabethan actors indicated to the audience through decipherable differences of voice and gesture the distinction between 'feigned' sorrow and 'real' sorrow. In *Hamlet*, Shakespeare takes the distinction further. As a man, the actor's 'real' sorrow is confined to his off-stage life. How 'real', then, is the feigned sorrow that makes the First Player weep for Hecuba? Stanislavsky would later advise actors to summon into the performance of passion the memory of personal emotion. It was – and is – a method of making real what is simulated. The Elizabethan actor would not so consciously have imported his experience into his character, but he was well aware of the distinction between the *true* and the *false* passion. Having acted a *true* sense of loss in his Hecuba speech, the First Player mimes a *false* grief in the dumb show:

> The Queen returns, finds the King dead and makes passionate action; the poisoner with some three or four comes in again, seeming to condole with her.
>
> (III.ii.146)

There is a distinction between the 'real' mimed passion of the queen and the 'seeming' of the poisoner. But the important contrast, the one that gnaws throughout the play, is between Hamlet and Claudius. Hamlet's performance of grief is 'real' but unimpressive; he cannot suit his actions to his words. The real *personation* of loss is not Hamlet's but the First Player's:

> What would he do
> Had he the motive and the cue for passion
> That I have?
>
> (II.ii.594–6)

Hamlet's use of theatrical metaphor is significant. If he can learn to act, to combine sorrow and its personation, he believes that he will be able to do the deed. But he has also to learn how to recognise seeming in others. He may recognise it in the dumb show poisoner, but Claudius is not so transparent. He avoids seeming by the simple device (subtle, too) of concentrating on his real responsibilities. The king is dead, long live the king – think positive, my boy – when I go the way of all flesh, you will be king. It is with thoughts like these that Claudius displays himself to the audience and to his nephew in I.ii. He is not feigning. He means what he says. For the audience, at this early point in the play, whatever feigning is going on in the outstandingly frank council meeting is probably Hamlet's. His sensitivity about his own performance is evident in the speed with which he counters his mother:

QUEEN: Thou know'st 'tis common all that live must die,
    Passing through nature to eternity.
HAMLET: Ay, madam, it is common.
QUEEN: If it be,
    Why seems it so particular with thee?
HAMLET: Seems, madam! Nay, it is; I know not seems.

> (I.ii.72–6)

That Hamlet passes for a seemer in the 'open' court of King Claudius is evident in the advice Polonius gives to Ophelia in the following scene:

> For Lord Hamlet,
> Believe so much in him, that he is young,
> And with a larger tether may he walk
> Than may be given you: in few, Ophelia,
> Do not believe his vows, for they are brokers,
> Not of that dye which their investments show,
> But mere implorators of unholy suits,
> Breathing like sanctified and pious bawds,
> The better to beguile.
>
> (I.iii.123–31)

His histrionic temperament is well established before he meets the Ghost, and before he resolves to put his antic disposition on. We may come to know, but we cannot immediately know, that both his sense of loss and his love for Ophelia are 'real'. It is an aspect of the topsy-turvydom of Denmark under Claudius that real feeling should present itself as seeming. The outstanding victims are Ophelia and Gertrude. Lacking the histrionic subtlety of the men who manipulate them, they have only their real selves, never the substituted 'seeming' self, to pit against the savage machinations of the court. By contrast with Hamlet's antic disposition, Ophelia's madness is terrifyingly real, and the queen's happiness – the queen herself – cannot survive the growing realisation that whatever is is *not* right. (The actively plotting ally of Hamlet is an invention of the bad quarto – an interesting one. Shakespeare's Gertrude feels the whips, but does not wield them.) John Russell Brown has shrewdly shown the theatrical shift that occurs after the play-within-a-play, when first Claudius and then the queen are seen, for the first time, separately.[21] The parting of their ways is a step towards their deaths. However her hasty remarriage may justify the Ghost's jibe at her 'seeming' virtue (I.v.46), Gertrude does nothing wrong during the play. She might otherwise have survived it.

The Hamlet of I.ii. may have *seemed* to the play's first audience to be over-acting grief. He may seem so to a modern audience, too. But if this personation of grief is a performance, it is a very unsubtle one. Hamlet's understanding of the scope of seeming is radically extended by the Ghost's revelations:

> O villain, villain, smiling, damned villain!
> My tables,[22] – meet it is I set it down,
> That one may smile, and smile, and be a villain;
> At least I'm sure it may be so in Denmark.
>
> (I.v.106–9)

The manifest villain is more at home in Shakespearean comedy than in his tragedies. A Claudius (or a Iago, or an Edmund) as transparent as Duke Frederick or Don John would be likely, unwittingly, to facilitate a happy ending, as the villain of melodrama usually does. The expertly deceptive Claudius has introduced seeming to the Danish court. The placing of the Players *as a healthy contrast* has to be seen as Shakespeare's serious claim for the moral value of 'true' acting. It is a debate that engages Christ as actor against the Devil as seemer. Polonius touches on it:

> We are oft to blame in this,
> 'Tis too much prov'd, that with devotion's visage
> And pious action we do sugar o'er
> The devil himself.
>
> (III.i.46–9)

Hamlet, more reflective and more extreme than Polonius, thinks not only of the human ability to disguise the devil, but also the devil's ability to disguise himself:

> The spirit that I have seen
> May be the devil: and the devil hath power
> To assume a pleasing shape.
> (II.ii.635–7)

The devil, disguised as a serpent or, perhaps, as the Ghost of Hamlet's father, is the supreme seemer. Whatever malignity there is in acting is his handiwork, a corruption of a benign craft.

If seeming is an aspect of the actor's function, watching is the audience's. But in Denmark the actors are also watchers, and the watchers also actors. Irresistibly during the play-within-a-play, but subtly throughout, the actual theatre audience is drawn into acceptance of a dual role as watchers and actors. It is because *Hamlet* tests and exploits the histrionic temperaments of those who read or watch it, demands a recognition of the way in which we understand our circumstances by silently dramatising them, that it has held its place for so long as the centrepiece of western theatre. Long before Stanislavsky gave it detailed expression, the need for accurate observation as a condition of effective performance was recognised by actors. The very 'purpose of playing', in Hamlet's famous words, 'was and is, to hold, as 'twere, the mirror up to nature; to show virtue her own feature, scorn her own image, and the very age and body of the time his form and pressure' (III.ii.25–8). The audience in a theatre is involved in the activity of watching from the moment the play starts. To pitch them straight into watching watchers, as *Hamlet* does, is to invite a preoccupation with theatricality. The observation of people in order to draw conclusions about them and in order to plan future strategies is the dominant activity of the play. Carried to absurdity by Polonius, who despatches Reynaldo to watch Laertes for no apparent purpose ('Observe his inclination in yourself' and 'Let him ply his music'. II.i.71 and 73) and who eavesdrops almost out of habit, it becomes an obsession for both Claudius and Hamlet. Bernardo, Marcellus, Reynaldo, Rosencrantz, and Guildenstern have no meaningful existence outside their function as observers. Shakespeare has created them in order to have them watch. The theatre audience might learn from the characters that accurate observation is not easy. We are as likely to see what we expect to see as what is actually there. Thus, Hamlet's behaviour confirms for Polonius that he is in love, for Rosencrantz and Guildenstern that he is ambitious, and for Claudius that he is dangerous. Hamlet himself is deceived by Claudius's 'act' of prayer. And, ominously for the play's after-life, Fortinbras – like old Hamlet, perhaps – is inclined to read more into 'acts' of war than is there. This final point requires a little development, by way of the strange scene, implanted in Act Four, that gives us our last glimpse of Hamlet on his way to England, and our first of Fortinbras on his way to Poland. It is an episode that invites our horror at the pointless, imminent carnage as eloquently as any poet of the First World War does. In the words of the nameless Norwegian Captain:

> We go to gain a little patch of ground
> That hath in it no profit but the name.
> To pay five ducats, five, I would not farm it.
>
> (IV.iv.18–20)

Hamlet's first response is one we might expect to share. It is a vital moment in the language of the play, when the imagery of disease merges with the theme of disguise to conjure up the rottenness that must be cured:

> This is the imposthume of much wealth and peace,
> That inward breaks, and shows no cause without
> Why the man dies.
>
> (IV.iv.27–9)

But out of his encounter, Hamlet, the observer, draws a dangerously simple-minded conclusion. It is the end of the soliloquy that follows the departure of the Norwegian soldiers:

> Rightly to be great
> Is not to stir without great argument,
> But greatly to find quarrel in a straw
> When honour's at the stake. How stand I then,
> That have a father kill'd, a mother stain'd,
> Excitements of my reason and my blood,
> And let all sleep, while, to my shame, I see
> The imminent death of twenty thousand men,
> That, for a fantasy and trick of fame,
> Go to their graves like beds, fight for a plot
> Whereon the numbers cannot try the cause,
> Which is not tomb enough and continent
> To hide the slain? O! from this time forth,
> My thoughts be bloody, or be nothing worth!
>
> (IV.iv.53–66)

To use the pointless slaughter of twenty thousand men as an exhortation to the killing of another one is silly. Hamlet here makes ill use of his powers of observation. For the Elizabethans, watching a play was a moral matter. There were lessons to be learned. Mere observation was not enough: the right conclusions must be drawn from it. Hamlet's act of revenge *may* be justified, but it is not Fortinbras who makes it so. Indeed, Hamlet's choice of so discreditable an *exemplum* threatens the justice of his cause, and encourages the audience to a livelier scrutiny of the whole concept of justifiable revenge. It is, after all, this same Fortinbras who will occupy Claudius's throne when Hamlet has brought his anger to its bloody end. The alert watcher in the audience will not accept unresistingly that justice has been well done.

It is with Fortinbras that we can begin our final exploration of *Hamlet* as a play with an unusual tendency to expose its characters as 'actors'. The royal family of Norway is one of the play's three main families, each of them containing members with a strong inclination to act their way through a crisis. Fortinbras provides no more – and no less – than the framework of the play. The first audience could have been forgiven for supposing that a conflict between Denmark and Norway would be the main theme. The appearance of the Ghost of old Hamlet in 'fair and war-like form' (I.i.47) cries out for some explanation, and the likeliest is soon furnished by Horatio in response to Marcellus's convenient question (it is one of those clumsy devices playwrights use to provide the audience with information that the questioner already knows) about the reasons for the stock-piling of munitions. Young Fortinbras, Horatio answers, is arming an invasion force to avenge the death of his father – despite the heroic propriety with which that death was brought about – and Denmark is taking defensive measures. The Ghost, perhaps 'privy to thy country's fate' (I.i.133) has been stirred by the preparations for war. The death of old Fortinbras, the cause of the dispute, sounds, in Horatio's version, like the outcome of martial histrionics:

> our last king,
> Whose image even but now appear'd to us,
> Was, as you know, by Fortinbras of Norway,
> Thereto prick'd on by a most emulate pride,
> Dar'd to the combat.
>
> (I.i.80–4)

and martial histrionics characterise the glimpses of young Fortinbras that the play affords us, culminating in the completion of the frame with the play's last lines:

> Let four captains
> Bear Hamlet, like a soldier, to the stage;
> For he was likely, had he been put on,
> To have prov'd most royally: and, for his passage,
> The soldiers' music and the rites of war
> Speak loudly for him.
> Take up the bodies: such a sight as this
> Becomes the field, but here shows much amiss.
> Go, bid the soldiers shoot.

Under the direction of young Fortinbras, and to the musical accompaniment of a dead march and the guns of Elsinore, Hamlet makes his last exit 'like a soldier'. The ceremony might better have suited his father; but the names and generations of Fortinbras and Hamlet merge.

The second family has also lost one member before the play begins. Unable to get a word in edgeways, perhaps, Polonius's wife has passed silently to the grave. Shakespeare introduces Polonius with some care. He is present for the first 130 lines of the council scene (I.ii.), but claims only four of them. Laertes has asked the king's permission to return to France. Has he his father's agreement, asks Claudius, with due decorum:

> He hath, my lord, wrung from me my slow leave
> By laboursome petition, and at last
> Upon his will I seal'd my hard consent:
> I do beseech you, give him leave to go.
>
> (I.ii.58–61)

It is a charmingly ironic economy in Shakespeare to have restricted the wordy Chamberlain to four lines, three of them superfluous. Polonius habitually acts out the scenes he plots and the events he describes. He provides Reynaldo, not only with a scenario for his spying, but also with the dialogue:

> POLONIUS: Take you, as 'twere, some distant knowledge of him;
> As thus, 'I know his father, and his friends,
> And, in part, him;' do you mark this, Reynaldo?
> REYNALDO: Ay, very well, my lord.
> POLONIUS: 'And, in part, him; but,' you may say, 'not well:
> But if't be he I mean, he's very wild,
> Addicted so and so;' and there put on him
> What forgeries you please.
>
> (II.i.13–19)

In telling Claudius and Gertrude of his attempts to obstruct Hamlet's love for Ophelia, he imitates an actor's care for his audience, and quotes his remembered lines:

> ... what might you
> Or my dear majesty, your queen here, think,
> If I had play'd the desk or table-book,
> Or given my heart a winking, mute and dumb,
> Or look'd upon this love with idle sight;
> What might you think? No, I went round to work,
> And my young mistress thus I did bespeak:
> 'Lord Hamlet is a prince, out of thy star;
> This must not be:' and then I precepts gave her.
>
> (II.ii.134–42)

Even in the queen's closet, in almost the last words he will ever speak, he is still trying to provide the dialogue:

> He will come straight. Look you lay home to him;
> Tell him his pranks have been too broad to bear with,
> And that your Grace hath screen'd and stood between
> Much heat and him.
>
> (III.iv.1–4)

With consistent ineptitude, Polonius performs his service to the state. Acting is his mode of being. He acts the father, just as he acts the loyal chamberlain. His performance is comic partly because it is unvarying. He is a single-style actor in a multi-styled play. Once he has become convinced that the good of Denmark is contingent on an understanding of Hamlet's behaviour, he initiates and stages two simple scenes, opting, himself, for the role of audience. For the first, he disposes Ophelia carefully on the platform:

> Ophelia, walk you here. Gracious, so please you,
> We will bestow ourselves. Read on this book,
> That show of such an exercise may colour
> Your loneliness.
>
> (III.i.43–6)

The directorial concern for detail is exemplary, if a little obvious. The property-book is a dramatic aid to a scene that might otherwise leave Ophelia too unprotected. The watchers do not learn enough from this encounter, and Polonius prepares a second. He has already boasted his love of acting in his greeting of the players. Now, in his second contrived eavesdropping, he is destined to re-enact the murdered role of Julius Caesar. His is the first death in the play. It is followed by his daughter's. Unlike the royal family of Denmark, the family of Polonius dies *seriatim*. Ophelia is first seen in a domestic context, wrapped in masculine advice, but wittily refusing to be smothered by it. She is so obviously a victim of the play's disguises that her own histrionic inclination can be easily overlooked. But the wording of her description of Hamlet's visit to her closet shows that she acts out the narration. The double use of 'thus' shows that the actor twice mimed Hamlet's behaviour; or that the whole speech was backed by imitation:

> He took me by the wrist and held me hard,
> Then goes he to the length of all his arm
> And with his other hand thus o'er his brow,
> He falls to such perusal of my face
> As he would draw it. Long stay'd he so;
> At last, a little shaking of mine arm,

And thrice his head thus waving up and down,
He rais'd a sigh so piteous and profound
That it did seem to shatter all his bulk
And end his being.

(II.i.87–96)

The boy who played Ophelia at the Globe was here performing both a dumb show and its commentary. He was giving 'seeming passion'. There is no *need* for Ophelia to act Hamlet. It is, on the contrary, a surprising thing for her to do, a reflection of Shakespeare's absorption in the idea of acting during the writing of *Hamlet*. Ophelia's final performance is involuntary. She does not act madness: she is mad. It is, as F. W. Sternfeld notes, a symptom of her derangement that 'she sings before an assembly of the Court without being encouraged to do so.'[23] That so much of what she sings is indelicate is a sign of something else. Ophelia has the good actor's ability to observe accurately. In the masculine world of Denmark, much of the conversation is bawdy – Polonius with Reynaldo, Hamlet with Rosencrantz and Guildenstern, and, shockingly, with Ophelia herself. In performing her mad songs, Ophelia is performing the rottenness of Denmark. The remaining member of his family, Laertes, is dangerously like Polonius in his facile admonitions to Ophelia, but his angry return to Denmark is not 'acted', nor his grief at Ophelia's funeral, for all that Hamlet charges him with 'seeming':

What is he whose grief
Bears such an emphasis? whose phrase of sorrow
Conjures the wandering stars, and makes them stand
Like wonder-wounded hearers?

(V.i.276–9)

The high-flown lamentations of Laertes are criticised by Hamlet as rhetorical tricks, and the graveyard confrontation becomes almost a competition of orators:

Nay, an thou'lt mouth,
I'll rant as well as thou.

(V.i.305–6)

It is, as we shall see, Claudius who draws Laertes into the theatricals of the Danish court, turning a posturing young man into a villainous role-player whose renunciation of 'foul practice' (V.ii.331) comes too late.

The third family, too, has lost a member before the play begins. His ghost commands our attention in the first scene. It is not a shy Ghost, skulking in corners, but a powerful marching figure, who should have died in battle, not poisoned in a garden. The Ghost, like young Hamlet, displays a fondness for the broad gesture and a whimsical sense of theatre.

138

But neither in the Ghost, nor in what we learn of old Hamlet, is there evidence of much subtlety. Claudius is the great seemer. Though never fully king, he is a masterful player of kingship – at least, until Hamlet mounts his challenge. His playing of the harder role of kinship is at its most effective in I.ii., and good enough to fool most of the people all of the time. Like a skilful, improvising actor, Claudius thinks on his feet. When Hamlet and Laertes scuffle in Ophelia's grave, he invents an *act* of mediation, already discerning a distant advantage. The impenetrable disguise that makes strenuous acting unnecessary is his theatrical costume, and indirectness is his mode of being. Unusual among villains, he conceals his villainy from the audience for much of the play. Piero, his equivalent in *Antonio's Revenge*, announces his crimes inside the first scene: 'Poison the father, butcher the son, and marry the mother; ha!' (I.i.105). This is not Claudius's style. Working at his best, as in the preparing of Laertes for the duel, he is actor, director, and dramatist in one. The duel, as he intends it to be played, is his own creation:

> For his death no wind of blame shall breathe,
> But even his mother shall uncharge the practice,
> And call it accident.
>
> (IV.vii.66–8)

It is the intuitive timing of a master-plotter that inspires him to interrupt the scheming by posing a question designed to allay Laertes's qualms: 'Laertes, was your father dear to you?' (IV.vii.107), and it is accurate observation that allows him to predict that Hamlet:

> Will not peruse the foils; so that with ease,
> Or with a little shuffling, you may choose
> A sword unbated, and, in a pass of practice,
> Requite him for your father.
>
> (IV.vii.136–9)

His mastery of detail, and the precision of the venomous phrase 'with a little shuffling', are in a different theatrical class from Polonius's simple planting of Ophelia with a book. As author of the duel/play, Claudius can scarcely have expected the help he gets from his leading actor, but he welcomes Laertes's addition of the poisoned blade, and compounds it with his own idea for a poisoned drink. The scenario improves as it is devised. Hamlet, though, is an elusive adversary and a fine actor. His 'antic disposition' is a substitution in the real world of Denmark of an assumed personality, a substitution designed to allow his real, abstracted personality to direct events comparatively unhindered. His plans are obstructed by both Polonius and Claudius; but with the elimination of Polonius, the real battle is joined. Rosencrantz and Guildenstern are incidental victims, as Hamlet explains to Horatio:

'Tis dangerous when the baser nature comes
Between the pass and fell-incensed points
Of mighty opposites.

(V.ii.60–2)

The image significantly anticipates the duel, facing Hamlet with his real adversary, Claudius, rather than his contrived one, Laertes. It is a confrontation that he strangely relishes, as he warns his mother in her closet: 'O! 'tis most sweet,/When in one line two crafts directly meet' (III.iv.209–10). The movement towards this meeting, however delayed by contrivances, is inexorable.

The meeting takes place at the fourth and final assembly of the Danish court. (The third was round Ophelia's grave.) Hamlet has agreed to take part in Claudius's 'play', though he has still in mind a contrary scenario of his own. The discipline and conduct of this duel would have been familiar to the play's original audience. Exhibitions of swordplay were staged in the Elizabethan open-air theatres, and there would have been vociferous criticism of clumsy swordsmanship in the Globe. It is not easy for us to interpret Osric's account of the proposed rules:

The king, sir, hath laid, that in a dozen passes between yourself and him, he shall not exceed you three hits; he hath laid on twelve for nine.

(V.ii.172–5)

In an extended discussion of the duel, Martin Holmes offers this gloss:[24]

Laertes, as admittedly the better swordsman, starts three down. If he can gain a clear lead of three in spite of this, he wins; if Hamlet can get up to nine before he attains this lead, Hamlet wins.

He also argues that, despite Laertes's preference for 'rapier and dagger' (V.ii.152), the likeliest form was single rapier, in which the weapon was used only for attack, parrying being done with the (usually gloved) left hand. Exchange of rapiers was always a possibility in this mixture of wrestling and fencing. A well-ordered duel was an image of harmony to its Elizabethan spectators, but Claudius and Laertes have scarred this image before the scene begins. This bout, carefully rehearsed by actors who knew how to fence, is an image of *disorder*. For Claudius, it promises an ending; for Hamlet, it is at best a means to an end. Using the same characters, each has plotted and acted in a different 'play' – but the queen's death figured in neither. We are left, when the stage has been cleared, with a sense that they have been collaborating in a greater play, in which their parts were written beyond their knowledge.

Hamlet investigates, with unique intensity, the power and the limitations of the actor, his invitation to the audience to recognise in life the interplay of illusion and reality. I would have liked, in this chapter, to have 'solved' the puzzle of Elizabethan acting, but no solution is possible. What the Elizabethan audience witnessed was a mingling of the vigorous, popular mediaeval tradition and the more refined styles encouraged by scholarly writers. The vital factor was the ability of skilful players to possess the platform and to engage the audience. *Hamlet* celebrates the solemnity of the actor's art without blinking its dangers. 'By his action', wrote Webster, 'he fortifies morall precepts with example.'[25] Our concern – it is the concern of *Hamlet* – is not only with how he stood, but with what he stood for. Unprotected – or unhindered – by a director, the Elizabethan actor was the leader of his profession. The help he needed most was the unsung labour of the stage-hands. Some of the demands made on them are the subject of the next chapter.

MACBETH FROM THE TIRING HOUSE

The reliance of Elizabethan playwrights on the actors with whom they worked – and, by implication, the trustworthiness of those actors – is the single, major contributing factor to the greatness of Elizabethan drama. But the actors, in their turn, relied on the playhouse servants to aid the visual and aural display that was so attractive a part of London life. Backstage activity in any theatre has its own rules and its own crescendo and diminuendo. What may be a quiet scene on the platform can call for hectic preparation in the tiring house. An actor's performance may depend on the precise timing of a sound effect, or the precise placing of a property. The job of the tireman was not ended when he had assembled the costumes. He would have to supervise changes, fix and remove beards for actors who were doubling roles, and make sure that everything was available when needed. Conspicuous display became increasingly a feature of the Jacobean theatre. We do not know whether the number of hired stage-hands increased, though it seems likely. We can, however, see that the demands made on them increased. A comparison of *Macbeth* with *Hamlet* will illustrate the change. It is not the aim of this chapter to make that comparison – though it ought to make itself – but rather, by a scene-by-scene analysis, to bring into focus the nature and the significance of the stage-hands' responsibilities during the first performances of *Macbeth*.

By the time Shakespeare began work on the play, probably in 1606, the problems of the English succession – those very problems that bubble beneath the surface of *Hamlet* – had been settled. (In Denmark, too, the king of a neighbouring country had filled the breach.) Sitting ungainly on the throne was the latest of the Stuart kings of Scotland, whose legendary ancestor was Banquo. As he wrote, Shakespeare kept beside him a copy of Holinshed's *Chronicles of Scotland*. He was well established as a company playwright, and the new monarch had seen fit to give that company his personal patronage. It was as poet to the King's Men that Shakespeare undertook the writing of *Macbeth*. He owed it to his colleagues to be tactful: the ice was thin. Knowing something by now of James I's greedy scholarship, and of his strong sense of himself as a part of Scottish history, the King's Men may have looked to Shakespeare to gratify their patron. They had come a cropper in 1604, when a play about the Gowry conspiracy had given offence; but Gowry was recent history, in which James had been personally involved. *Not* to perform something in which James might see his own reflection could have been viewed as a sin of omission, a failure to compensate for the *faux pas* of the Gowry piece; and the history of Scotland in the eleventh century was safer cover than a six-year dead conspiracy. Even so, Shakespeare made assurance doubly sure by a wise editing of Holinshed. He suppresses, for instance, the statement that Macbeth was for ten years so just a king that 'he might well have been numbered amongst the most noble princes that anie where had reigned', muffles any hint of Banquo's collaboration in the killing of the king, and sensibly avoids any reference to the disreputable career of Fleance after his flight to Wales. There is some force in the claims that *Macbeth* was prepared for presentation at Hampton Court before James I and Christian IV of Denmark in August 1606. The decision to make the allies of the traitorous 'merciless Macdonwald' (I.ii.9) Norwegians instead of Danes, as they are in Holinshed, is particularly persuasive evidence: and there is no doubt that *Macbeth* is sprinkled with deliberate flattery of the Stuart dynasty. Some high-minded critics have been offended by this, regretting the discovery of their idol's feet of clay. The King's Men must have been glad: a house playwright without clay feet would be an embarrassment. What is much less certain, and really not very important, is the subsidiary claim that *Macbeth* was *first* performed at court. Like all the plays that remained in the repertoire of the King's Men, it was written for ready adaptation to presentation anywhere. That is not to deny features in the text, particularly its reliance on darkness, that make it particularly suitable for indoor performance. It can be presumed to have held a proud place in the Blackfriars repertoire after 1609, and it may be that the Folio text, our only authority, contains not only what Shakespeare wrote, but also a lot of what subsequently happened to what Shakespeare wrote. Whatever the location of the world première, the only recorded production in Shakespeare's lifetime took place on 20 April 1611 – at the Globe.

Simon Forman was there, and wrote about it in his *Book of Plays*. Since contemporary comment on performances is so rare, and since the Forman account has caused considerable controversy it is worth quoting in full:

> There was to be observed, first, how Macbeth and Banquo, two
> noble men of Scotland, riding through a wood, there stood before
> them three women fairies or nymphs, and saluted Macbeth, saying,
> three times unto him, hail Macbeth, king of Codon; for thou shalt
> be a king, but shalt beget no kings, etc. Then said Banquo, What all
> to Macbeth and nothing to me? Yes, said the nymphs, hail to thee
> Banquo, thou shalt beget kings, yet be no king. And so they departed

and came to the court of Scotland to Duncan king of Scots, and it was in the days of Edward the Confessor. And Duncan bade them both kindly welcome, and made Macbeth forthwith Prince of Northumberland, and sent him home to his own castle, and appointed Macbeth to provide for him, for he would sup with him the next day at night, and did so. And Macbeth contrived to kill Duncan, and thoro' the persuasion of his wife did that night murder the king in his own castle, being his guest. And there were many prodigies seen that night and the day before. And when Macbeth had murdered the king, the blood on his hands could not be washed off by any means, nor from his wife's hands, which handled the bloody daggers in hiding them, by which means they became both much amazed and affronted. The murder being known, Duncan's two sons fled, the one to England the [other to] Wales, to save themselves; they being fled, they were supposed guilty of the murder of their father, which was nothing so. Then was Macbeth crowned king, and then he for fear of Banquo, his old companion, that he should beget kings but be no king himself, he contrived the death of Banquo, and caused him to be murdered on the way as he rode. The next night, being at supper with his noblemen whom he had bid to a feast to the which also Banquo should have come, he began to speak of noble Banquo, and to wish that he were there. And as he thus did, standing up to drink a carouse to him, the ghost of Banquo came and sat down in his chair behind him. And he turning about to sit down again saw the ghost of Banquo, which fronted him so, that he fell into a great passion of fear and fury, uttering many words about his murder, by which, when they heard that Banquo was murdered they suspected Macbeth.

Then Macduff fled to England to the king's son, and so they raised an army, and came into Scotland, and at Dunston Anyse overthrew Macbeth. In the meantime while Macduff was in England, Macbeth slew Macduff's wife and children, and after in the battle Macduff slew Macbeth.

Observe also how Macbeth's queen did rise in the night in her sleep, and walked and talked and confessed all, and the doctor noted her words.

What the account makes clear is that Forman, as much as the less scholarly members of the audience, was primarily there to receive a story. What is less immediately obvious is that he has relied on Holinshed to supplement, if not sometimes to replace, Shakespeare. Some critical energy has been expended on the discrediting of Forman's evidence as a guide to Jacobean performance in general, and as an indication of what happened when *Macbeth* was played at the Globe in particular.[1] It is comparatively easy, though, to say what you cannot safely deduce from his account. You cannot, for instance, as Dennis Bartholomeusz does,[2] use it as evidence that Macbeth and Banquo made their first entrance on horseback – though you cannot entirely rule out the possibility, either. It is more important, and less open to witty disparagement, to try to make something of Forman. What seems most to have commanded his attention does not encapsulate the King's Men's performance, but it may illuminate it. Forman recalls:

i) the first meeting between Macbeth and Banquo and the Witches in I.iii. (He does not refer to the traditionally spectacular second meeting in IV.i., nor at all to Hecate.)

ii) that 'it was in the days of Edward the Confessor'. (It may have been his reading of Holinshed that reminded him of this; but the orientation towards English history may reflect a preoccupation of the Globe audience.)

iii) that the murdered Duncan was Macbeth's *guest*. (This is not an emphasis in Holinshed, whose account of the murder of Malcolm Duff by Donwald has been transposed by Shakespeare.)

iv) that prodigies were seen that night and the day before. (Astrology was one of Forman's many interests.)

v) the impossibility of washing the blood of Duncan from the hands of Macbeth and Lady Macbeth. (This suggests that there was some detailed work on stage business here.)

vi) the death of Banquo, and, much more vividly, the appearance of his ghost at the feast. (Forman's account here comes close to defining the theatrical timing of the scene.)

vii) the activities and sufferings of Macduff – but only in the broadest terms. (Even so, his memory is of Shakespeare. In Holinshed, Macduff's flight to England *follows* the slaughter of his family.)

viii) in significant afterthought, Lady Macbeth's sleep-walking, and the doctor taking notes.

The last of these is, emphatically, the recollection of vivid performance. On the other hand, Banquo's impetuously self-interested questioning of the Witches is more likely a culling from Holinshed than evidence of Shakespearean dialogue omitted from the Folio text, and the terms 'fairies' and 'nymphs' are plucked directly from the *Chronicles*. It would be as foolish to claim utter reliability for Forman as to neglect him altogether. As we go through the play considering the contrivance of its spectacle by the stage-hands, his particular recollections will be of service.

Act One Scene One

Sound effect   – thunder
Lighting effect – lightning
Properties   – uncertain

The opening scene of *Macbeth* poses in the theatre a problem that the
scholarly critic need never resolve. The text of the play leaves the precise
nature of the 'Witches' uncertain. Equivocation is their medium. There is
no solution in Holinshed. He first calls them 'three women in strange and
wild apparel, resembling creatures of elder world', but later takes refuge
in 'the common opinion' that 'these women were either the weird sisters,
that is (as ye would say) the goddesses of destinie, or else some nymphs
or feiries, indued with knowledge of prophesie by their necromanticall
science.' Shakespeare further confuses Holinshed's confusion by ascribing
to his three sisters powers of prophecy that Holinshed variously attributes
to 'certeine wizzards' and to 'a certeine witch, whome hee had in great
trust.' Without any clear scruple, Shakespeare exploits the fears and super-
stitions about witchcraft and demonic possession that were current at the
time. It is only the diligence of later scholars that has sought to distinguish
between, or to equate witches, fairies, nymphs, weird sisters, even the
classical Furies and the Scandinavian Norns. Within the play, they both
set the fashion for, and feed off, the characteristic *Macbeth* ellipsis. By
saying less, Shakespeare implies more. But ambiguity, a happy hunting
ground for the critic, is no help to the tireman. Even reticence is an
indulgence for him. He has to dress the Witches in something, and he has
to apply the appropriate make-up. The indication in Banquo's speech
(I.iii.39–47) is startlingly specific:

> What are these
> So wither'd and so wild in their attire,
> That look not like th' inhabitants o' the earth,
> And yet are on't? Live you? or are you aught
> That man may question? You seem to understand me,
> By each at once her choppy finger laying
> Upon her skinny lips: you should be women,
> And yet your beards forbid me to interpret
> That you are so.

Made up as withered, bearded, rough-fingered, and thin-lipped, and
dressed in extravagant defiance of contemporary fashion, they are discern-
ibly earthly women. They cannot have been played by boys – an unhelpful
incongruity would have been the result – which suggests that whoever
acted them would have had other parts in the play as well. (The Murderers
of III.iii. have a dangerously 'modern' appropriateness: they might equally
well have served as attendant lords, the Old Man of II.iv., or Seyton and

the Seywards in Act Five.) One way or another, they set the tireman a problem.

It was widely enough believed that witches could raise storms for Reginald Scot to feel the need to deny it.[3] Shakespeare may not have dug so far into witchcraft as James I had, but he does nothing in *Macbeth* to contradict the superstitious. It is natural to associate the storm that loudly opens the play with the Witches, and to see them also as creators of the 'fog and filthy air' (I.i.10). The thunder effect was an easy one. After the trumpet had prepared the Globe audience, the play began impressively with the release of the cannonball along the thunder-run above the stage. The lightning of the opening stage direction is more of a problem. Was it, perhaps, restricted to indoor performance? We know from the stage direction to the dumb show at the opening of V.iii. in *The Revenger's Tragedy* that the King's Men had a 'blazing star' effect, and *The Second Maiden's Tragedy*, probably performed by the King's Men in 1611, depends on light for one of its spectacular moments:

> On a sudden, in a kind of noise like a wind, the doors clattering, the tombstone flies open, and a great light appears in the midst of the tomb.
>
> (IV.iv.42)

but there is no certainty that such effects were used at the Globe. We are moving into the ambience of the elaborate court masques in which James's queen took such extravagant delight. The Blackfriars would accommodate the leaning towards spectacle more easily than the Globe. It would have needed a knowledge of the properties of coal gas or, better still, of quicklime to make any impression in the daylight.[4]

We cannot know whether properties were used for this scene. Something could, of course, have been pre-set – a cauldron or an open fire – and small objects associated with the conjuring of evil spirits might well have been carried on by the actors. But nothing is *necessary* if sound-effect, costume, and performance can be relied on to meet the challenge of doing so much in so few lines. What we are actually watching seems to be the conclusion of a sabbat.[5] The victim has been selected; all that remains to be decided is the time and the trysting-place.

Act One Scene Two

Sound effect – alarum
Properties – Duncan's colours (the royal banner of Scotland)
(N.B. Here and throughout, I have made no attempt to itemise the weaponry carried by the actors.)

The change of scene is signalled by a sound effect. An alarum was played on drums – the tucket, sennet, and flourish were played on trumpets. In its context, the sound of the drums would have contrasted effectively with the rumbling thunder from the Heavens of the previous scene. It is a human imitation of elemental noise. As the Witches leave the stage (the Folio's *exeunt* does not ask for a flying ballet of a departure), the bleeding soldier enters alone at a stage door to begin his walk, or stagger, downstage. It may not yet be clear which scene he is in. This is a subtle point of timing, and must have depended on the cue to the drummers. What they announce is not the entrance of the lonely soldier, but the parade of Duncan with attendant lords. It is a nice production point that only costume and stage grouping can distinguish Donalbain as one of the king's sons. He has no words either here or in I.iv. Duncan and the wounded soldier provide the focus for the first half of the scene, Ross and Duncan for the second half: but the subject is Macbeth. Shakespeare has notably departed from his source in describing the death of the traitor, Macdonwald:

> For brave Macbeth – well he deserves that name –
> Disdaining fortune, with his brandished steel,
> Which smoked with bloody execution,
> Like valour's minion carved out his passage
> Till he faced the slave –
> Which ne'er shook hands nor bade farewell to him
> Till he unseamed him from the nave to the chops,
> And fixed his head upon our battlements.
>
> (ll.16–23)

In Holinshed, 'Makdowald':

> being overcome, and fleeing for refuge into a castell (within the which his wife & children were inclosed) at length when he saw how he could neither defent the hold anie longer against his enimies, nor yet vpon surrender be suffered to depart with life saued, hee first slue his wife and children, and lastlie himselfe, least if he had yeelded simplie, he should haue beene executed in most cruell wise for an example to other. Makbeth entring into the castell by the gates, as then set open, found the carcasse of Makdowald lieng dead there amongst the residue of the slaine bodies, which when he beheld, remitting no peece of his cruell nature with that pitifull sight, he caused the head to be cut off, and set vpon a poles end, and so sent it as present to the king.

This, following that of the Witches, is the play's second reference to Macbeth. For the audience, there is some irony in his disdaining of the 'fortune' we have just seen preparing a trap for him. Nor should we miss the recognition that his unseaming of Macdonwald, whilst it may be an act of heroism, is also an act of butchery. This is not the cruel Makbeth of Holinshed (not yet, anyway), but it is an unnerving story, told by a bloody man about a man of blood. It is a trite but unavoidable point that the image will be stronger if the tireman has done the soldier's make-up well.

Act One Scene Three

Sound effects – thunder
                     drum
Special effect – vanishing
Properties   – Pilot's thumb, otherwise uncertain

If the previous scene does not end with a trumpet flourish, it must be because the Witches' thunder comes in fast on the concluding words. Duncan and his party exit into thunder as the Witches enter. What we watch next is, more explicitly than I.i., part of a sabbat. It begins with a recital of exploits undertaken since the previous sabbat, and with an elaboration on the one that is not yet completed. This elaboration describes a characteristically trivial act of vengeance, arbitrarily directed, not at the woman who would not share her chestnuts, but at her sailor-husband. There may be obscene implications, and a convincing case can certainly be made for some oblique reference to James I's adventures with the North Berwick witches during the winter of 1589–90. One of the witches, accused of having raised the storms which threatened James's ship, confessed that they had sailed out to sea in a sieve (cf. 1.8) to drown a cat. James had taken part in the subsequent examination and trial of the accused. He would not have been slow to pick up any allusions. What may be more important than the nature of the ceremony is the First Witch's apparent confession of her limited powers over the sailor:

> Though his bark cannot be lost,
> Yet it shall be tempest-tost.
> (ll.24–5)

But it is difficult to take literally anything the Witches say. The audience is drawn into the atmosphere of the scene by the hypnotically rhyming short lines and the ecstatic accompanying movement they demand. The off-stage sound of Macbeth's drum takes the ceremony to the point where ritual dance is used in the casting of a spell over the selected victim. The timing of the drumbeat is important to the rhythm of the incantatory verse. The cueing of sound effects is an exacting job in *Macbeth*.

When the generals make their first appearance, the Witches are significantly grouped at the peak of their dance – 'the charm's wound up' (l.37). It was said of Sir Henry Irving that he would never accept a play in which he was required to be on stage at the first raising of the curtain: he liked a build-up. The build-up for Macbeth's first entrance has been elaborate: to squander it would be theatrically inexcusable. The tension between the unsuspecting figures at the stage door and the weird sisters in their ominous group is held in the minds of the audience as Banquo and Macbeth pick their way across the platform. The Witches' repeated chants in sequence imply a simultaneous sequence of movements, a grotesque dance, perhaps, circling the two generals until, according to the peremptory stage direction, they vanish. There is no certainty that the Globe stage was trapped, but a disappearance downwards is more appropriate to the demonic sisters than a flying up and out. Flying effects, even indoors, could not be rapid.

Act One Scene Four

Sound effect – flourish of trumpets twice
Properties – Duncan's colours

This is a straightforward scene, in which the trumpet flourish announcing the king's entrance covers the exit of Macbeth and Banquo. The only curious feature is Macbeth's lonely exit five lines before the conclusion of the scene. It is well enough motivated – he is going to prepare for Duncan's visit to Inverness – but it remains conspicuous, drawing closer attention to Macbeth's unease at the naming of Malcolm as Duncan's heir. The passage from the king's presence to the stage door cannot be completed unobtrusively, particularly if, as seems likely, Macbeth has moved to the edge of the platform to deliver his speech aside (ll.48–53). This speech and Macbeth's exit is covered in the stage grouping by a convention of 'unheard conversation'.[6] Duncan's 'True, worthy Banquo' (l.54) is a response to an observation that the audience has not heard. The convention blends naturalism – actors in search of a pretext, not wishing to stand like dummies – with stylisation – the convention of inaudibility. The mixture was not felt to be anomalous.

Act One Scene Five

Property – a letter

The entrance of Lady Macbeth has a fuller impact if it is slightly delayed. Duncan has been taken off stage by a trumpet flourish. The transition is to the play's first indoor scene, and the first to begin unannounced by a sound-effect. The silence that follows the flourish makes more impressive the arrival – alone, with a letter – of Lady Macbeth. Momentarily, the rush of short, busy scenes is stilled, and the audience sees the stage, for the first time, occupied by a single figure, for whose astonishing words nothing has prepared us. The property letter, like virtually all hand-properties, invites 'natural' acting, and there is a marked tonal contrast between the words read and Lady Macbeth's responsive rhetoric.

The unnamed Messenger is the fourth to have appeared in the play already – the bleeding soldier and, twice, Ross and Angus had preceded him. Add to that the letter itself, and the impression grows of vital information hunting down its appropriate recipient. The rapid succession of exits and entrances accelerates the passage of time, so that Lady Macbeth's, 'I feel now / The future in the instant' (ll.58–9) is a vocalising of the audience's anticipation.

Act One Scene Six

Sound effects – hautboys
                    bird-song (?)
Lighting effect – torches

The dignity, almost the languor, of the opening speeches promises a slackening of the tempo as Duncan approaches the castle where he will die, until Lady Macbeth increases it in the tumbling rush of her two welcomes. The Folio stage direction is a puzzle. It may well have been mistakenly carried forward, in the printing, from the head of the following scene. If not, the oboes provide an aptly ominous counterpoint to the comfortable words of Duncan and Banquo. They will be heard by Macbeth much later in the play (IV.i.), when he, too, is facing his future. Editors generally assume that this is a 'daylight' scene, and that the torches are further proof of the compositorial error. But the text does not specify a time. Does the 'temple-haunting martlet' (l.4) sing? Frances Shirley believes that bird-song was among the off-stage sounds in Shakespeare's theatre,[7] and it would certainly have provided an attractive background to Banquo's speech. But it does not help firmly to establish the time of day. Even the house-martin will sing at night, when disturbed by oboes! A torchlight arrival at the castle of Inverness is what is implied by the stage direction as it stands in the Folio.

Act One Scene Seven

Sound effect – hautboys
Lighting effect – torches
Properties – dishes and service

The pacing of a play in performance will depend, often uncomfortably, on the exact timing of sound effects and the efficient deployment of properties. When this scene begins, the murder of Duncan is uncertain. When it ends, the murder is imminent. The pace of the action is independent of the time it takes, but not independent of its technical support.

The hautboys here, for instance, add to their threatening shrillness a traditional association with feasts and sumptuousness. They both establish and undermine an atmosphere. The torches light a scene of ordered efficiency – not at all like the below-stairs phrenzy of *Romeo and Juliet* I.v. It is Macbeth who is out of place. The servants move in and out of the two stage doors, lit by torches and accompanied by music. Macbeth's lonely entrance breaks the pattern they have established. We expect a servant and we see the host. His downstage move, in an indoor theatre, takes him away from the light. It is the first time we have seen him alone, and the soliloquy draws us towards that sense of complicity that is a mighty force in our experience of the killing of Duncan. The 'overheard' quality of Macbeth's soliloquies invites careful staging. They are not, as Hamlet's are, an open confiding in the audience. It would be interesting to know whether Burbage instinctively stopped short of the platform's edge. 'My worthy lord,/Your noble friends do lack you', Lady Macbeth warns in the play's second broken feast (III.iv.83–4). In this one, too, the music of the hautboys is a reminder that Macbeth has offended custom. Has the king asked for him? 'Know you not, he has' (l.30). It is a scene that ends in stasis – violence coiled. We are hurried on.

Act Two Scene One

Sound effect   – bell
Lighting effect – torches
Properties   – diamond
                    'that' (handed by Banquo to Fleance in l.5. Fleance already has Banquo's sword. His hands are full!)

There is no pause between this and the previous scene. Macbeth and Lady Macbeth go out through one stage door in 'darkness'. Banquo and Fleance enter at the other in torchlight. They are talking about the time, focusing the audience's awareness of threat. It is the hour at which the Ghost of Hamlet's father walked in Elsinore, just after midnight. The alternate pools of torchlight, Banquo's and Macbeth's, invite indoor staging. In the Globe, the effect depends upon a Jacobean perception of visual metaphor. The diamond, presented by Duncan to his hostess, is Shakespeare's refinement of a detail in Holinshed, who tells how Duncan distributed general largesse on the night of his murder. A diamond is not a shy property. It, too, should reflect the light.

The supreme effect in this scene, though, is the off-stage bell. Macbeth has instructed his servants:

> Go bid thy mistress, when my drink is ready
> She strike upon the bell.
>
>   (ll.31–2)

He has shrouded the killing of the king in euphemisms. It is 'this business' (I.vii.31), 'this terrible feat' (I.vii.80), 'the bloody business' (II.i.48). Now the very sound of the bell is a ghoulish euphemism. Macbeth's 'drink' is ready:

> The bell invites me.
> Hear it not, Duncan; for it is a knell
> That summons thee to heaven or to hell.
> (ll.62–4)

Act Two Scene Two

Sound effects   – owl
                crickets (?)
                knocking (four times)
Lighting effect – none specified
Special effects – Macbeth's entrance 'above'
                blood on the hands of Macbeth and Lady Macbeth
Properties   – two daggers

This climactic scene is dominated in the theatre by sounds and silence. The owl, demonic bird, hoots from the north, the devil's side. The knocking is at 'the south entry' (l.67), God's side. Macbeth's first words are spoken from the gallery, above the stage doors at the back of the stage. Lady Macbeth, by contrast, is at the front of the stage. The impression must be that the Globe is full of noises, from all its compass points. Macbeth, and even the resolute Lady Macbeth, dwindle against the orchestration of the night. The retributive process of what Dr Johnson called 'their own detection' has already begun. The knocking is an audible guarantee that the public world is about to burst in on a scene of private murder. Might it also, as J. W. Spargo suggests, have reminded its first audiences of the knocking at the gate in time of plague, during the search for dead bodies?[8]

Act Two Scene Three

Sound effects – knocking (six times)
               bell
Special effects – use of stage door

Both the associations and the location of the knocking change in this scene. The Porter's language invited the Jacobean audience to remember the old pageants of the harrowing of Hell, and the knocking at Hell-gate that presages heavenly judgment. That was less immediately the concern of the stage-hands than the different quality of sound required. The knocking 'within' – some distance away at the south entry – has to become a literal knocking at one of the stage doors, disturbing enough to bring the drunken porter staggering through the other. It is an aural equivalent of the shift from long-shot to close-up, a telescoping of space represented by sound alone.

A vital feature of the scene is the rapid punctuation of its exits and entrances. The affective change in the volume and source of the knocking is followed by the entrance of the Porter alone. Macduff and Lennox bring the on-stage number to three. It remains three when Macbeth replaces the Porter, drops to two with Macduff's exit, reverts to three with his horrified return, drops to one when Macbeth and Lennox leave, rises to two with Lady Macbeth's entry (as if conjured by the alarum bell), to three with Banquo's arrival, to six with the return of Macbeth and Lennox, now joined by the silent Ross, and finally to eight when Malcolm and Donalbain provide the focus for the broken grouping. Each time the number changes, the arrangement of actors on the platform changes, almost with the formality of a dance. Such exploitation of the stage and its doors is theatrically thrilling, not least because of the weight it throws on to the image of the dead king. More than almost any other of Shakespeare's plays, *Macbeth* invites the audience to relate the activity and the locations that it sees to activity and locations that it does not see. The stage is an island in a threatening world.

The conclusion of the scene depends on the accurate positioning of Malcolm and Donalbain. They are the focus of the final fifty lines. By drawing the attention of the other actors when she faints (l.125), Lady Macbeth permits them their first private conversation. It is completed when they are left alone on stage. This scene contains Donalbain's first and only lines. The actor may be needed again, but Donalbain is not.

Act Two Scene Four

This choric scene brings to an end the first movement of the play. (Duncan is dead. The next movement will see the elimination of Banquo.) It makes no technical demands on the Globe's stage-hands. There is no good evidence that the Globe broke its performances with intervals: but the shift to the Blackfriars, with its fondness for entr'acte music during the occupation of the Children of the Revels, may well have encouraged the practice. If *Macbeth* is to have two intervals, now is the time for the first of them.

Act Three Scene One

Sound effect – sennet
Properties   – throne (perhaps two thrones)

This is the first time we have seen Macbeth as king. Either during an interval, or as a significant start to a new phase in the play, the throne of state was probably lowered from the Heavens. For the opening ten lines, Banquo is on stage alone, the first time he has been seen in isolation. It marks the beginning of the movement of which he is the main theme. The trumpet sennet is Macbeth's confident assertion of his kingship, and the formal assembly of the Scottish court provides him with an audience for a performance almost as impressive as Claudius's at the Danish council in I.ii. of *Hamlet*. The first part of this scene is occupied by Macbeth's persuading Banquo to attend the royal feast. His soliloquy (ll.48–72) then functions as a theatrical colon, both separating the first part of the scene from, and linking it with, the last, in which Macbeth tries to ensure that Banquo will *not* attend the feast. He manipulates the Murderers rather as Claudius manipulates Laertes, breaking off at a crucial time to remove their qualms with the jabbing reminder: 'Both of you/Know Banquo was your enemy' (ll.114–15). The scene's antithetical shape would have been reinforced at the Globe by the contrast in staging between the courtly formality of the first part and the ragged intimacy of the last. The Folio records no exit for Lady Macbeth. Presumably she leaves with the courtiers (l.44). It is the first physical sign of the progressive estrangement of Macbeth and his wife, and the significance should not be fudged in the staging. The move from mighty words to the vulnerability of a boy-actor in women's clothes begins here.

Act Three Scene Two

Properties – thrones remain

There is no need for a change of location in this scene, and no call for a pause. A shift in the shape of the story is marked by Macbeth's exit through one stage door, and Lady Macbeth's almost-simultaneous entrance through the other. To reach her husband now, she has to send a servant for him. The scene is full of echoes from the one that has just ended. Macbeth's apprehension that 'To be thus is nothing;/But to be safely thus' (III.i.48–9) is shared now by his wife:

> Nought's had, all's spent.
> Where our desire is got without content.
> 'Tis safer to be that which we destroy
> Than by destruction dwell in doubtful joy.
> (ll.4–7)

On the one hand 'nothing/nought', on the other 'safety' – even under the barrage of theatrical performance, the audience will recall Macbeth's identical contrast less than five minutes before. But the effect is to emphasise the split between the accomplices. Macbeth has a new plan: Lady Macbeth, like Racine's Hermione is plotless, 'errante et sans dessein'.[9] And Macbeth has begun to deceive her. As in the previous scene, he seems anxious to make provision for Banquo at the feast at the same time as he is determined that he shall miss it. What is new here is his taunting of his wife with secret knowledge and with endearments grotesquely inappropriate to his true purposes.[10]

Act Three Scene Three

Sound effect   – horses' hooves
Lighting effect – torch
Properties   – thrones flown out before scene begins (?)

For effective presentation, this scene must have depended on a free and adventurous use of the open stage. It is, perhaps, the darkest scene in the play, although 'the west yet glimmers with some streaks of day' (1.5), and there is no need for elaborate concealment. The Murderers are 'invisible', even in full view of the audience. Nevertheless, it would be simplest to hold them upstage of the pillars, under cover of the Heavens, and to have Banquo and Fleance enter at a stage door and begin their walk around the pillars. The Murderers are not at first sure that it is Banquo and Fleance whose horses they have heard. Neither should the audience be. This is a scene that draws the eyes of the spectators towards the stage doors in nervous anticipation. There is no reason why Fleance should not make his escape through the audience. Whatever he does cannot be half-hearted. The savage killing of Banquo ('Twenty trenched gashes on his head', III.iv.27) is only half of the stage picture. The escaping Fleance carries Macbeth's doom with him.

Act Three Scene Four

Sound effect – hautboys (?)
Special effect – Banquo's ghost
Properties   – throne (possibly two thrones)
                  table fully spread with food and wine

The scene of Banquo's murder gives just about enough time for some intensive preparation in the tiring house. The table has to be prepared and brought out, and the actors have to be called to stand by for their massed entry. The absence of any reference to music in the Folio stage direction is surprising. A royal feast without instrumental accompaniment would not be normal, and Macbeth is concerned that everything should look as normal as possible. Perhaps Shakespeare intended that the feast should be obviously false from the start – or perhaps the Folio fails to record what happened on stage.

Each of the three preceding scenes in Act Three has pointed forward to the feast, and the repetition here of Macbeth's contradictory hopes that Banquo should attend the event *and* that he should be prevented provide the context for the appearance of the ghost, equivocally answering both of Macbeth's demands. There is no doubt that the ghost was a palpable physical presence on the Globe stage, played by the actor of Banquo. He needed no further disguise than blood – a love of significant pattern would have recommended that he be made to look like the bloody soldier who appeared before the last king shortly before his death. We can only guess at the effect the ghost was intended to have on the audience. The probability is that no special tricks were used, no concealed entry or sudden emanation through a trapdoor, since an upstage entry through the stage door would be more impressive. That would have involved the 'corpse' of Banquo in a seen-but-not-seen resurrection at the end of III.iii. – back into the tiring house for a hurried application of blood by the tireman.

Emrys Jones, having drawn attention to the play-within-a-play qualities of the feast, describes the effect on Macbeth of the apparition:[11]

What happens in terms of the play-within-a-play is that Macbeth is put out of his part. The dramatic effect – the effect on the audience of *Macbeth* – is extraordinarily intense. For just as at a real-life performance of a play the experience of seeing an actor forget his part can be quite unforeseeably jarring, so the spectacle of Macbeth lapsing into helpless confusion arouses a feeling of acute tragic embarrassment.

This is an acute observation. The whole scene is set up by Macbeth as a performance, with the moves written in. It is clear, for instance, that as the feast starts Macbeth mingles with his guests, whilst Lady Macbeth advertises her apartness by remaining seated in her throne of state. His own place is 'i' the midst' (l.10), and it is to that central position that the ghost will make its way. The ragged inset, when Macbeth talks with the Murderer, must be set apart from the formal grouping of the feast. It is an uncomfortable hiatus for the feasters, who can eat and drink nothing until Macbeth has given the cheer (l.33). How did the actors at the table pass the twenty lines of Macbeth's dialogue with Banquo's killer? The 'unheard conversation' convention is a possibility, but the sense is rather of embarrassed silence that will be felt with even greater intensity when Macbeth addresses the invisible ghost. It is the critical moment in Macbeth's fortune. He may pull himself together, but he can never again hope to pull his court together. A piece of stage business that became traditional in later productions of *Macbeth* may well have originated with Burbage. We have to picture the moment when the host raises his glass:

Now good digestion wait on appetite,
And health on both!

(ll.38–9)

Steeling himself against the disappointment of Fleance's escape, Macbeth has turned back to the feast to play the part of genial host – and suddenly Banquo is there. Fingers numbed, Burbage lets the glass slip from his hand. Is it to this that Jasper, his face mealed in grotesque imitation of a ghost, refers in Beaumont's *The Knight of the Burning Pestle* (1607)?

> When thou art at thy table with thy friends,
> Merry in heart, and fill'd with swelling wine,
> I'll come in midst of all thy pride and mirth,
> Invisible to all men but thyself,
> And whisper such a sad tale in thine ear
> Shall make thee let the cup fall from thy hand,
> And stand as mute and pale as Death itself.

(V.i.22–8)

The resemblance is unmistakable. Beaumont is surely referring to a famous moment in Burbage's performance of Macbeth – one of those hair-raising 'natural' touches that put the audience in touch with the real world without breaking their concentration on the world of the play.

Act Three Scene Five

Sound effects – thunder
                music and a song (within)
Special effect – flying exit for Hecate (if thrones are to be flown out from the previous scene, Hecate could not fly in as well.)

The Hecate scenes are gaining defenders, so that we can no longer take for granted that they were non-Shakespearean playhouse interpolations. But even if Shakespeare wrote them, we cannot be sure when he wrote them. Had Hecate been included in the cast of the 1611 Globe performance, Forman would probably have remembered her. This scene is nothing if it is not theatrically impressive. Its inclusion in the Folio text proves only that it was part of the playhouse book by 1623. It is a 'reminder' scene – 'meanwhile the Witches . . .' – that takes further the theatrical, or more particularly masque-like, element in the play. Macbeth, who believes himself in charge of the plot, is subservient to it. The demonic decorators of the stage have a place for him.

However persuasive the arguments, doubts about the scene cling. The superbly compressed 'Banquo' movement has reached its climax in the feast, a climax so exact and exacting that it makes this spectacular interlude seem loose and approximate. It is an 'entertainment' thrust into a tragedy. The off-stage song (the only other song is in the other Hecate scene, IV.i.: like this one, it seems to have been borrowed from Middleton's *The Witch* (produced between 1610 and 1616?) but may have been part of a common stock) was probably sung by a choir of boys, a financial extravagance at the Globe, less so at the Blackfriars. It is a splendid example of the 'impurity' of popular drama that such a scene should be nudged in at such a point, but there are excuses for cutting it in performance. All that happens, after all, is that an overbearing, and presumably gorgeously costumed, Hecate scolds her inferiors and promises to stir up trouble for Macbeth, before heading off (and up) to a foggy cloud (l.35).

Act Three Scene Six

Another choric scene, making no technical demands, brings to an end the second movement of the play. The share taken in the dialogue by 'another lord', less shaded even than Lennox, is a reminder of Shakespeare's willingness to subject character to function in *Macbeth* – a far remove from *Hamlet*. The majority of the actors have only to deliver or to recapitulate a story. The final speeches, with their reference to Macduff's meeting with Malcolm in the English court of Edward the Confessor, project us towards the play's final 'Macduff' movement. A second interval would have been appropriate here.

Act Four Scene One

Sound effects – thunder
               music and a song
               music for a dance
               hautboys
               galloping of horses

Special effects – Three apparitions
               entrance and exit (flying) of Hecate
               dumb show of eight kings and Banquo
               mirror effect
               vanishing of witches

Properties   – cauldron
               ingredients of cauldron (twenty-four are mentioned)
               severed head (Macbeth's)
               branch of a tree
               eight crowns
               ten orbs
               twelve sceptres

The list of theatrical prerequisites for this scene makes its own point. It is a nightmare for the stage-hands and a pantomime for the audience. If we assume, as I think we must, that the Hecate episode is an indoor theatre interpolation, we can ignore the clumsy flying mechanism of the Globe. The Folio text's insistence that the three apparitions 'descend' may also refer to the more elaborate trap-doors of the Blackfriars or the second Globe. If the first Globe had traps amenable enough to spectacular descents and ascents for the effective presentation of the three apparitions and the vanishing Witches, it is surprising that the extant Globe plays made so little use of them. We simply cannot be sure that the performance of *Macbeth* seen by Forman employed any of the vanishing and appearing tricks called for in the Folio stage directions. Much more challenging is the reconstruction of the business implied by the dumb-show mirror, 'the last king with a glass in his hand' (l.111). Macbeth describes the effect from his point of vantage:

> And yet the eighth appears, who bears a glass
> Which shows me many more.
>
> (ll.119–20)

But an effect that is visible only to the actor is not an effect at all. There is a fascinating possibility that, in the Hampton Court performance of 1606, the silent presenter of the eighth king held the mirror in front of James I himself, the latest guarantee of the continuing Stuart line; but it would take some clever handling of the mirror on the Globe stage to contrive for the audience a sight of the reflected seven kings preceding the mirror-carrier. Such a refinement looks forward to Pepper's awe-inspiring nineteenth-century stage ghost.

The three apparitions probably made lesser demands. The first presents the severed head of Macbeth, carried by a boy actor. It is a property that will be needed again. The second seems to represent Macduff, and the third Malcolm, but it is only by suggestive costuming of the boys who walk on in their place that the point could have been clearly made: another job for the tireman. The dumb show of kings, introduced by the ominous playing of hautboys, was probably a parade round the stage, brought to a halt in a static line prior to a final exit through the other stage door.

The opening of the scene is another 'quotation' from the spell-casting section of a sabbat. It is unlikely that each of the mentioned ingredients was faithfully imitated by the property makers. The theatrical stress is less on the objects than on the words, and on the ritualistic, rhythmic dance for which the words provide the music. The later, probably interpolated, dance would have required much more elaborate choreography. It is a theatrical show rather than a dramatic necessity.

The final sound effect is of the galloping of horses. Since Macbeth tells us that *he* hears them, *we* do not need to. But there is evidence that this was an off-stage noise often heard in the Elizabethan and Jacobean theatres, and it has a nice ambiguity here. It *could* be the sound of the vanishing

Witches – 'Infected be the air whereon they ride' (l.138) – but it *is* the sound of messengers bringing news that Macduff has fled to England.

Act Four Scene Two

The spectacular scene is followed by an indoor – almost a parlour – scene. The various visitors to Lady Macduff are ushered, or break, into intimacy. The actor of Lady Macduff has a strange job to do. This is her only scene, and she stands in necessary contrast to Lady Macbeth. She is emphatically a mother – which Lady Macbeth is not – and she is also the wife of a good man; but, far from being heroic, her opening words to Ross are petulant and ill-considered. She accuses Macduff of lacking the 'natural touch', of deserting her and his children. Like Banquo, but unlike Macbeth, Macduff is fertile; but he stands accused of being a bad father. One modern director, George Roman, has told me that he found it helpful to the actress of Lady Macduff to play the part as if in the late stages of pregnancy, giving her ill temper a source in her physical discomfort. It is a sophisticated touch, that serves to highlight a dramatic contrast between the fertile and the barren. What is of more importance in the construction of the play is this scene's reference forward to the next, when Macduff's 'nature' will be tried and proved. This, in theatrical terms, is a stage door scene. Ross carries the tensions of Macbeth's court into Lady Macduff's house – 'I dare not speak much further' (l.17) – and the unnamed messenger who next appears at a stage door might, for all the audience knows, be a murderer. The arrivals in this scene are soundless and sudden. It ends with the shrieking exit of Lady Macduff at one stage door, and the entrance of her husband at the other.

Act Four Scene Three

Properties – Macduff's hat

Together with the previous scene, this one forms a unit in which Macduff's humanity is fully explored. Like the previous one, this scene is composed of visits, with Ross, the first visitor to Lady Macduff, the final visitor to her husband. The only 'sound' effects, both carefully emphasised, are Macduff's two silences, the first (l.137) after Malcolm has revealed his true integrity and his plans to liberate Scotland from its tyrant, the second when Ross has brought the news of the savage slaughter of Macduff's wife and children:

> What, man! Ne'er pull your hat upon your brows.
> Give sorrow words: the grief that does not speak
> Whispers the o'erfraught heart and bids it break.
> (ll.208–10)

The business with the hat is a fine example of the difficulty of distinguishing between 'natural' and 'formal' acting. It may refer to a conventional gesture of grief, but it could be Shakespeare's way of illuminating particularity. It seems unlikely that every member of the King's Men, given the cue for grief, pulled his hat down – but it is not impossible.

Act Five Scene One

Sound effect   – knocking (?)
Lighting effect – taper
Properties   – table
                 notebook

This is the only eavesdropping scene in the play. The staging convention at the Globe would have been well established. (It is important that the Doctor's note-taking should be strikingly visible: Forman remembered it.) If the Doctor and the Waiting-Gentlewoman positioned themselves upstage of the pillars, Lady Macbeth would have had the rest of the stage to walk. The taper's pool of flickering light is an indoor effect, closely parallel, though with vastly different emotional force, to the torchlight that leads Banquo to his death. It is not impossible that an audible knocking accompanied Lady Macbeth's reference in 'To bed, to bed; there's knocking at the gate' (ll.71–2). No stage direction supports it, and it is certainly sufficient to 'hear' the sound in Lady Macbeth's head as the dagger was 'seen' in Macbeth's. But the fondness for broad effects in the Globe is worth stressing.

There is always a practical theatrical dimension in Shakespeare's writing. The taper, for example, represents Lady Macbeth's bid to keep at bay the demon Nightmare, nocturnal relative of the Witches – 'she has light by her continually' (ll.25–6) – but that would be of less significance to the stage-hands than the need for a table to stand it on, so that she can rub her hands without burning herself.

Act Five Scene Two

Sound effect – drum
Costume   – armour
Properties   – colours

The plunge to damnation is relentless through the short, military scenes of Act Five. The armies of Act One have re-assembled, but with new purpose. For the actors of the King's Men, the conventions of the armed procession were familiar. There is, though, an interesting uncertainty about the colours carried in this scene by the 'loyal' rebels. If Macbeth has usurped the Scottish colours, Malcolm may have borrowed the English (a point about the uniting of the countries under James VI and I would not be missed). Whose colours does this makeshift army carry?

Act Five Scene Three

Costume   – armour
Properties – notebook

It seems unlikely that the Doctor would come on to the platform without the tell-tale notebook. It carries some of the vital evidence towards the apocalypse. This scene is notable for a speech which requires of Burbage a 'natural' ability to talk to the Doctor whilst, at the same time, instructing his armourer. The timing and the visualising of the on-stage activity implicit in the writing are demandingly exact:

> Throw physic to the dogs; I'll none of it.
> Come, put mine armour on; give me my staff.
> Seyton, send out. – Doctor, the thanes fly from me. –
> Come, sir, dispatch. – If thou couldst, doctor, cast
> The water of my land, find her disease
> And purge it to a sound and pristine health,
> I would applaud thee to the very echo
> That should applaud again. – Pull't off, I say –
> What rhubarb, senna, or what purgative drug
> Would scour these English hence? Hear'st thou of them?
>   (ll.47–56)

The actor of Seyton had to be disciplined. Shakespeare could not have written this speech if he had no confidence in a preparedness to rehearse detail.

Act Five Scene Four

Sound effect – drum
Properties   – colours
                branches

The short scenes alternate from side to side of the imminent battle. Malcolm's army marches on, joined now by the Scottish rebels of V.ii., carrying its distinctive colours. By the time the soldiers march off, they may be already carrying the branches from Birnam Wood that will destroy Macbeth's security. John Holloway has drawn attention to a likely image in the minds of the Globe audience:[12]

The single figure, dressed in his distinctive costume (one should have Macbeth in his war equipment in mind) pursued by a whole company

163

of others carrying green branches, was a familiar sight as a Maying procession, celebrating the triumph of new life over the sere and yellow leaf of winter.

Even the sceptical G. K. Hunter concedes that this is 'presumably the clearest "anthropological" moment in the play'.[13]

Act Five Scene Five

Sound effects – drum
                 cry of women
Properties   – colours

As one army leaves, the other enters. The symmetry of the Globe stage, the product of its pillars and stage doors, accommodates and clarifies armed conflicts. The scenes of Act Five, after Lady Macbeth's sleep-walking, are not in any real sense, separate from each other. The episodes contribute to a single action, the inevitable defeat and understood damnation of Macbeth. To that action, the eerie off-stage cry of women adds its own terror. Macbeth's inability to feel the loss of his wife is a sign of his lost manhood. It has to be set against the anguish of Macduff, and against the repeated metaphorical quest for manliness that has stiffened Macbeth's resolve and mocked his failures throughout the play.

Act Five Scene Six

Sound effects – drum
                 alarum
Properties   – colours
                 branches

The stage direction specifies that Malcolm's army marches on 'with boughs'. Macbeth's colours would not have been removed at the end of the previous scene. The battle will take place against a background of the Scottish colours on one side of the stage and the English colours on the other.

The final stage direction calls for 'continued' alarums. The drummers must have a clear view of the action during the battle. Their timing has to be precise, more precise than could be achieved by any cueing system. There seems no reason to doubt that the drummers, costumed in light armour, stood on the platform, with the actors.

Act Five Scene Seven

Sound effects – alarums
     retreat and flourish (both trumpet calls)
     flourish (twice more)
     drum
Special effects – two duels in armour
Properties – severed head (Macbeth's)
     Jewelled crown

The killing, or would-be killing, of sons is Macbeth's barren assault on heredity. Young Seyward, like young Macduff, receives his wounds 'before'. Seyward's benediction, 'Why then, God's soldier be he' (1.76), reminds us that his killer has become the devil's general. The combat between Macbeth and young Seyward was probably brief. The King's Men would be sure to make the confrontation of Macbeth and Macduff the centre of the scene. The Folio stage direction creates a puzzle: 'Exeunt fighting. Alarums. Enter fighting and Macbeth slain.' If Macbeth dies on stage, we have an answer to Kenneth Tynan's complaint: 'it fails in the last analysis as a tragedy for this very reason – that tragic heroes do not die off-stage in battle.'[14] But it is not at all clear what the Folio text envisages. Many modern editors see fit to omit all reference to the re-entry, defending themselves on the ground that the stage directions are not Shakespeare's. Against that, they are as accurate a representation of playhouse practice as we can hope to find. It may be that we have here the barest indication of a spectacular duel, covering the whole platform, and including an exit through one door and a bursting back through the other, a shameless piece of Errol-Flynnery. But what happens to Macbeth's corpse? Young Seyward's may remain on stage, among the small number of the slain described in his father's, 'by these I see / So great a day as this is cheaply bought' (ll.65–6), but Macbeth's cannot – unless Macduff is seen to behead it before his exit. If the Folio is accurate, Macbeth gains an on-stage death: if we could be certain that it is wrong, we would be spared a mystery.

One thing is certain. However apologetic the chorus of *Henry V*, the King's Men specialised in effective battle scenes, combining skilful sword-play and impressive costume with a convention of well-choreographed stage-formations. There is no *need* for any of the battle scenes in Shakespeare. The Greek stage had excluded them. So would Corneille and Racine. But English audiences relished them. They are taken straight from the popular drama, from Mummers plays and the Robin Hood stories that provided seasonal entertainment in towns and villages the length and breadth of England. Critics who claim that *Macbeth* ends whimperingly have failed to take account of the taste of its original audience, and the technique of its original performers. Only after the tumult has died down does Macduff enter with the severed head of the erstwhile King of Scotland. From it, his words imply, he takes the jewelled crown, and places it on the head of Malcolm:

> Hail, King! For so thou art. Behold where stands
> The usurper's cursed head. The time is free.
> I see thee compassed with thy kingdom's pearl,
> That speak my salutation in their minds,
> Whose voices I desire aloud with mine. –
> Hail, King of Scotland!
>
> (ll.83–8)

The actor who played Macduff at Hampton Court would have known how, by a graceful gesture, to include both the king on the stage and the king in the audience.

8

TWO PLAYHOUSES

Since the publication of the first edition of this book in 1983, there have been significant advances in our understanding of theatrical conditions in Shakespeare's England. The 1989 Bankside excavations have been the most conspicuous, earning the veteran C. Walter Hodges's generous acknowledgment that 'the Rose has thrown all our established working premises and assumptions into disarray. It hasn't made them necessarily wrong in themselves, but they've all had to shove over to make room for another piece in the game'.[1] I have incorporated in this new edition some observations on the Rose, though all such observations are, at this stage, necessarily of an interim nature. New questions – about capacity, the orientation of the stage, the location of the Lord's Room, the tiring-house facade, the viability of the Vitruvian *ad triangulam* theory of playhouse construction, the application of the alternative *ad quadratum* theory, even about drainage – have certainly to be asked; but we cannot expect definitive answers in a hurry. Meanwhile, Sam Wanamaker's splendid dream, the International Shakespeare Globe Centre on the Bankside, is on the edge of becoming a reality, within easy walking distance of an uncovered segment of the foundations of the original Globe that will silently criticise some of its architectural assumptions. Less sensational, but equally challenging, are the accumulating revelations of the *Records of Early English Drama* series of volumes. One of the things we are learning from these is that provincial touring by the London companies needs to be reassessed. Like many other scholars, I have too easily assumed that such touring was a plague-driven necessity rather than a regularly calculated financial venture. It is, however, to a third area of theatrical enquiry that this short chapter addresses itself.

On 29 March 1608, the licence of the Children of the Queen's Revels to perform plays in the Blackfriars was terminated. James Burbage had purchased the Parliament Chamber of the old monastery as long ago as 1596, converted it almost at once for use as an indoor playhouse and then had his ambitions frustrated by a successful petition from the Blackfriars residents, who opposed the establishment of a public playhouse in their privileged precinct. The immediate fate of the proscribed indoor theatre is not known. It was not until 1600 that Richard Burbage, who had inherited it from his father in February 1597, negotiated its 21–year lease to the Children of the Chapel Royal. There is no record of opposition from local residents to the prospect of irregular performances by boy players in the Blackfriars, but we cannot assume, despite the evidence of *Hamlet*, that the 'little eyases' carried all before them. In 1604, Henry Evans and others, on behalf of the renamed Children of the Queen's Revels, negotiated with Richard Burbage for the termination of their lease after only four years. Mindful, perhaps, of the 1596 petition, Burbage did not respond. How, then, do we account for his change of attitude in 1608, when Evans again approached him? To be sure, the Boys' Companies were in disarray in 1608, and their adult rivals may have wished to capitalise on that, but the King's Men had nothing to gain unless they could be sure that the Blackfriars residents would not repeat their successful obstructiveness. In the absence of hard evidence, we are forced to speculate. J. Leeds Barroll has opened up for me a number of fruitful lines of enquiry:[2]

1 Richard and Cuthbert Burbage had property interests in the Blackfriars. They made a purchase there in 1601, even while the Children of the Chapel Royal were in confident possession of the Parliament Chamber, and further purchases in 1610 and 1614, when the indoor playhouse was leased to the King's Men. Their intention may well have been to convert, or simply to lease, premises to wealthy citizens in search of a desirable environment. It is just possible, though Leeds Barroll does not suggest this, that their initial willingness to terminate Evans's lease reflected a landlord's determination to improve the precinct. If they could not be sure of housing the King's Men in the playhouse, they could at least prevent any other companies from performing there and thus legitimise a raising of their rent-demands.

2 The bitter winter of 1607/8, the beginning of Europe's 'little ice age', had provided a sharp reminder of the hazards of outdoor playing. The disbanding of the Children of the Queen's Revels in March 1608 gave the Burbages a chance to reflect, and perhaps to canvas the opinion of the present Blackfriars residents, on the future of the deserted playhouse.

3 Henry Evans had failed, despite the terms of his lease, to keep the Blackfriars playhouse in good repair. Without prompt action on the Burbages' part, the value of this portion of their Blackfriars property would decline.

4 The historic rights to self-determination of the Blackfriars residents were soon to be ended. Arrangements were under way throughout 1608 for its status as a Liberty under the Crown, and therefore exempt from City of London jurisdiction, to be changed. A charter of 20 September

1608 formally surrendered the Blackfriars precinct (along with that of the Whitefriars) to the civic authorities. The Burbages, then, had less to fear from local opposition in 1608 than they had had in 1596 or 1604; but their new, and potentially formidable, problem was the hostility of successive Lord Mayors.

It is surprising, particularly in respect of the last of these points, that Shakespeare agreed, along with Heminges, Condell and William Sly, to sign a lease on the Blackfriars playhouse on 9 August 1608. And the fact that, at the time, there was no immediate prospect of performing there increases the sense of surprise. The delay was not a result of the need to carry out internal repairs, but of the professional players' old enemy, plague. Because the King's Men took possession of the Blackfriars in 1608 Shakespearean scholars have tended to assume that their playwright's last plays, from *Pericles* onwards, were intended primarily for the indoor stage. It is a view that must be modified in the light of Barroll's researches. What now seems clear is that there were very few performances in London's playhouses between July 1608 (i.e. before the King's Men signed the Blackfriars lease) and February 1610. That is not to say that there were few performances elsewhere, at court or in the provinces. We know that the King's Men received £40 in April 1609, a gift from their royal patron to reward them 'for their private practice in the time of infection', and £30 a year later to compensate them for 'being restrained from public playing within the City of London in the time of infection during the space of six weeks in which time they practised privately for his Majesty's service'. There is no reason to suppose that the Blackfriars was immune from either the plague or the desperate legislation that aimed to impede its spread. By a sad historical accident, Shakespeare and his colleagues were denied access to their new playhouse for the first eighteen months of their leasehold. Although the acquisition of an indoor playhouse marks a watershed in the history of the King's Men, it was not that acquisition that brought to an end the Globe's glorious decade, but a particularly virulent outbreak of the bubonic plague.

There is nothing strange, of course, in the company's decision to re-possess the second Blackfriars playhouse in 1608. However astonishing their achievement during the Globe decade, their preference for indoor performance, particularly during the winter months, need surprise no one who has been frozen or drenched in a grey London. Much more striking is the decision to go on performing at the Globe as well. There was nothing sentimental about it, we can be sure of that. If it was not a commercial gamble, it was a commercial necessity. It may be, though there is no evidence to prove it, that there was no prospect of year-round performance at the Blackfriars, either because the residents of the precinct were felt to be powerful enough to prevent it, or because the potential audience declined too far in the summer, when the Inns of Court were on vacation and the wealthy citizens left town. The second of these possibilities makes a dangerously easy assumption about the composition of the Blackfriars audience; the first finds support in the success of the 1596 petition, but leaves us wondering why, if the residents were still strong enough to obstruct performances for part of the year, they were not strong enough to obstruct them altogether.

The possession of two playhouses was a sign of the supremacy of the King's Men, and we must assume that the combined profitability was felt to be a deciding factor in the decision to maintain both. It is a reasonable assumption, but not more than that, that the Globe was the summer headquarters. Using Sir Humphrey Mildmay's diary and account book as a source, Irwin Smith has suggested that the Globe season covered the five months from the middle of May to the middle of October, and that the King's Men transferred to the Blackfriars for the remaining seven months of the year.[3] We should note, however, that Mildmay was writing in the 1630s. The original practice, and even the original intention, was probably not so clear-cut. The suggestion that the King's Men thought in terms of two repertoires, one for the 'popular' Globe and one for the 'private' Blackfriars, cannot be entertained for a minute. They promised, as would any theatre company at the peak of success, business as before. The cold historical fact is that the plague hit both their houses before the twin operation could be tested. The conjunction of dates is of more than passing interest:

28 July 1608	– plague deaths reach fifty in a week.
9 August 1608	– Richard Burbage executes leases to his fellow-sharers in the Blackfriars.
13 August 1608	– William Sly, one of those sharers, dies, perhaps of the plague.
20 September 1608	– Blackfriars (and Whitefriars) pass into the jurisdiction of the City of London.
29 September 1608	– plague deaths peak at 147 in a week.

Surrounded by the evidence of plague, with the theatre already closed, and knowing of the city's bid for jurisdiction over the Liberty of the Blackfriars, Burbage and his colleagues committed themselves, each to a one-seventh share in the pitch and toss of a new theatrical enterprise.

Other than that of Evans, the Welsh scrivener turned theatrical lessee to whom Richard Burbage had rented the Blackfriars for £40 per year in 1600, there are no new names among the housekeepers: Cuthbert and Richard Burbage, Shakespeare, Heminges, Condell and Sly. Of the actors who had worked together in the early years at the Globe, Pope and Phillips were dead, and the thin man, John Sincler, too. The untimely death of William Sly was a severe blow. He had been one of the players in *The Seven Deadly Sins*, acted by Lord Strange's Men nearly twenty years before. Just when he joined the Chamberlain's Men is not known. His purchase from Henslowe of 'a jewel of gold set with a white sapphire' in 1594 gives us a glimpse of a young actor determined to make an impression, and his ability to carry a costume proudly is implicit in the reference, in the 1598 wardrobe inventory of the Admiral's Men, to 'Perowe's suit, which William Sly wore'.[4] He had left the Admiral's Men some time before the inventory was drawn up, and was certainly with the Chamberlain's Men before the opening of the Globe, being admitted to a share after the death of his friend, Augustine Phillips. A decade's loyalty was nothing unusual in the King's Men, nor the dying in harness, but the tour forced on the company by the plague – Coventry and Marlborough are among the recorded venues – was saddened by the loss of a friend. John Lowin was the most valued of the new members, an expert dancer at a time when the audience demand for dancing was high, particularly at the 'private' theatres.

There is no hint in surviving records of any major redesigning of the Blackfriars stage by the King's Men, though maintenance and repairs would have pinched the sharers' pockets during 1609, when the continuance of plague kept the theatres closed until well into the winter. When, none too soon, playing began again at the Blackfriars, conditions had changed little from those to which the 'little eyases' of the Children of the Revels had been accustomed. The Duke of Stettin-Pomerania had seen one of their performances on 18 September 1602. Like so many foreign visitors to English theatres, he saw the strangeness of what the regular audience took for granted:

> Whoever wishes to see one of their performances must give as much as eight shillings of our coinage; and yet there are always a good many people present, and even many respectable women. . . . They act all their plays by [artificial] light, which produces a great effect. For a whole hour before the play begins, one listens to a delightful instrumental concert.

He draws our attention to four features which would have continued to distinguish the Blackfriars from the Globe during the tenancy of the King's Men:

1 The greater cost of admission. (Translating Stralsund coinage into English terms gives us an admission price for the duke of one shilling. He would have had to pay a further sixpence for the privilege of a stool on the stage.)

2 The 'respectability' of the audience. This is protected by the cost of admission, since the possession of wealth, however it has been

accumulated and provided that it is sometimes conspicuously spent, is what the world generally considers 'respectable'.

3 The lighting of stage and auditorium by candles. Probably gathered in branched candelabra operable by pulleys, these must have been impressive when seen for the first time. There were problems – the 'mending' of the candles by tireman and stage-hands, called for in the Induction to Jonson's *The Staple of News,* had to be repeated several times in every Blackfriars performance – but it was evidently felt to be worth shuttering the windows against the afternoon light.

4 The use of music. A weight of evidence suggests that, though the King's Men may have reduced the quantity of music, they continued to employ it much more than had been their custom at the Globe. It was a music-house as well as a playhouse, and it would have been unnecessarily provocative of the King's Men to disappoint the expectations of their patrons. Those great crowd-pleasers, Beaumont and Fletcher, found space for entr'acte music and dance more readily than Shakespeare. They were writers of the Blackfriars generation.

Since the Blackfriars is not the subject of this book, I may be excused for o'erleaping conjecture. There is still scholarly debate about the kinds of change that were brought about by the King's Men's purchase of an interest in an indoor theatre, or whether, indeed, there were any changes at all. It needs to be constantly borne in mind that the Globe was run in tandem, and that when, in June 1613, it was burned to the ground, a second Globe was promptly erected on the site. But it has generally been true, in the history of the theatre, that a playhouse can change its actors more quickly than it can change its audience. In daring to challenge the judgment of 1596 that no 'common playhouse' should be inflicted on the citizens of Blackfriars, the King's Men must obviously have hoped for a recognised status closer to that of the 'private' theatres. That is of much greater significance in the history of the theatre in England than the effect, or lack of it, on Shakespeare or any other writer. By assuming a private face, the country's leading group of players carried further the drift from the popular theatre of the Middle Ages towards the minority theatre with which we are familiar today. There was no sudden change in acting styles. None would have been expected. Voices have a different resonance indoors, but the King's Men were no strangers to that; nor to the kind of adjustment an actor makes when all his audience is seated. We would need to know more than we can about the behaviour of the patrons who bought their sixpenny right to a stool on the stage before we could hope definitely to determine the effect on performance of the absence of the Globe's standing audience. The self-assertiveness of these gallants, judging from the references we do have, is an uncomfortable contrast to the penny-plain humour of the less prosperous groundlings. Writers' complaints about the 'magistrates of wit' who sat in judgment and self-regard on the Blackfriars stage (chapter six of Dekker's *The Gull's Hornbook* is the *locus classicus*) may be exaggerated, but they cannot be ignored. Against the possibility that the seated audience at the Blackfriars brought a new sophistication to Jacobean public performance has to be set the contrary possibility that what it brought was a new kind of rivalry, one that lacked the jocularity of the actor–audience relationships in the popular theatre. The loss of performance space to the stool-holders must also have had an effect on performance. Glynne Wickham, following some of the arguments of Richard Hosley, proposes for the Blackfriars stage a practical acting area 19 feet in width and almost the same in depth, not much larger than a square front-room in a commodious modern house.[5]

We have no sure indication of what Shakespeare felt about all this. He was forty-four when he joined the Blackfriars syndicate, a fine and private man whose adaptation to new circumstances had always been intuitive rather than formulated, after the style of his friend John Fletcher, or combative, after the style of Ben Jonson. The plays he wrote with an eye to performance at the Blackfriars may not have been written as they were *because* they would be performed there, but it would be strange if they were utterly unaffected. He had spent his working life in the conversion of plots to plays, knowing that his own prosperity, as well as that of the actors, depended on their pleasing an audience. One significant shift was an increased reliance on music. Shakespeare had long shown his willingness to write songs to suit the talent of Robert Armin, but in the romantic comedies from *Pericles* to *The Tempest* there is a new interest in unaccompanied atmospheric music. The King's Men, at this time, exploited the melodic gifts of James I's lutanist, Robert Johnson. Johnson's compositions were probably best served by indoor acoustics, and his collaboration with Shakespeare is among the most persuasive evidences that the late plays were written with an indoor audience increasingly in mind. But these plays could be, and were, performed at the Globe. If there is a distinctive Blackfriars play, it may be the late collaboration with Fletcher, *Henry VIII*, or their lost *Cardenio*. (Bardolaters find this collaboration slightly shameful.) There is presumptive evidence that Shakespeare spent a growing proportion of his time at Stratford, in which case his purchase for £140 of the upper floor of one of the Blackfriars gate-houses may have been intended to provide him with a convenient *pied-à-terre* in London, about one hundred yards from his company's winter theatre. There is a real possibility that this deal, completed in March 1613, cost him his share in the Globe. He contracted to pay down £80, and to cover the remaining £60 with a mortgage, to be repaid by the following Michaelmas. But the burning of the Globe on 29 June intervened. As a sharer in the rebuilding scheme, he was probably asked for a further £60 in a hurry. Could he afford both? In his will, he bequeathed the Blackfriars gate-house to his daughter Susanna. There is no mention of any Globe shares. It would be a travesty of theatrical truth if Shakespeare forsook his interest in the Globe for the sake of a flat in the Blackfriars.

APPENDIX A

The inventory taken of all the properties for my Lord Admiral's Men the 10th of March 1598 (=1599)

Item,	1 rock, 1 cage, 1 tomb, 1 Hell mouth.
Item,	1 tomb of Guido, 1 tomb of Dido, 1 bedstead.
Item,	8 lances, 1 pair of stairs for *Phaeton.*
Item,	2 steeples, & 1 chime of bells, & 1 beacon.
Item,	1 hecfor¹ for the play of *Phaeton,* the limes [? limbs] dead.
Item,	1 globe, & 1 golden scepter; 3 clubs.
Item,	2 marchpanes, & the city of Rome.
Item,	1 golden fleece; 2 rackets; 1 bay tree.
Item,	1 wooden hatchet; 1 leather hatchet.
Item,	1 wooden canopy; old Mahomet's head.
Item,	1 lion skin; 1 bear's skin; & Phaeton's limbs, & Phaeton's chariot; & Argus's head.
Item,	Neptune's fork & garland.
Item,	1 crozier's staff; Kent's wooden leg.
Item,	Iris's head, & rainbow; 1 little altar.
Item,	8 vizards; Tamburlaine's bridle; 1 wooden mattock.
Item,	Cupid's bow, & quiver; the cloth of the sun & moon.
Item,	1 boar's head & Cerberus's 3 heads.
Item,	1 caduceus; 2 moss banks, & 1 snake.
Item,	2 fans of feathers; Belin Dun stable; 1 tree of golden apples; Tantalus's tree; 9 iron targets.
Item,	1 copper target, & 17 foils.
Item,	4 wooden targets; 1 greave armour.
Item,	1 sign for Mother Redcap; 1 buckler.
Item,	Mercury's wings; Tasso's picture; 1 helmet with a dragon; 1 shield with 3 lions; 1 elm bowl.
Item,	1 chain² of dragons; 1 gilt spear.
Item,	2 coffins; 1 bull's head; and 1 vulture [or philtre?]
Item,	3 tumbrils, 1 dragon in *Faustus.*

Item,   1 lion; 2 lion heads; 1 great horse with his legs; 1 sack-butt.
Item,   1 wheel and frame in the *Siege of London.*
Item,   1 pair of wrought gloves.
Item,   1 pope's mitre.
Item,   3 Imperial crowns; 1 plain crown.
Item,   1 ghost's crown; 1 crown with a sun.
Item,   1 frame for the heading in *Black John.*
Item,   1 black dog.
Item,   1 cauldron for the Jew.

APPENDIX B

Extract from the contract for building the Fortune in 1599/1600

The frame of the said house to be set square and to contain four score foot of lawful assize every way square without, and fifty-five foot of like assize square every way within, with a good sure and strong foundation of piles, brick, lime and sand both without and within, to be wrought one foot of assize at the least above the ground; and the said frame to contain three stories in height, the first or lower storey to contain nine foot of lawful assize in height; all which stories shall contain twelve foot and a half of lawful assize in breadth throughout, besides a jutty forwards in either of the said two upper stories of ten inches of lawful assize, with four convenient divisions for gentlemen's rooms, and other sufficient and convenient divisions for twopenny rooms, with necessary seats to be placed and set, as well in those rooms as throughout all the rest of the galleries of the said house, and with suchlike stairs, conveyances & divisions without & within, as are made and contrived in and to the late erected playhouse on the Bank in the said parish of St. Saviours called the Globe; with a stage and tiring house, to be made, erected & set up within the said frame, with a shadow or cover over the said stage, which stage shall be placed & set, as also the staircase of the said frame, in such sort as is prefigured in a plot thereof drawn,[1] and which stage shall contain in length forty and three foot of lawful assize, and in breadth to extend to the middle of the yard of the said house; the same stage to be paled in below with good, strong, and sufficient new oaken boards, and likewise the lower storey of the said frame withinside, and the same lower storey to be also laid over and fenced with strong iron pikes; and the said stage to be in all other proportions contrived and fashioned like unto the stage of the said playhouse called the Globe; with convenient windows and lights glazed to the said tiring house; and the said frame, stage and staircases to be covered with tile, and to have a sufficient gutter of lead to carry & convey the water from the covering of the said stage to fall backwards.

APPENDIX C

Petition by the inhabitants of Blackfriars to the Privy Council, 1596

To the right honorable the Lords and others of her Majesties most honorable Privy Councell, – Humbly shewing and beseeching your honors, the inhabitants of the precinct of the Blackfryers, London, that whereas one Burbage hath lately bought certaine roomes in the same precinct neere adjoyning unto the dwelling houses of the right honorable the Lord Chamberlaine and the Lord of Hunsdon, which romes the said Burbage is now altering and meaneth very shortly to convert and turne the same into a comon playhouse, which will grow to be a very great annoyance and trouble, not only to all the noblemen and gentlemen thereabout inhabiting but allso a generall inconvenience to all the inhabitants of the same precinct, both by reason of the great resort and gathering togeather of all manner of vagrant and lewde persons that, under cullor of resorting to the playes, will come thither and worke all manner of mischeefe, and allso to the great pestring and filling up of the same precinct, yf it should please God to send any visitation of sicknesse as heretofore hath been, for that the same precinct is allready growne very populous; and besides, that the same playhouse is so neere the Church that the noyse of the drummes and trumpetts will greatly disturbe and hinder both the ministers and parishioners in tyme of devine service and sermons; – in tender consideracion wherof, as allso for that there hath not at any tyme heretofore been used any comon playhouse within the same precinct, but that now all players being banished by the Lord Mayor from playing within the Cittie by reason of the great inconveniences and ill rule that followeth them, they now thincke to plant them selves in liberties; – That therefore it would please your honors to take order that the same roomes may be converted to some other use, and that no playhouse may be used or kept there; and your suppliants as most bounden shall and will dayly pray for your Lordships in all honor and happines long to live.

NOTES

CHAPTER 1   THE LORD CHAMBERLAIN'S SERVANTS

1 The nomadic life of the Tudor actor brought the profession under the terms of the Poor Law legislation. The 1572 act was further amended in 1576, 1584–5, and 1597–8.

2 The 1597 order has been examined in detail by Glynne Wickham. See *Early English Stages*, Vol. Two, Part II, pp. 9–29.

3 The earliest mention dates from 1580. It seems likely that this theatre was demolished after the 1597 order.

4 It may seem a little hard on the Middlesex justices to ask them to investigate on the Surrey side, but it was accepted practice. See, for example, Middleton, *A Chaste Maid in Cheapside*, II.ii.67.

5 He is thus described by Meercraft in Jonson's *The Devil Is an Ass*, II.viii.75.

6 *Ram Alley*, ed. P. Corbin and D. Sedge, Nottingham, 1981, l.1596.

7 J. F. D. Shrewsbury, *A History of Bubonic Plague in the British Isles*, Cambridge, 1971, p. 177.

8 By William A. Ringler, Jr., 'The Number of Actors in Shakespeare's Early Plays', in *The Seventeenth-Century Stage*, ed. G. E. Bentley, Chicago, 1968.

9 T. W. Baldwin, *The Organization and Personnel of the Shakespearean Company*, Princeton, NJ, 1927.

10 Alison Gaw argues this case in 'Jon Sincklo as one of Shakespeare's actors', *Anglia*, XLIX, 1926, pp. 289–303.

11 'The Letting of Humours Blood in the Head-Vaine', Satire iv.

12 The phrase comes from the chamber accounts of Elizabeth I, where it refers to a performance of the Admiral's Men in February 1589. Two years later, Strange's Men, of whom Phillips was one, followed a play with 'other feates of Activitye'.

13 That the word was a virtual synonym for 'acrobatics' is implied by the reference in note 12, above.

14 The relationship of Edward Alleyn to the Admiral's Men is interestingly parallel to and different from Burbage's to the Chamberlain's Men. Alleyn was related (by marriage, not by blood) to the manager/owner of the Rose, Philip Henslowe. He joined in the management of this theatre while still the leading actor of the company. However, he retired from the stage in 1597, and devoted the rest of his life, with the exception of one or perhaps two short comebacks, to business ventures, not all of them theatrical, and good works. Richard Burbage remained with his company throughout his working life, dying in harness in 1619.

15 It has led to the suggestion – no more than a suggestion – that the Earl of Southampton provided Shakespeare with the money to buy himself in.

16 The dating of Shakespeare's plays is difficult. This list should be taken with a pinch of salt, but not more than a pinch.

17 *Early English Stages*, Vol. Two, Part I, p. 157.

18 M. C. Bradbrook, *The Rise of the Common Player*, London, 1962, p. 48.

19 It was, in fact, vigorously questioned by Giles Allen, in law suits that continued until 1602.

20 *Early English Stages*, Vol. Two, Part II, p. 20.

CHAPTER 2   BALANCING THE BOOKS

1 According to Henslowe's *Diary*, the 1595 season, for example, opened at the Rose on 25 August.

2 The quotations are from, respectively, *The Rise of the Common Player*, p. 97 and *Early English Stages*, Vol. Two, Part I, p. 16.

3 J. F. D. Shrewsbury, *A History of Bubonic Plague in the British Isles*, Cambridge, 1971, p. 306.

4 R. A. Foakes and R. T. Rickert (eds), *Henslowe's Diary*, Cambridge, 1961, 1971, p. 130.

5 The reiterated defence of public performances – that they were a rehearsal for court performances – was not simply, though it was partly, a convenient fiction. The royal command was not confined to the Christmas period.

6 This is an argument pursued at some length by Glynne Wickham in *Early English Stages*, Vol. Two, Part II, to which the reader is referred.

7 The phrase is from *Early English Stages*, Vol. Two, Part I, p. 197.

8 See *Diary*, p. 22.

9 *Diary*, p. 9.

10 *The Overburian Characters*, Percy Reprints XIII, Oxford, 1936, p. 68. We can be certain that Overbury did not himself write the character of 'A Water-man', but we do not know who did. Webster is among the likeliest names proposed.

11 Alfred Harbage, *Shakespeare's Audience*, New York, 1941, pp. 24f.

12 Harbage, op. cit., p. 23.

13 Ann Jennalie Cook, *The Privileged Playgoer*, Princeton, NJ, 1982. The book provides some important corrections to Harbage.

14 Martin Holmes, *Shakespeare and His Players*, London, 1972, p. 15.

15 The figures are from P. J. Finkelpearl, *John Marston of the Middle Temple*, Cambridge, Mass., 1969, p. 5. His exact count is 1,040 in the year 1600, or 1,703 if the Inns of Chancery are included.

16 Estimates of the numbers of people under direct jurisdiction at the Court of Elizabeth I and James I vary from 1,100 to 1,500 but not all of these would have been 'cultured'.

17 The quotation is from Finkelpearl, op. cit., p. 48. The inference is my own, but Finkelpearl would not, I think, dissent from it.

18 *Diary*, p. 13.

19 R. A. Foakes and R. T. Rickert, *Henslowe's Diary*, pp. xxxii–xxxiii.

20 These are earlier than any of Henslowe's own entries. John Henslowe died before 1592. Philip presumably found the largely empty folio in its limp vellum wrapper, and liked the look of it.

21 In 1599, when the Earl of Nottingham published a fixed-price list for his forces quartered in London, he included:

A full quart of the best ale or beer	1d.
Seven eggs, the best in the market	2d.

    A fat pig the best in the market   16d.

Even allowing for some inflation, Ben Jonson's Ursula is being exorbitant when she addresses the disguised Adam Overdo: 'five shillings a pig is my price, at least; if it be a sow-pig, sixpence more: if she be a great-bellied wife, and long for 't, sixpence more for that'. (*Bartholomew Fair*, II.ii.109–12).

22 See *Shakespeare's Audience*, Ch. Two, for Harbage's detailed discussion of average attendances.

23 *Diary*, p. 186. The spelling is modernised here, because the original is contorted to the point of obscurity.

24 *Diary*, pp. 104 and 35.

25 *Diary*, p. 99.

26 *Diary*, pp. 291–4.

27 See Appendix A and *Diary*, pp. 319–21.

28 Henslowe sometimes refers to him by his name – Steven Magett.

29 *Diary*, p. 11.

30 For example, by E. K. Chambers, and by V. C. Gildersleeve, *Government Regulation of the Elizabethan Drama*, London, 1908, Ch. Two.

31 *Diary*, pp. 241 and 167.

32 *Diary*, pp. 238–9.

33 E. K. Chambers, *The Elizabethan Stage*, Vol. II, Oxford, 1923, pp. 62–71. A one-sixteenth interest in the Blackfriars at the same time was worth £45.

34 We know that Shakespeare acted in *Sejanus* in 1603 or 1604, but nothing later than that is supported even by gossip. For three reasons, I consider it likely that he played Sir Adam Prickshaft in Dekker's *Satiromastix* in 1601. All of them rely on the veiled allusions of which Elizabethans were so fond: i) Adam is the part that Shakespeare is believed to have played in *As You Like It*; ii) Prickshaft is bald. Shakespeare seems to have been so, too; iii) the name is the kind of bawdy pun on Shakespeare's own that the audience would have enjoyed.

CHAPTER 3 'THIS LUXURIOUS CIRCLE': THE GLOBE THEATRE

1 Tourneur, *The Revenger's Tragedy*, III, v. 22.

2 For a strongly worded argument against the suitability of baiting arenas as playhouses, see Oscar Brownstein, 'Why didn't Burbage lease the Beargarden?', in *The First Public Playhouse*, ed. Herbert Berry, Montreal, 1979.

3 *The First Public Playhouse*, p. 56.

4 Ibid., p. 35.

5 Ibid., p. 58.

6 Andrew Gurr with John Orrell, *Rebuilding Shakespeare's Globe*, London, 1989, p. 113. The excavated segment of the Globe has led archaeologists to project an external diameter for the whole building of 80 feet, exactly the same as the specified dimensions of the Fortune.

7 For a discussion of the possibility that the actors used the yard, see Allardyce Nicoll, 'Passing over the Stage', in *Shakespeare Survey*, 12 (1959).

8 De Witt explained his interest in the Swan to Van Buchell: 'Since its form seems to resemble that of a Roman structure, I have made a drawing of it.'

9 Bernard Beckerman makes this claim for the Globe, conceding with a dangerous willingness that the sight-lines were poor. See *Shakespeare at the Globe*, New York, 1962, p. 129.

10 C. Walter Hodges, *Shakespeare's Second Globe*, London, 1973, Ch. Six. (See also the same author's *The Third Globe*, 1981.)

11 J. L. Styan has calculated that the actor 'could perambulate for up to fifty feet,

as in a diagonal entrance, or for up to seventy feet, as in an entrance carrying him downstage and across'. See *Shakespeare's Stagecraft*, Cambridge, 1967, p. 69.

12 I am quoting from King's summary of his findings in *The Elizabethan Theatre III*, ed. David Galloway, Toronto, 1973, p. 9. King's book, *Shakespearian Staging, 1599–1642*, Cambridge, MA, 1971 is a very thorough survey of available evidence.

13 Since *The Malcontent* was not originally written for the Globe, although it was played there, we have to be cautious about using this stage direction over-literally. The reference in *Pericles*, IV.iv.23 – 'Enter Pericles at one door with all his train, Cleon and Dioniza at the other' – is firmer evidence of what must, nevertheless, remain an assumption rather than a certainty.

14 See *Every Man out of His Humour*, IV.ii.75–84. Shakespeare focuses our attention on a stage door with sudden intensity in *Hamlet*, IV.v, when Laertes and his 'rabble' clamour for entry, break in, and then agree to leave the stage to Claudius and Laertes alone. 'Sirs, stand you all without', says Laertes (l.112) and the rabble move into the tiring house, but still with only the door between Claudius and revolution.

15 See note 7, above.

16 See *Shakespeare's Stagecraft*, p. 16.

17 See Appendix A.

18 *Early English Stages*, Vol. Two, Part I, p. 220. Wickham argues that, because the throne had always to occupy a theatrically valuable central position, it was flown out when not needed. Other properties and furniture, he argues, could be left onstage throughout – a rock, a mossy bank, etc. – since they could be spread about in such a way as not to impede the performers. All we can say is that this would have been acceptable practice. We do not know what was the norm, nor what convention allowed.

19 For a recent review of the evidence for a 'discovery-space', see Richard Hosley's chapter in *The Revels History of Drama in English*, Vol. III, London, 1975, especially pp. 182–8.

20 *Shakespeare at the Globe*, pp. 92–3.

21 Ibid., p. 192.

22 *Revels History*, Vol. III, pp. 192–3 and 196.

23 *We Saw Him Act*, ed. H. A. Saintsbury, London, 1939, p. 105.

CHAPTER 4   THE GLOBE PLAYS

1 Fynes Moryson, *Itinerary*, 1617, p. 476.

2 G. E. Bentley, *The Profession of Dramatist in Shakespeare's Time*, Princeton, NJ, 1971, p. 196.

3 Quoted in *The Profession of Dramatist*, p. 52.

4 We do not even know where the prompter was positioned, nor does he figure in any of the disguised impromptus that Ben Jonson particularly, but not only Ben Jonson, liked to present as Inductions to his plays. But no company could stage ten plays in a fortnight without a reliable system of prompting. Common sense must stand in for evidence.

5 *Diary*, pp. 182 and 137.

6 G. E. Bentley concludes from available evidence that 'as many as half of the plays by professional dramatists incorporated the writing at some date of more than one man,' *The Profession of Dramatist*, p. 199. Bentley is concerned with the period 1590 to 1642. The proportion of collaborative work between 1599 and 1608 was greater.

7 'Palladis Tamia' was published in 1598. It is Meres's only substantial claim to fame. He surveys the work of 125 English writers since Chaucer, comparing each one with a Greek, Latin or Italian writer.

8 *Diary*, p. 73.

9 G. E. Bentley records the buying of old playbooks for £2, *The Profession of Dramatist*, p. 84.

10 David Wiles, *Shakespeare's Clown*, Cambridge, 1987, p. 146.

11 Quoted in I. H. Jeayes, *Descriptive Catalogue of Charters and Muniments at Berkeley Castle*, Bristol, 1892, p. 323.

12 i.e. Augustine Phillips, from whose deposition before Chief Justice Popham and Justice Fenner this quotation is taken.

13 See S. T. Bindoff, *Tudor England*, Harmondsworth, 1950, p. 303.

14 John Manningham, *Diary*, ed. John Bruce, 1868, p. 130.

15 For an account of Fletcher's career, see Sir James Fergusson, 'The English Comedians in Scotland', in his *The Man Behind Macbeth*, London, 1969.

16 See Rosalind Miles, *Ben Jonson*, London, 1986, p. 100.

17 For a lively comparison of Jonson and Shakespeare, see Alexander Leggatt, *Ben Jonson: His Vision and His Art*, London, 1981, pp. 227–32.

18 There is a lucid account of the provenance of the *Apology* in an essay by J. H. Hexter in *For Veronica Wedgwood These*, ed. Richard Ollard and Pamela Tudor-Craig, London, 1986.

19 J. R. Tanner (ed.), *Constitutional Documents of the Reign of James I*, Cambridge, 1930, p. 222.

20 See Plate 10.

21 Glynne Wickham, *Early English Stages*, Vol. Two, Part II, London, pp. 146–85.

22 *Volpone*, New Mermaid Edition, London, 1968, p. xxv.

23 Sir John Harington, *Nugae Antiquae*, London, 1769, Vol. 1, pp. 349–50.

24 Madame de Verneuil, created marquise by Henri IV after some years as his mistress, cherished hopes of becoming his queen. Her involvement in the Biron conspiracy was never proved.

25 The 1616 Deposition refers to 'Thomas' Evans. I am assuming that this is a mistake or the record of wilful deception.

26 *The Profession of Dramatist*, Ch. Six.

CHAPTER 5 *TWELFTH NIGHT* AND PLAYHOUSE PRACTICE

1 Jean Cocteau makes the distinction in his Preface to *Les Mariés de la Tour Eiffel*, Paris, 1921.

2 B. L. Joseph, *Shakespeare's Eden*, London, 1971, p. 307.

3 And thereby, of course, hangs a tale. Was it customary to provide title-boards for locations in the Elizabethan theatre? We cannot rely on Sidney's reference here. He is alluding to a practice that may have died out by the end of the sixteenth century. The distinction on the mediaeval stage between the unspecified *platea* and the specific *locus* may have been aided by title-boards. The possible bearing on Elizabethan theatre practice of the *platea/locus* distinction is interestingly explored by Robert Weimann in *Shakespeare and the Popular Tradition in the Theatre*, Baltimore and London, 1978, pp. 73–85 and 215–24.

4 It should be noted that *Histriomastix*, from which this is a quotation, was not published until 1632. Prynne was born in 1600, more or less when Shakespeare was writing *Twelfth Night*.

5 Mary Chan, *Music in the Theatre of Ben Jonson*, Oxford, 1980, pp. 36–7.

6 'Shakespeare and the Music of the Elizabethan Stage', in *Shakespeare In Music*, ed. Phyllis Hartnoll, London, 1964, p. 23.

7 M. C. Bradbrook, *Shakespeare the Craftsman*, London, 1969, p. 68.

8 Ibid., p. 57.

9 Emrys Jones, *Scenic Form in Shakespeare*, Oxford, 1971, pp. 24–7.

10 I agree with T. W. Craik (Arden Edition, p. xxxiv) that 'for a Twelfth Night play there could be no title more barren than *Twelfth Night*', but cannot as happily as he reject all the associations that the title carries with it.

11 T. Baldwin, *The Organization and Personnel of the Shakespearean Company*, Princeton, NJ, 1927, inserted table of actors and their roles (between pp. 228 and 229).

12 *The Merry Wives of Windsor* comes closest to the practice of *Twelfth Night* in this respect, eight actors having 150 lines or more, but even there the responsibility is much less evenly shared. *Julius Caesar* relies heavily on four actors – which might be further evidence that it was written as a 'safe' play. *As You Like It* and *Hamlet*, though they have six and seven parts respectively in the over-150 line range, rely heavily on about four actors.

13 The quotation is from M. M. Mahood's Introduction to her New Penguin edition of *Twelfth Night*, p. 39. It follows a discussion of the isolation of Antonio, not of the substitution of the song for a dance. Professor Mahood would not necessarily accept my application of it here.

14 Stubbes, *The Anatomie of Abuses*, pp. 154–6. I am indebted to Alan Brissenden's *Shakespeare and the Dance*, London, 1981, not only for this quotation, but also for much information on Elizabethan dancing.

15 *Scenic Form in Shakespeare*, p. 41.

16 J. L. Styan, *Shakespeare's Stagecraft*, Cambridge, 1967, p. 45.

17 This stage direction, like the whole Induction, is parodic: but parody requires a recognisable reality behind it.

18 B. Beckerman, *Shakespeare at the Globe*, New York, 1962, p. 78.

CHAPTER 6 *HAMLET* AND THE ACTOR IN SHAKESPEARE'S THEATRE

1 M. C. Bradbrook, *Shakespeare the Craftsman*, London, 1969, p. 129.

2 We know from a reference in *Antonio's Revenge*, II.i.30, that it was the tireman who made the beards for the Paul's Boys. He may well have performed the same service for the Chamberlain's Men.

3 *Shakespeare the Craftsman*, p. 130.

4 Ibid., p. 135.

5 This seriousness was an outstanding feature of Peter Quince's players in Peter Brook's famous 1970 production of the play.

6 M. Shapiro, *Children of the Revels*, New York, 1977, pp. 38f.

7 The phrase is from R. A. Foakes, 'Tragedy at the Children's Theatres after 1600', in *The Elizabethan Theatre II*, ed. David Galloway, Toronto, 1970, p. 45.

8 Anne Righter, *Shakespeare and the Idea of the Play*, London, 1962, p. 13.

9 *The Overburian Characters*, Percy Reprints xiii, Oxford, 1936, pp. 76–7.

10 S. T. Coleridge, *Table Talk*. The comment was recorded in 27 April 1823, and is most easily located in the various editions by looking for that date.

11 See *King Richard III: Edmund Kean's Performance as recorded by James H. Hackett*, ed. Alan S. Downer for the Society for Theatre Research, 1959.

12 For some further discussion of this point, see Andrew Gurr, 'Who Strutted and Bellowed?', in *Shakespeare Survey*, 16, 1963, pp. 95–102.

13 'To Edward Allen', *Epigrammes* LXXXIX, Herford and Simpson, Oxford, 1925–52, VIII, pp. 56–7.

14 *Revels History of Drama in English*, Vol. III, London, 1975, p. 114.
15 B. Beckerman, *Shakespeare at the Globe*, New York, 1962, p. 129.
16 J. L. Styan, *Shakespeare's Stagecraft*, Cambridge, 1967, p. 45.
17 Nigel Alexander, *Poison, Play, and Duel*, London, 1971, p. 22.
18 J. Dover Wilson, *What Happens in Hamlet*, Cambridge, 1935, p. 158.
19 The illustration is reproduced in Martin Holmes, *The Guns of Elsinore*, London, 1964.
20 *The Guns of Elsinore*, p. 51.
21 J. R. Brown, *Shakespeare's Plays in Performance*, London, 1966, pp. 139–41.
22 Burbage may well, at this point, have written down the observation in his 'tables', after the contemporary fashion of noting memorabilia. As a piece of stage-business, this was well established by the eighteenth century.
23 F. W. Sternfield, *Music in Shakespearean Tragedy*, London, 1963, p. 55.
24 *The Guns of Elsinore*, pp. 165–79.
25 *The Overburian Characters*, p. 77.

CHAPTER 7 *MACBETH* FROM THE TIRING HOUSE

1 An effective summary of the limitations of Forman's evidence is Leah Scragg, 'Macbeth on Horseback,' in *Shakespeare Survey*, 26, 1973, pp. 81–8.
2 Dennis Bartholomeusz, *Macbeth and the Players*, Cambridge, 1969, pp. 1–13.
3 See Reginald Scot, *The Discoverie of Witchcraft*, 1584, Book III, chapter xiii.
4 For a discussion of theatrical lighting techniques, see Terence Rees, *Theatre Lighting in the Age of Gas*, 1978.
5 Thirteen is the normal number for a sabbat, but the magic number three would be acceptable theatrical shorthand.
6 An outstanding example of the 'unheard conversation' convention is in *Julius Caesar* II.i.101–11, when we do not hear how Cassius persuades Brutus to join the conspiracy.
7 Frances Shirley, *Shakespeare's Use of Off-Stage Sounds*, Lincoln, NE, 1963. The book is lively and learned.
8 Cited in G. K. Hunter, '*Macbeth* in the Twentieth Century', *Shakespeare Survey*, 19, 1966, p. 11.
9 Racine, *Andromaque*, V.i.3.
10 Here and elsewhere in this chapter, I am indebted to the work of Emrys Jones in chapter seven of *Scenic Form in Shakespeare*, Oxford, 1971.
11 *Scenic Form*, pp. 116–17.
12 John Holloway, *The Story of the Night*, London, 1961, p. 66.
13 G. K. Hunter, op. cit., p. 8.
14 Kenneth Tynan, *He that Plays the King*, London, 1950, p. 81.

CHAPTER 8 TWO PLAYHOUSES

1 Quoted in Christine Eccles, *The Rose Theatre*, London, 1990, p. 146.
2 Professor J. Leeds Barroll provided me with a copy of his unpublished paper, 'The Second Blackfriars Reconsidered – Again'. I am grateful to him for this example of his well-known generosity to fellow Shakespeareans.
3 Irwin Smith, *Shakespeare's Blackfriars Playhouse*, London, 1966, p. 258.
4 *Diary*, pp. 35 and 322 respectively.
5 Glynne Wickham, *Early English Stages*, Vol. Two, Part II, London, 1972, p. 180.

APPENDIX A

1 'hecfor' is unexplained. Perhaps 'heifer'.
2 'chain of dragons' is also unexplained.

APPENDIX B

1 Unfortunately this drawing is lost.

SELECT BIBLIOGRAPHY

GENERAL STUDIES

Beckerman, Bernard, *Shakespeare at the Globe*, New York, 1962.
Chambers, E. K., *The Elizabethan Stage*, 4 vols. Oxford, 1923.
— *William Shakespeare*, 2 vols. Oxford, 1930.
Gurr, Andrew, *The Shakespearean Stage*, Cambridge, 1970.
Hattaway, Michael, *Elizabethan Popular Theatre*, London, 1982.
Reese, M. M., *Shakespeare: His World and His Work*, London, 1953.
Revels History of Drama in English, Vol. III, London, 1975.
Schoenbaum, S., *William Shakespeare: A Documentary Life*, Oxford, 1975.
Sturgess, Keith, *Jacobean Private Theatres*, London, 1987.
Weimann, Robert, *Shakespeare and the Popular Tradition in the Theater*, ed. Robert Schwartz, Baltimore, 1978.

THE GLOBE THEATRE

Berry, Herbert, *Shakespeare's Playhouses*, New York, 1987.
Gurr, Andrew with John Orrell, *Rebuilding Shakespeare's Globe*, London, 1989.
Hodges, C. Walter, *The Globe Restored*, London, 1953.
— *Shakespeare's Second Globe*, London, 1973.
Hosley, Richard, 'The Playhouses and the Stage', in *A New Companion to Shakespeare Studies*, ed. Kenneth Muir and S. Schoenbaum, Cambridge, 1971.
— 'A Reconstruction of the Fortune Playhouse', in *Elizabethan Theatre VI*, 1978 and *Elizabethan Theatre VII*, 1980.
Nagler, A. M., *Shakespeare's Stage*, trans. R. Manheim, Yale, 1958.
Orrell, John, *The Quest for Shakespeare's Globe*, Cambridge, 1983.
Wickham, Glynne, *Early English Stages*, Vol. Two: 1576 to 1660, Part I, London, 1963, and Part II, London, 1972.

THE LORD CHAMBERLAIN'S MEN

Baldwin, T. W., *The Organization and Personnel of the Shakespearean Company*, Princeton, NJ, 1927.
Bentley, G. E., *The Profession of Player in Shakespeare's Time*, Princeton, NJ, 1984.
Bevington, David, *From 'Mankind' to Marlowe*, Cambridge, MA, 1962.
Booth, Stephen, 'Speculations on Doubling in Shakespeare's Plays', in *Shakespeare: The Theatrical Dimension*, ed. P. C. McGuire and D. A. Samuelson, New York, 1979.

Bradbrook, M. C., *The Rise of the Common Player*, London, 1962.
Carson, Neil, *A Companion to Henslowe's Diary*, Cambridge, 1988.
David, Richard, 'Shakespeare and the Players', in *Studies in Shakespeare*, ed. Peter Alexander, London, 1964.
Holmes, Martin, *Shakespeare and Burbage*, London, 1978.
Hosking, G. L., *The Life and Times of Edward Alleyn*, London, 1952.
Hotson, Leslie, *Shakespeare's Motley*, London, 1952.
Jamieson, Michael, 'Shakespeare's Celibate Stage', in *Papers Mainly Shakespearian*, ed. G. I. Duthie, Edinburgh, 1964.
Mason, Alexandra, 'The Social Status of Theatrical People', in *Shakespeare Quarterly*, XVIII, 1967.
Nungezer, Edwin, *A Dictionary of Actors*, Yale, 1929.
Ringler, William A., 'The Number of Actors in Shakespeare's Early Plays', in *The Seventeenth-Century Stage*, ed. G. E. Bentley, Chicago, 1968.
Rutter, Carol, *Documents of the Rose Playhouse*, Manchester, 1984.
Thomson, Peter, 'Playhouses and Players in the Time of Shakespeare', in *The Cambridge Companion to Shakespeare Studies*, ed. Stanley Wells, Cambridge, 1986.

ACTING STYLES

Armstrong, William A., 'Actors and Theatres', in *Shakespeare Survey*, 17, 1964.
Bethell, S. L., 'Shakespeare's Actors', in *Review of English Studies*, n.s. I, 1950.
Brown, John Russell, 'On the Acting of Shakespeare's Plays', reprinted from the *Quarterly Journal of Speech*, XXXIV, in G. E. Bentley, *The Seventeenth-Century Stage*, Chicago, 1968.
Foakes, R. A., 'The Player's Passion', in *Essays and Studies*, n.s. VIII, 1954.
Gurr, Andrew, 'Who strutted and bellowed?', in *Shakespeare Survey*, 16, 1963.
—— 'Elizabethan Action', in *Studies in Philology*, LXIII, 1966.
Joseph, B. L., *Elizabethan Acting*, 2nd edn, London, 1964.
Marker, Lise-Lone, 'Nature and Decorum in the Theory of Elizabethan Acting', in *The Elizabethan Theatre*, II, ed. David Galloway, Toronto, 1970.
Rosenberg, Marvin, 'Elizabethan Actors: Men or Marionettes?', in *PMLA*, XLIX, 1954.
Seltzer, Daniel, 'The Actors and Staging', in *A New Companion to Shakespeare Studies*, ed. K. Muir and S. Schoenbaum, Cambridge, 1971.
—— 'Prince Hal and the Tragic Style', in *Shakespeare Survey*, 30, 1977.
Wiles, David, *Shakespeare's Clown*, Cambridge, 1987.

SHAKESPEARE'S AUDIENCE

Cook, Ann Jennalie, *The Privileged Playgoer*, Princeton, 1982.
—— 'The Audience of Shakespeare's Plays: a Reconsideration', in *Shakespeare Studies*, VII, 1974.
Gurr, Andrew, *Playgoing in Shakespeare's London*, Cambridge, 1987.
Harbage, Alfred, *Shakespeare's Audience*, New York, 1941.
Wright, Louis B., *Middle-Class Culture in Elizabethan England*, Chapel Hill, NC, 1953.

MUSIC IN THE ELIZABETHAN THEATRE

Baskervill, C. R., *The Elizabethan Jig*, Chicago, 1929.

Chan, Mary, *Music in the Theatre of Ben Jonson*, Oxford, 1980.

Ingram, R. W., 'Music as a Structural Element in Shakespeare', in *Shakespeare 1971*, ed. Clifford Leech and J. M. R. Margeson, Toronto, 1972.

Long, John H., *Shakespeare's Use of Music*, Gainsville, FL, 1971.

Seng, Peter J., *The Vocal Songs in the Plays of Shakespeare*, London, 1967.

Sternfeld, F. W., *Music in Shakespearean Tragedy*, London, 1963.

—— 'Shakespeare and Music', in *A New Companion to Shakespeare Studies*, ed. K. Muir and S. Schoenbaum, Cambridge, 1971.

Stevens, John, 'Shakespeare and the Music of the Elizabethan Stage', in *Shakespeare in Music*, ed. Phyllis Hartnoll, London, 1964.

COSTUME IN THE ELIZABETHAN THEATRE

Jones, Eldred, *Othello's Countrymen*, Oxford, 1965.

Linthicum, M. C., *Costume in the Drama of Shakespeare and His Contemporaries*, Oxford, 1936.

LIGHTING IN THE ELIZABETHAN THEATRE

Dessen, Alan, 'Night and Darkness on the Elizabethan Stage', in *Renaissance Papers 1978*, 1979.

Graves, R. B., *English Stage Lighting, 1557–1642*, Unpublished Ph.D. thesis at Northwestern University, 1976.

—— '*The Duchess of Malfi* at the Globe and Blackfriars', in *Renaissance Drama*, n.s. 9, 1978.

PROPERTIES IN THE ELIZABETHAN THEATRE

Dessen, Alan, 'Elizabethan Audiences and the Open Stage', in *Yearbook of English Studies*, 10, 1980.

Habicht, Werner, 'Tree Properties and Tree Scenes in Elizabethan Theater', in *Renaissance Drama*, n.s. 4, 1971.

Jones, Marion and Wickham, Glynne, 'The Stage Furnishings of George Chapman's *The Tragedy of Charles, Duke of Biron*', in *Theatre Notebook*, 16, 1962.

Smith, Warren D., *Shakespeare's Playhouse Practice*, Hanover, NH, 1975.

CHILDREN'S COMPANIES

Davies, W. Robertson, *Shakespeare's Boy Actors*, London, 1939.

Foakes, R. A., 'Tragedy of the Children's Theatres after 1600', in *The Elizabethan Theatre* II, ed. David Galloway, Toronto, 1970.

Gair, Reavley, *The Children of Paul's*, Cambridge, 1982.

Hillebrand, H. M., *The Child Actors*, Urbana, IL, 1926.

Shapiro, Michael, *Children of the Revels*, New York, 1977.

ELIZABETHAN STAGECRAFT

Bradbrook, M. C., *Themes and Conventions of Elizabethan Tragedy*, Cambridge, 1935.

Brown, John Russell, *Shakespeare's Plays in Performance*, London, 1966.

— *Free Shakespeare*, London, 1974.

Dessen, Alan, *Elizabethan Drama and the Viewer's Eye*, Chapel Hill, NC, 1977.

Greenfield, Thelma, N., *The Induction in Elizabethan Drama*, Eugene, OR, 1969.

Homan, Sidney (ed.), *Shakespeare's 'More than Words Can Witness'*, Lewisburg, PA, 1980.

King, T. J., *Shakespearean Staging, 1599–1642*, Cambridge, MA, 1971.

Mehl, Dieter, *The Elizabethan Dumb Show*, London, 1965.

Reynolds, G. F., *The Staging of Elizabethan Plays at the Red Bull Theatre, 1605–1625*, New York, 1940.

— *On Shakespeare's Stage*, Boulder, CO, 1967.

Saunders, J. W., 'Staging at the Globe, 1599–1613', in *Shakespeare Quarterly*, 11, 1960.

Seltzer, Daniel, 'The Staging of the Last Plays', in *Later Shakespeare*, ed. John Russell Brown and Bernard Harris, London, 1967.

Styan, J. L. *Shakespeare's Stagecraft*, Cambridge, 1967.

The following books have been useful in the writing of particular chapters:

CHAPTER 1 THE LORD CHAMBERLAIN'S SERVANTS

Shrewsbury, J. F. D., *A History of the Bubonic Plague in the British Isles*, Cambridge, 1971.

Stone, Lawrence, *The Crisis of the Aristocracy, 1558–1641*, Oxford, 1965.

Wilson, F. P., *The Plague in Shakespeare's London*, Oxford, 1927.

CHAPTER 2 BALANCING THE BOOKS

Burnett, John, *A History of the Cost of Living*, London, 1969.

Finkelpearl, P. J., *John Marston of the Middle Temple*, Cambridge, MA, 1969.

Gildersleeve, V. C., *Government Regulation of the Elizabethan Drama*, London, 1908.

Holmes, Martin, *Shakespeare and His Players*, London, 1972.

Klein, David, 'Did Shakespeare Produce His Own Plays?' in *Modern Language Review*, LVII, 1962.

CHAPTER 3 'THIS LUXURIOUS CIRCLE': THE GLOBE THEATRE

Berry, Herbert (ed.), *The First Public Playhouse*, Montreal, 1979.

Eccles, Christine, *The Rose Theatre*, London, 1990.

Hodges, C. Walter, *The Third Globe*, London, 1981.

Nicoll, Allardyce (ed.). *Shakespeare Survey*, 12, 1959.

CHAPTER 4 THE GLOBE PLAYS

Akrigg, G. P. V., *Jacobean Pageant*, London, 1962.

Bentley, G. E., *The Profession of Dramatist in Shakespeare's Time*, Princeton, 1971.

Bindoff, S. T., *Tudor England*, Harmondsworth, 1950.

Byrne, M. St Clare, *Elizabethan Life in Town and Country*, London, 1925.

Dusinberre, Juliet, *Shakespeare and the Nature of Women*, London, 1975.

Fergusson, Sir James, *The Man Behind Macbeth*, London, 1969.

Hyde, Mary Crapo, *Playwriting for Elizabethans*, New York, 1949.

Leggatt, Alexander, *Ben Jonson: His Vision and His Art*, London, 1981.
Ordish, T. F., *Shakespeare's London*, 1897.

CHAPTER 5 *TWELFTH NIGHT* AND PLAYHOUSE PRACTICE

Bradbrook, M. C., *Shakespeare the Craftsman*, London, 1969.
Brissenden, Alan, *Shakespeare and the Dance*, London, 1981.
Hotson, Leslie, *The First Night of Twelfth Night*, London, 1954.
Jones, Emrys, *Scenic Form in Shakespeare*, Oxford, 1971.
Joseph, B. L., *Shakespeare's Eden*, London, 1971.

CHAPTER 6 *HAMLET* AND THE ACTOR IN SHAKESPEARE'S THEATRE

Alexander, Nigel, *Poison, Play, and Duel*, London, 1971.
Holmes, Martin, *The Guns of Elsinore*, London, 1964.
Morsberger, R. E., *Swordplay and the Elizabethan and Jacobean Stage*, Salzburg, 1974.
Righter, Anne, *Shakespeare and the Idea of the Play*, London, 1962.

CHAPTER 7 *MACBETH* FROM THE TIRING HOUSE

Bartholomeusz, Dennis, *Macbeth and the Players*, London, 1969.
Harris, Anthony, *Night's Black Agents*, Manchester, 1980.
Holloway, John, *The Story of the Night*, London, 1961.
Muir, Kenneth (ed.), *Shakespeare Survey, 19*, 1966.
Shirley, Frances, *Shakespeare's Use of Off-stage Sounds*, Lincoln, NE, 1963.
Tynan, Kenneth, *He That Plays the King*, London, 1950.

CHAPTER 8 TWO PLAYHOUSES

Smith, Irwin, *Shakespeare's Blackfriars Playhouse*, London, 1966.

INDEX OF PLAYS

193

GENERAL INDEX

INTRODUCTORY REMOTE SENSING:

Remote sensing h   Earth, and our
place on it. The a   ht significant
advances in a wid   o urban planning, environmen   rmation and a
deeper understanc   e sensing is a
complex subject.

Introductory Rem   oth the theory
and application of   addresses four
key questions: Wł   e sensing data
obtained? What a

Chapter 1 intro   olution – from
aerial platforms an   f today. Chapter 2 presents deta   equired before
a clear understanc   g platforms –
including Landsat   examines and
illustrates many o

A unique Webs   n, for users of
Netscape 3/Intern

- over 45 full col   orology, geol-
  ogy, vegetatior   spanning the
  world's major r   alasia, Sudan,
  Oman, Wester
- image exercises
- questions and a
- an online gloss   online, and a
  preview of the

Access the accon

Please return/renew this item by the last date shown

Tillibh/ath-chlaraidh seo ron cheann-latha mu dheireadh

Paul J. Gibson is Senior Lecturer in Remote Sensing, Department of Geography and **John Keating** is Lecturer in Computer Sciences, both at the National University of Ireland, Maynooth, Ireland. **Clare H. Power** is Senior Lecturer in Remote Sensing, School of Environmental and Earth Sciences, University of Greenwich, UK.

THE COMPLETE
INTRODUCTORY REMOTE SENSING
TEACHING AND LEARNING PACKAGE

Introductory Remote Sensing: Principles and Concepts is published alongside a companion textbook to present a complete introductory package for those studying or working with remote sensing. The companion textbook, *Introductory Remote Sensing: Digital Image Processing and Applications*, explains how digital images can be processed, presents detailed case study illustrations, and includes a practical exercise manual to support the unique CD-ROM which accompanies the textbook. Containing fully functioning image processing software and over 70 satellite digital datasets, the CD-ROM enables hands-on image processing by students.

Both textbooks include features specifically designed for students, bringing topics alive and enabling closer student interaction with images, and a clearer understanding of key topics. Each textbook includes:

- full illustration throughout with explanatory diagrams and drawings, black and white images, and large numbers of full-colour images in the books and on the Web
- boxes to highlight key concepts, examples and more advanced topics
- end-of-chapter summaries, further reading lists, and self-assessment tests
- appendices: a glossary of terms, explanation of acronyms, sources of remote sensing information, self-assessment test answers, comprehensive further reading list
- dedicated Website.